THE DUAL NATURE OF ISLAMIC FUNDAMENTALISM

JOHANNES J.G. JANSEN

The Dual Nature of Islamic Fundamentalism

Cornell University Press
Ithaca, New York

First published in the United States 1997 by Cornell University Press

International Standard Book Number 0-8014-3338-X (cloth)

Library of Congress Cataloging-in-Publication Data

Jansen, Johannes J.G.
The dual nature of Islamic fundamentalism/Johannes J.G. Jansen.
p. cm.
Includes bibliographical references (p.) and index.
ISBN 0-8014-3338-X
1. Islamic fundamentalism. I. Title.
BP 166.14.F85J36 1997 96-9729
297' .09'04–dc20 CIP

Printed in Hong Kong

'*lā budda* [a] *li-'l-islām an yaḥkum* [Inevitably Islam shall rule]'

—SayyidQuṭb, *Ma'rakat al-Islām wa'-l-Ra'smāliyya,* 7th edn, Cairo 1980, 55

'An existing High Culture...to be endowed with a political roof worthy of it....'

—Ernest Gellner, *Conditions of Liberty: Civil Society and its Rivals*, London 1994, 115

CONTENTS

PREFACE

Modern governments of modern states in modern times want to be legitimate. It would, of course, be best if modern elections were to supply modern legitimacy. However, in a number of countries this is not possible.

The reasons vary. It may be socially unacceptable to oppose the government and its infinite wisdom. The ruling regime may have created an atmosphere in which whoever opposes the government does not or cannot vote. Voters may be intimidated into not voting for the opposition, but without being won over by the government. Chaotic circumstances or lack of experience of the necessary procedures may make proper elections an improbability. Also, the results of elections, if they are held, could be undesirable in the eyes of the regime or of international public opinion. Election results may also be expected to preclude the holding of another free election – *one man, one vote, one time* – ever in the future. Whatever the case may be, modern governments that do not have legitimacy through elections want to find it from some other source.

Demand creates supply. It would be contrary to human nature if religions did not supply what rulers, in such cases, want to find. Religion, Islam not excluded, is in many ways a mystery, but both scholars and believers agree on one important point, namely that religion satisfies a desire which the world leaves unfulfilled. The most common example of such a desire is the wish for life after death. Seldom, however, are human aspirations which the world cannot fulfill as grandiose as the resurrection of the body and life eternal.

In a fiercely competitive society the dominant religion may preach that the greatest virtue is to love one's neighbour. The religion of a group which over the centuries has become marginalised may, on the other hand, preach that God has exclusively and explicitly chosen those who follow His commandments, and this group may come to believe that it plays a central role in the history of God and His creation. Another example: in a society where the law is not much more than an interesting but highly theoretical matter, the major religion may proclaim that following God's laws is the only way to put things right.

Modern times have changed human life. The demands which man makes upon his religions have changed too. Health care, for instance, is not demanded from churches, monasteries and saints but from hospitals and doctors. To invoke religion where science can provide an answer is simply not done, and to do so when effective science is available is usually frowned upon, even by believers. Pious parents today not only pray for their children, but take them to the hospital as well.

Similarly, in societies where political authority and the power of the state are based on the results of elections, or the overwhelming power of the police and the military, people see no need to call upon religion and its functionaries to justify the existence and the presumed omnipotence of the worldly powers that be. Here the power of the state is self-explanatory. No individual sceptic can argue against election results or rough police procedures. This is even beyond the ability of a platoon of experienced terrorists. When, on the other hand, no earthly justification for the power of the state can be found, if only because the ruling regime, for whatever reason, is unable or unwilling to organise proper elections, it is unavoidable that religion should be called upon to find a justification for the authority of the state.

Religious functionaries are usually willing to respond to such demands from the state, and on the whole they give the state their blessing, but at a price: when the state asks religious leaders for their recognition, should it not be obliged to return the favour? When the state receives its legitimacy partly or wholly from religious leaders, should it not pay them salaries and give them some influence over current affairs? Should it not also protect their position and prestige when (inevitably) reformers attack them, give them the right to censure all publications that concern religion, and perhaps even attempt to carry out some of the precepts which that religion recommends, such as (in the case of Islam) the ban on interest, or the imposition of fixed punishments for theft, adultery etc?

What should religious functionaries do when their religion has a developed system of law and is asked to supply legitimacy to a modern state that has the power to promulgate laws? Should they demand that the state executes the laws that their religion imposes? Or should they merely be content with their salaries and positions? What must believers do in such a situation – demand from the state the implementation of some or all of the rules of their religion? Religious functionaries can be manipulated, individually if need be, once they are in league with the government, but how about ordinary believers? What could possibly keep in check their religious and political enthusiasm, and their ardour for the Kingdom of Heaven? It should not be surprising that such a situation gives rise to movements which merge politics and religion into fundamentalism.

Islamic fundamentalism is both politics and religion. It has a dual nature. When it is analysed as if it were a movement that has a political nature only, mistakes are made because fundamentalism is fully religion at the same time. When it is analysed as if it were a movement that has a religious nature only, mistakes are made too, because fundamentalism is fully politics at the same time.

For over a century, since Al-Sayyid Ğamāl al-Dīn al-Afghānī (d. 1897), an intra-Islamic debate has been in progress concerning the dilemmas created by this modern fusion of religion and politics. This debate has not always been carried on in public, and often has hardly been visible or audible. The only country in which the debate has been clearly visible for more than a century is Egypt. There, as in all Islamic countries, this debate has been strongly influenced by local circumstances. This is unavoidable and natural, but it does not mean that the outcome of the Egyptian debate is not – subject to some limitations – highly relevant for other regions of the Islamic world.

Because there are a number of advantages when a discussion is visible over a long period, much in the following pages is derived from Egyptian sources. However, this book is not about Egypt. It is about a discussion. Because of the intellectual dominance of Egypt in the Islamic world, Egyptian thinkers inevitably play a central role in a report on this discussion.

All over the Islamic world, from Tangier to Yogjakarta, books written by Egyptian writers – sometimes in translation – are sold. Islamic thinkers from many Islamic countries have their books printed in Egypt, and distributed from there. There can be no study of Islam in which Egypt and things Egyptian do not figure prominently.

In April and March 1851, the Dutch governor-general of what was then the Netherlands East Indies visited Egypt on his way to his vast kingdom in South-East Asia. It is difficult to prove but easy to illustrate anecdotally that in his eyes, and in those of his contemporaries, the differences between the Muslim Middle East and the West were not very large. Nevertheless these differences are large now, and in a number of fields are continually getting larger.

The governor-general's wife wrote a letter from Suez, dated 4 April 1851, addressed to her sister in the Netherlands, in which she described her stay in Alexandria, Cairo and Suez in considerable detail.[1] She repeatedly expressed her surprise at the sometimes biblical scenes she and her husband witnessed while travelling, but little or no surprise at the social circumstances they met with. For instance, the distance between the servants and the élite, or the rulers and the ruled, obviously did not strike the couple as unusual or remarkable. Egypt at that time was not yet very different socially from the Europe they came from and were familiar with. The governor-general's wife was delighted to meet the Egyptian diplomat Nubar Pasha[2] and his wife. Nubar, she wrote, 'is an Armenian, so [he is] of the Greek religion. Nevertheless, [he] follows the Turkish ways in dress and custom.' When the two eminent couples met for lunch, Nubar 'kept [his] head covered with a red cap', even during the meal.

At the end of the twentieth century it is not the male headdress worn during lunch that would impress a visitor as the most striking difference between the Arab world and Western Europe. These two parts of the world are becoming more and more different from each other, both socially and culturally. Even the élites do not mix as easily as they did a century and a half ago. Momentous change has taken place in Western Europe and North America in the past 150 years. Although great changes have also touched the Middle East,[3] they are not the same, especially where religion

[1] Letter from Maria I. Duymaer van Twist-Beck to her sister Cecilia Beck, dated Cairo/Suez 4 April 1851, in the collection of the Cost Budde Foundation, Diepenveen (Netherlands).

[2] Premier of Egypt 1878-9, 1884-8 and 1894-5.

[3] 'Middle East' is used as a geographical designation. The term has to be preferred to a number of alternatives because unlike, e.g., 'the Arab world' or 'the Muslim world', it

is concerned. Inhabitants of the Middle East and Western Europe are both subject to the attractions of secularisation, revival and cult formation,[4] but the consequences of the pull of these forces are not, and cannot be, the same in the two territories. The religious and political contexts are radically different, and this, in its turn, deeply influences the outcome of these all-important and continuous processes.

To begin with, religion in the Middle East does not operate in a free market: apostasy from Islam is either socially impossible or legally forbidden, often both. Secondly, while political freedom may not always be completely absent everywhere, it certainly is less than that taken for granted in Europe or North America. All this has a number of consequences.

Many of the people quoted in this book are still alive. I have talked with many of them, and wish to thank and salute them from these pages. Nevertheless, I have not quoted their often interesting and sometimes controversial oral statements, but have relied on examples of their views that I could find on the printed pages of their publications, using the interviews they granted me as a lamp to illuminate their writings, not as a mirror of their thought. This may have impoverished the book, but how could I possibly use an interview that ended with the great reformer showing me the gramophone record *The Classics Made Modern by the Great Maestro James Last,* the reformer at the same time explaining to me that he wanted to be the one that made Islam more modern? – or an interview in which a great thinker who, when asked during Ramaḍān about the meaning of Ramaḍān, clapped his hands and shouted for coffee, thus effectively breaking his fast, and then ignored the question?

Can one use an interview in which a famous Koran commentator

intends to be religiously and ethnically neutral. What the Middle East is to the East of is obvious: that can only be the West. However, someone who travels eastwards from France, Germany or Britain would not arrive in the Middle East but pass to the North of it and end up in Kazakhstan. The term 'Middle East' was invented as recently as 1902 by a naval historian to designate the area between Arabia and India, but its present use nevertheless appears to reflect the pre-colonial predominance of the Mediterranean world, as do the terms 'Orient', 'Anatolia' and 'Levant', which mean 'sunrise', in Latin, Greek and Italian respectively. See, e.g., Lewis, *The Middle East,* 25; and on the origin and precise definitions of the term the references mentioned in Lewis, *The Shaping of the Modern Middle East,* 3-4.

[4] See Rodney Stark and William Sims Bainbridge, *The Future of Religion: Secularization, Revival and Cult Formation,* Berkeley: University of California Press 1985.

states that he 'does not care about Islam' but 'only about the Koran'? – or a statement by a leading Muslim who assures me, albeit late at night during a conference far removed from the social realities of the Middle East, that 'Islam has always been a violent half-fascist theocracy in the first place'? How seriously should one take an internationally known scholar of Muslim law who denies that Islam ever prescribed the death penalty for apostasy? What about a famous Muslim scholar who has published many pages in a variety of languages about an even greater variety of subjects, the Koran not excluded, who, it turns out, can speak only the most rudimentary Arabic, or, if one leaves aside niceties and euphemisms, does not speak or understand Arabic at all?

It may be that my intuitions are always right, and that I am able to select competently from the many oral statements I heard the ones that are authentic. However, I have opted for another approach altogether: to use only statements that I could find in written, published sources. I assume that when a Muslim thinker addresses his own public in his (and their) own language he preaches what he believes to be true and important. This approach nevertheless has its limitations. Certain axioms are sometimes not expressed because they are common assumptions, shared between the preacher and his audience. Here I have attempted to supply the cultural ellipsis, trusting my intuitions, although I may have drawn the wrong inferences. It is much easier for the reader to follow me in this case than if I were subjectively selecting material obtained in interviews.

Islamic fundamentalism is a amalgam of religion and politics. Politics, furthermore, cannot exist without violence; hence, Islamic fundamentalism fuses politics, religion and violence – and is certainly not the first and only movement in the history of mankind that can be so characterised. It is a movement which threatens the existing order in the Muslim world, and which holds the West spellbound. Can outsiders understand Islamic fundamentalism in its own human context? What do the fundamentalists of Islam aspire to? Are their aspirations understandable in human terms, given the axioms from which Muslim fundamentalists have to start, and the social context in which they have to operate? What is the tenor of their ideology? In what terms is it couched? How did it develop? How is Islamic fundamentalism linked to the history of Islamic thought?

Maybe these questions cannot be answered without a detailed chronicle of the struggle between Islamic fundamentalism and the powers that be in the Middle East. However, such a chronicle does not yet exist, and may never come into existence, since the archives on which it would have to be based may never become accessible. In the mean time the success and the failure of Islamic fundamentalism nevertheless raise a number of urgent questions concerning the relationship between politics and religion in the world of Islam, and at least an attempt to formulate and answer these questions cannot be postponed.

From the viewpoint of philosophy, fundamentalism does not present much of a problem after Ernest Gellner's lucid analysis of it.[5] According to Gellner (d. 1995), where objective truth is concerned, there are three possible relationships: (1) I may believe that the truth exists, and that I know it (+ +). (2) I may believe that the truth exists, but that I am not absolutely certain that I know it, i.e. that I do not know it (+ –). (3) I may believe that the truth does not exist, and that I consequently do not know it(- -). The third possibility is the postmodernist position, all too common in universities and in politics, which leads to humourless cynicism, to hermeneutic, 'emic' relativism, to political correctness, to anti-colonial subjectivism, to the appearance of profundity, and to metatwaddle. It has, however, one advantage: it saves us from the inconveniences of trying to find things out. We can always study our own reactions to, e.g., another person's religion, rather than studying the other person's religion.

The second possibility is the traditional academic outlook, which may be dying out. It is also the philosophical starting point of most Western political parties and of most mainstream Christian churches, and the traditional attitude of Muslim professional religious leaders, the 'Ulamā'. It is widely known that they teach that there are a number of different *madhāhib*, schools of Islamic law; they put their faith in a saying ascribed to the Prophet of Islam: *ikhtilāf ummatī raḥma*, 'differences of opinion in my community are a blessing'. Moreover, their *fatwās* always end with the formula *Wa-'llāhu A'lam*, 'God knows best', or perhaps even 'God knows better'. The first possibility, however, is the fundamentalist position, a position from which death sentences are

[5] Ernest Gellner, *Postmodernism, Reason and Religion*, London 1992.

easily passed and as easily executed. And why should its representatives hesitate to kill, since they know they are right? Are truth and falsehood equally entitled to live?

Ernest Gellner found that within the world of Islam low culture became contaminated by high culture, among other things through the spread of literacy. This contamination he sees as one of the prime causes of the strength of fundamentalism in the modern world of Islam. The ideas and values of Islamic high culture, once the monopoly of a small minority of intellectuals, suddenly appeared to be within reach of the half-literate majority. Action, of the most sanguinary kind, replaced contemplation. Theories reflected upon for centuries in libraries were suddenly turned loose on semi-literates in poor overcrowded run-down neighbourhoods of Arab cities. This new and enthusiastic breed of radicals could see no reason why God's good news should not be applied immediately.

Koran 2:31 reveals how God 'taught Adam all the names'. In this Koranic perception, language is not a human invention as it is in the opening chapters of the Bible[6] but a divine creation. In the same way law, in the perspective of many Muslims, should not be a human invention. The law of the land should conform to the laws revealed by God.

Muslim fundamentalists have made a far-reaching interpretation of this view. In their own words, they believe that

> ....to carry out God's prescripts [is] an obligation for the Muslims. Hence, the establishment of an Islamic State is obligatory.. because something without which what is obligatory cannot be carried out itself becomes obligatory. If such a state cannot be established without war, then this war is an obligation as well.... The laws by which the Muslims are ruled today are [not the laws of Islam but] the laws of Unbelief.... The rulers of this age are [hence] in apostasy from Islam.... An apostate has to be killed even if he is unable to carry arms and go to war.[7]

It is this unusual combination of logic, religion, politics and violence that we are forced to attempt to understand.

The longer one lives, the more numerous become one's debts

[6] Genesis 2:20.

[7] Taken from Farağ, *Fariḍa*, §§ 16, 21 and 25.

to others. I am grateful to Leiden University for making it possible for me to write. I am grateful to a number of wise old men for telling me how to write. I am grateful to my family for allowing me to write. I am grateful to the publishers of this book for taking care of a great number of things.

Leiden/Zwolle
January 1996

JOHANNES J.G. JANSEN

1

THE DUAL NATURE OF ISLAMIC FUNDAMENTALISM

Islamic fundamentalism is both fully politics and fully religion. This is disturbing. Not to respect the boundaries between religion and politics goes against a basic tenet of the modern world.[1] Fundamentalism, so many moderns believe, has to be either political or religious – if it wants to be both at the same time, it should simply not exist. If it is political, it can be fought. If it is religious, constitution or conscience dictate that it should be tolerated. By being both, Islamic fundamentalism forcefully demonstrates the weakness of a cherished modern belief, if not of the modern world itself.

Islamic fundamentalism has already deeply influenced large parts of the world, and may become of even greater significance in the future. Some of the scholarship about it may be reducible to a seven-second soundbite like 'Islamic fundamentalism is the Islamic religious tradition reduced to a power-hungry anti-modern ideology'. Such a characterisation looks convincing, but even though it may be true, it does not do justice to the messianic, religious dream of which Islamic fundamentalism is an integral part.[2] Fundamentalism is a religion narrowed down to an ideology – but it is undeniably a religion too.

It is admittedly important to distinguish between religion and ideology, but the distinction raises a serious problem. It is well known that ideology and religion are both based on propositions that can not be tested. Ideologies demand specific political action,

[1] For a quick introduction to the way in which the churches and the state have worked out an accommodation in Europe and in the United States, see Ruthven, *Supermarket*, 303-15. However, in the history of mankind religion and politics have not always been so neatly separated (Chidester, *Salvation*, 165). See, e.g., Burridge, *New Heaven/New Earth*.

[2] Bruce B. Lawrence, *Defenders of God*, is an erudite but verbose statement of the politically correct position that fundamentalism is a reduction of religion into ideology.

and religions are supposed not to do so. Nevertheless, religions also demand a particular kind of behaviour from believers. They ask people to do certain things: to fast, pray or visit holy places. Why, a philosopher might well ask, is this different from admonishing them to do certain other things, like helping to build the nation or supporting the proletariat in its class-war against capitalism? Why is asking for racial equality or equal opportunities different from asking for application of the Koranic punishments? Is the demand for the Islamisation of a society a religious or a political-ideological demand?

To discount and disqualify Islamic fundamentalism as religion because it is an ideology that requires action may thus be problematic, since Islam itself, like any other religion, also requires deeds. Fundamentalists do aspire to come to power.[3] However, power in the perception of Islamic fundamentalism is not something that can be divided or shared with other groups, persons or institutions. Fundamentalists, perhaps in imitation of the secular regimes they want to replace, see power as indivisible. The different fundamentalist movements want the very power which the governments they oppose exercise: total power, complete power, supreme power, over anyone or anything that even contemplates resisting them.

Whereas in the West modern elections have often created situations in which powerful rulers had to reconcile themselves to a sharing of power, this has rarely happened in the Arab world. Hence, the belief in the indivisibility of power is general and absolute, among both the fundamentalists and many of those who hold power at the present time. This makes a compromise between the present regimes and the Islamic fundamentalists difficult to envisage. It may make sense to ascribe to the fundamentalists a belief in the indivisibility of the power of the modern nation-state, but there may be another contributing factor that has to be considered. The mere acceptance of the existence of the modern nation-state is something relatively new in the world of Islam. In the Middle East nation-states only came into being at the end of the colonial period, and at first the character of such states was not generally appreciated by their subjects.

Even around 1980 it was widely discussed in the Kuwaiti press

[3] On Christian fundamentalism and its desire for power, Ruthven, *Divine Supermarket*, ch. 10, esp. p. 206.

whether real Islam, *al-islām* al-*ḥaqīqī*, did not prescribe the rule of an individual, *ḥukm al-fard*. Many believed that the rejection or acceptance of democracy was the real issue of these discussions.[4] Although the Kuwaiti ruling family, not known for its love of democracy, must have had a strong interest in the outcome of the debate, the deeper issue of the polemic appears to have been whether Islam and the nation-state are compatible at all. In past centuries, the Islamic world has known many movements that called for either the reform of an existing imperfect, traditional Islamic state or the enthronement of an alternative just ruler and messiah. However, since its foundation in the late 1920s the Muslim Brotherhood demanded something different and much more sophisticated. While assuming modern political forms and processes, it called for an *Islamic form of the nation-state*:[5] a state where, in one form or another, Islamic law would be the law of the land. It may well have been the first Islamic organisation to do so.

In such a perspective Islamic fundamentalism may be interpreted as an attempt at Islamisation of the modern nation-state. It would certainly not be the first Islamisation attempt in history. Historians are aware that Islam absorbed the systems of law which existed in the Middle East before the advent of the Muslim invaders. The Islamic sharīʿa represents the successful Islamisation of the pre-Islamic legal systems of the region. The same is true of Islamic philosophy. Muslim philosophers have Islamised the Greek philosophical tradition. Even today Aristotle cannot be studied without Ibn Sīnā (d. 1037) and Ibn Rushd (d. 1198), two Muslim philosophers better known in the West by their Latin names Avicenna and Averroes. Similarly a variety of pre-Islamic religious phenomena were successfully Islamised by generations of Islamic thinkers.

The process of Islamisation of the modern nation-state appears to have been started by Ḥasan al-Bannā and the Muslim Brotherhood. Since the 1930s and '40s, the Brotherhood has grown into three different things. First, it ripened into a regular parliamentary opposition, as the Egyptian elections of 1984 showed. It also became a movement of social engineering that occupied itself with, among other things, Islamic banking. Thirdly, a number

4 Fu'ād Zakariyyā, *Ṣaḥwa*, 114.

5 Zubaida, *Islam*, 155; Jansen, 'Preaching', 192.

of revolutionary groups that subsided into primitive rebellion also have to be seen as a continuation of the Muslim Brotherhood. None of these changes may be anything more than specific cases of general socio-economic political processes[6] which are also observable elsewhere.

The 1979 Islamic Revolution in Iran, despite its anti-Western rhetoric, similarly accepted the existence of the modern Western nation-state as legal – its use of the word 'republic' betrays this. Up till the twentieth century, the world of Islam was ruled by dynasties, whose rule was accepted – or not accepted – by Muslim religious leaders, the 'Ulamā' and Āyatollāhs. In founding an *Islamic republic* Khomeini carried out his most daring and perhaps most lasting innovation.[7]

The fundamentalists in the Middle East imitate their enemies, the existing regimes, in more ways than one. Apart from the belief in the indivisibility of power, making no distinction between long-term and short-term goals is a conspicuous characteristic of the fundamentalist ideologies. The fundamentalist worldview generally does not distinguish between long-term aspirations, ideals or a grand design on the one hand, and short-term detailed policy goals on the other.[8] To be effective, the aspiration to achieve power, like wanting to become rich, should be subdivided into smaller, humbler goals that are attainable. Such goals might include creating a party from which a future cadre might be selected, trying to agree on the first social and economic revolutionary measures, or forming a broadly-based coalition that might serve as a transitional government. The tendency of Islamic fundamentalist movements not to believe in the need to distinguish between ideal far-away goals and realistic immediate goals in the pursuit of power may contribute to internal conflicts once they achieve power. Again the fundamentalist movement may have taken this position in imitation of its enemies, the secularist regimes which it wants to supplant. These regimes too – for example, in their conflict with Israel – have for many years kept to the position that both grand design and immediate policy should be focused on the destruction of Israel. Such unity of abstract design and

[6] Zubaida, *Islam*, 123.
[7] Cf. Zubaida, *Islam*, 59.
[8] Cf. Harkabi, *Fateful Hour*, 2.

concrete policy is difficult to sustain in politics, as it is in private life.

Since the Islamic fundamentalists so fervently hope to achieve power, one has to assume that their day-to-day activities are being closely watched by a variety of secret services. The personnel of such services have received sophisticated training, but only rarely has this training included theology. Nevertheless, we need a theologian's outlook to understand what fundamentalism is about. Fundamentalism is not a protest against being poor. To think so is simply unsophisticated. Nevertheless, the tenacity of the unsophisticated approach does great honour to the intellectual influence of Marxism, but people do not turn fundamentalist because they are destitute. Poverty cannot cause fundamentalism. Prosperity does not cure it. Moreover, Islamic fundamentalism is not about taking the scriptures literally. It is a set of beliefs that draws modern political power into the realm of religion; it offers a religious approach to political power. It wants power in order to coerce mankind into obeying God's commands; it even wants to enforce the advent of the Kingdom of God itself. In such a Kingdom the literal truth of the revealed divine book will be a minor, self-evident detail.

Islamic fundamentalism is very much a creation of an Islamic religious imagination. Nevertheless, it is also an ideology, but as such it differs in an important way from ideologies like nationalism, feminism or communism. These profane ideologies may, one has to admit, impress outsiders as being partly religious in character. They may occasionally employ primordial religious techniques, and may have adapted religious techniques of persuasion. Among their supporters such ideologies may evoke strong emotions, which to outsiders which have the unmistakable look of being religious. They may even have created congregations which the believers themselves innocently call parties. Such a party may, for instance, employ a canon of songs or scriptures, and may posses the equivalent of monks, martyrs, popes and bishops. Its members may firmly believe in a revolutionary Day of Judgement. They may even believe that they are the Elect.

Nevertheless, such ideologies remain this-worldly. They are not concerned with the Hereafter, and do not rise above the observable world or concern themselves with an existence that is not of this world. Even when they contain religious elements they are not a universal religious dream or a part of such a dream. However, Islamic fundamentalism is a religious dream. It is concerned with the observable world and has designs for it, but it is also very much concerned with the Hereafter. Islamic fundamentalism heavily depends on Islam, but is *not* identical to it although in several ways they are similar. For instance, Islamic fundamentalism classifies individuals as human or subhuman in the same way as Islam does. Like Islam, it sentences subhuman persons (apostates) to death. However, it goes several steps further than Islam: as the recent history of Algeria and Egypt shows, it actually executes those sentences.

Like Islam itself, Islamic fundamentalism demands application of the prescripts of Islamic law, the sharī'a. However, Islam demands for its representatives, the 'Ulamā', the right to censure a Muslim ruler who does not apply the sharī'a properly.[9] Islamic fundamentalism, on the other hand, demands much more – namely the authority to oversee the application of the law of the land which, as a matter of course, has to conform to the sharī'a. It wants to exercise supreme political power, and leaves no room for a *sulṭān*, whether he calls himself president or king.

A number of authorities believe that it is not possible to make a valid distinction between mainstream Islam and Islamic fundamentalism. If one does exist between these two, they suggest, it is only a matter of degree. Does this mean that Islam itself can be blamed for the violence ascribed to the Islamic fundamentalists? Some argue that, regrettably, it can not be denied that some violence has indeed been used by Islamic fundamentalists, but they hint that this could have merely been counter-violence against an aggressive government that wanted to suppress the truth. The Egyptian journalist Fahmī Huwaydī thinks Islam and violence can never be separate, nor should they be. Islam, he believes, needs a state, and states use violence. He quotes with approval Ibn Ḥazm (d. 1064) who is believed to have written that all Muslim denominations have always agreed that it is obligatory to have an *Imām*: *ittafaq al-ğamī' 'alā wuğūb al-imāma*. 'To have an Imām', Fahmī Huwaydī argues, nowadays means nothing, and today this has to be translated as setting up a state, *iqāmat dawla*.

The separation between politics and religion which the West,

[9] Cf. e.g., Olivier Roy, *Failure*, 29.

according to Fahmī Huwaydī,[10] wants to force upon the Middle East, is a lie because it does not even exist in Europe itself: all over Europe Christian parties are active and even hold power, and in England the monarch is the 'supreme head' of the church. In Poland, South Africa and Latin America the churches are deeply involved in political struggles, the Pope is (so Fahmī Huwaydī argues) head of the Vatican state, and Archbishop Makarios ruled Cyprus as ethnarch and president. The force of Huwaydī's argument is weakened a little by a proposition he expounds on the next page of his book: that the basic difference between Islamic and Western culture is the separation between religion and the state. In the West, he explains, this separation has been the natural result of a long and bloody struggle which was not necessary in the world of Islam.

Fahmī Huwaydī believes that it is not difficult to justify the use of force in the service of Islam and that one of the most exciting aspects of the Islam solution[11] is the slogan 'to command the laudable and to forbid the disreputable', *al-amr bi-'l-ma'rūf wa-'l-nahy ani 'l-munkar.*[11] This is not a slogan, he boasts, made up by an extremist ayatollah, but a phrase in the Koran, 'which means that it comes from God and His messenger, peace be upon him'. This slogan is the 'essential key to the solution, and its cornerstone', *al-miftāḥ al-asāsī li-'l-ḥall wa-ḥağar al-zāwiya fīhi.*

The authoritative medieval theologian Abū Ḥāmid Al-Ghazālī (d. 1111), Fahmī Huwaydī proudly explains,[12] already called the duty to command to do the laudable the 'summit of religion', *al-quṭb fī 'l-dīn;* God has sent his Prophets for this purpose. In Koran 3:104 it becomes clear that the command to do what is laudable imposes a collective duty on the Muslim community. This means that when some execute it, others do not have to do so. In other words, once the members of an Islamic government command, others can rest assured that the Islamic duty to command is not neglected. The text of the relevant verse from the Koran runs: 'Let there be formed of you a community inviting to good, commanding what is laudable, and restraining [others] from what is disreputable.' To command others without having authority over them is laughable; therefore, modern Muslims need an Islamic

10 Huwaydī, *Tadayyun*, 79.

11 Ibid., 83-7.

12 Huwaydī, *Tadayyun*, 84.

government and a modern, powerful Islamic state. It is this government alone which will fulfill the duty to command its subjects to do what is laudable, and forbid them to do what is disreputable. Muslim religious leaders will define and decide what is laudable and what is disreputable.

Fahmī Huwaydī addresses an Arab public, many of whom might be convinced by his arguments. His book went through several editions. However, some readers of his apologetics might be tempted to overlook the exegetical embellishments. They may be reminded of the criminal lawyer who argued that his client did not commit violence; and that *if* he did, he was forced to, and if he was *not* so forced, he was after all fully entitled to commit violence. Even if one accepts the validity of Fahmī Huwaydī's arguments, it is difficult to see how they can be sustained in a modern industrial multi-ethnic multi-religious multicultural society.

Also non-Muslim observers sometimes argue that no valid distinction exists between Islam and Islamic fundamentalism.[13] However, it is the understanding of the ideal role of the 'Ulamā' which visibly separates the two. In a fundamentalist state the measures the government takes or proposes to take cannot be subject to criticism by the 'Ulamā', whereas in the Muslim world such criticism is commonplace. An over-publicised example of such censure is the constant spate of rumours emanating from Saudi Arabia[14] about frictions between the Saudi royal family and the Saudi 'Ulamā', between *umarā'* and *'ulamā'*, 'princes' and 'scholars'. Such rumours are not an indication that 'in reality' Saudi Arabia is an Islamic fundamentalist state or would soon become one – if its present government did not suppress Islamism. On the contrary, such frictions between government and clergy indicate that Saudi Arabia is to a certain extent a traditional Muslim state[15] where the hierarchy of the government and the religious hierarchy both have their own aspirations, their own spaces, their own buildings and their own institutions.

Of course, the alleged Saudi sponsorship of fundamentalist movements outside Saudi Arabia needs to be explained. Would the

13 E.g. Moshe Sharon, 'The Islamic Factor'.

14 Saïd K. Aburish, *The Rise, Corruption and Coming Fall of the House of Saud*, London 1994, gives an interesting but not always fully convincing picture of Saudi Arabia.

15 Cf., e.g., Sandra Mackey, *The Saudis*, New York 1987, 96.

Saudi rulers rather live with fundamentalism than with democracy? Does their regime naively hope to control and eventually deradicalise modern Islamic fundamentalism? An American observer suggests that this is so.[16] Nasser's sponsorship of revolutionary unrest outside Egypt supplies an interesting parallel. Egypt in the days of Nasser was internally one of the most orderly countries in the world, but his regime at the same time supported attempts to create unrest elsewhere.

Some of the Saudi family plenipotentiaries may argue that their freedom of action is somewhat curtailed by the United States. They do not really mind this, and are willing and able to live with this American supervision, but if religious unrest in the region – outside Saudi Arabia, of course – keeps the Americans busy, the Saudi policy-makers would not see this as a problem. On the contrary, it might even make the Americans more appreciative of the support the House of Saud gives to their interests.

Modern dictatorships like those of Syria and Iraq, unlike the Saudi regime, do not trust that eventually the Ulema will collaborate with the government in power. For a start, dictatorships do not allow anyone to criticise their own infinite goodness. Therefore they also suppress the criticism which emanates from the circles of the 'Ulamā'. Several examples show that this creates considerable tension and may easily lead to unpredictable explosions of Islamist action.[17] Especially when there is even a modest decline in a country's prosperity,[18] situations can deteriorate and quickly become destabilised. Such sudden changes usually benefit the Islamic fundamentalists.

Mainstream Muslims and fundamentalist Muslims have little or no difference of opinion over belief and its content, or over the proper forms of worship and devotion. The fundamentalists, however, will not attribute great importance to these dimensions of Islam, or to knowledge and understanding of the central elements of its religious culture, which 'have no need for much study'.[19] But they appear to emphasise another dimension of islam. They reproach mainstream Muslims for underestimating the importance

[16] Edward G. Shirley, 'Iran's Present', 43.

[17] E.g. Hama in Syria in 1982.

[18] Algeria's GNP went down, but only slightly, in 1986. Disturbances followed on 5-9 October 1988 that were ruthlessly suppressed.

[19] Cf. Farağ, *Farīḍa*, 64, in Jansen, *Neglected Duty*, 189.

of *ǧihād*, the armed struggle against unbelief, and for not attaching great value to waging war against the enemies of God. To true fundamentalists, the other, more spiritual meanings of *ǧihād*[20] are unimportant, or at least much less important than the specific martial meanings of the term.

Islamic fundamentalists hold a radically different view on how to behave towards the world in which they live. They expect a better world to come, which they believe can only be reached through armed struggle. Consequently, they are at war with the world and may well die waging war against it and its unbelief. If they do, they will be compensated by being blessed in paradise and obtain an exceptional place in the other world. The belief in a heavenly reward for martyrdom existed in Judaism and Christianity as well[21] but has long since been forgotten. Its persistence in modern fundamentalist Islam is one of the main reasons why the public perceives the latter as alien and threatening.

Islamic fundamentalists do not agree with mainstream Islam over Islamic religious organisation and the position of the 'Ulamā'. They do not recognise the special authority of the 'Ulamā', whom they regard as not modern enough to play a role in the Islamisation of the modern world, and as being corrupted by the un-Islamic governments that must be replaced by the fundamentalist visionaries. When individuals from among the 'Ulamā' bless the actions of the fundamentalist activists and sanction them by giving a *fatwā* to that effect, the fundamentalists feel joy, but if such help is not forthcoming their fighters will go ahead anyway.

On the position of the 'Ulamā', Iranian Shī'ī fundamentalists hold opposite views to those of their Arab Sunnī friends and colleagues. According to them the 'Ulamā' and the Ayatollahs, as the representatives of Islam, are not inept and irrelevant; on the contrary, they are the supreme authority in the universe, and state and politics fall entirely within the sphere of their absolute, divinely ordained authority. This view, popularly ascribed to Khomeini, became known as the *Wilāyat al-faqīh* doctrine.[22] This illustrates that over Islamic religious organisation the Shī'ī Iranian

[20] Like struggle against one's own soul or against the Devil, see Farağ, *Farīḍa*, 88, in Jansen, *Neglected Duty*, 200.

[21] Cf. Stark and Bainbridge, *Future*, 9-10; and Wensinck, 'Martyrs', 111.

[22] Cf. Khomeini, *Al-Ḥukūma al-Islāmiyya*, 3. *Wilāya*: supremacy. *Wilāyat:* the supremacy of. *Al-faqīh*: scholar of Islamic law.

fundamentalists and Sunnī Arab fundamentalists disagree with each other and with mainstream Islam. The functions which in these three perspectives have to be fulfilled by the Islamic men of religion differ considerably. But does this provide sufficient grounds to claim that Islamic fundamentalism is a new religion, distinct from Islam?

Whether Islamic fundamentalism is distinct from Islam is an important question for citizens of the Arab world and the professionals who police them. For the former it is not simply a matter of an academic definition: it may decide the rather existential question of whether they will be hanged, imprisoned or left alone. It is also an important question for the European and American academic thought-police who have appointed themselves to pass judgement on political correctness: obviously Islam, like Christianity and Judaism, is a religion that has to be tolerated in an open society, but does this tolerance extend to Islamic fundamentalism too? It may have to do so if Islamic fundamentalism is a legitimate form of Islam, but not if it is a separate religion, or not a religion at all but an ideology.

To those for whom such concerns are not of immediate relevance it is clear that Islamic fundamentalism shares its corpus of holy texts and its systems of belief and worship with Islam, but its systems of behaviour and organisation are not the same. Does this make it into a separate religion? Whatever the correct answer to this question, it is obvious from considerations like these that by all conceivable standards Islamic fundamentalism is a religion and not a mere political ideology. It is a religion concerned with earthly power. At the same time, it is also a political movement and an ideology. Modern political science categories do not fit and are irrelevant.

Islamic fundamentalism, as it has been manifested since the mid-1970s, is new if only because it is concerned with the modern state. The modern state did not come into being until the nineteenth and twentieth centuries, and it would be absurd to argue that fundamentalism pre-existed its object. Its object, however, does not merely exist; the modern state has become omnipresent, omniscient and omnipotent. How could an entity possessing these three properties avoid becoming the object of a religion and being fervently worshipped, especially when its existence is beyond any doubt?

Most Muslims and most orientalists agree that the political and religious spheres were not separate in the golden age of Islam, the period of Mohammed (d. 632) and his immediate successors, the rightly guided Caliphs (632-61).[23] According to Jean-Claude Barreau,[24] Mohammed was culturally a contemporary of Abraham, the Patriarch who leaves Haran (Genesis 12) for the land that God will show him. The type of world in which we have to imagine Abraham, Barreau tells us, was so primitive that no distinction between politics and religion could have made sense there, and the same holds true, he suggests, for the world of Mohammed and his successors in Medina.

This may be true, but there is a difference between Mohammed's situation in Muslim tradition and Abraham's situation as portrayed in the Book of Genesis. The biblical text does not picture Abraham as a military leader or as a leader of more men than his own immediate household. Mohammed, however, leads many more men than his immediate household, and much of his time is taken up with military matters. If his society has to be equated with a society described in biblical episodes, it is the Book of Judges which comes to mind. The Judges lead military campaigns against the enemies of the believers, they are God's prophets, and they lead many more men than their own household.

However this may be, in the decades after Mohammed's arrival in Medina in 622, supreme religious and political authority went together in the same way as in the days of the Judges. This idyllic situation did not last: the Caliphs, after some time, lost their religious authority to the Ulema and their political authority to the Sultans.[25] This did not invalidate the paradigm of the Golden Age in Medina, since it is a religious paradigm. Its historicity is hardly relevant.

However, it does mean that during the many centuries preceding the European conquest of the Muslim world, the world of Islam effectively knew a separation of politics and religion;[26] these enjoyed their own spaces, even though as a matter of course they recognised

[23] See the discussion in Ira Lapidus, 'The Separation of State and Religion in the Development of Early Muslim Society', *International Journal of Middle East Studies*, 1975, 363-85.

[24] Barreau, *De l'Islam*, 30.

[25] Patricia Crone and Martin Hinds, *God's Caliph*.

[26] Cf. Ira Lapidus, 'Separation' (1975); and, e.g., Ann K.S. Lambton, 'Quis Custodiet Custodes?', *Studia Islamica*, V, 1956, 125-48; Kerr, *Reform*, 48.

each other's existence and influenced each other. Islam has created a world in which society exists more or less independently of the state.[27] It goes without saying that to the inhabitants of such a world politics and religion are distinct abstractions.

Islamic fundamentalism wants to undo this time-honoured separation, to bring politics and religion together in the way that things were in the exemplary days of the Prophet. It not only *wishes* to do so: its activists and thinkers have carried on fierce struggles against the existing regimes and the regimes have fought back. The situation in Egypt in the early 1960s, culminating in the execution of Sayyid Quṭb in 1966, did not get much international attention at the time but according to many observers came close to being a civil war. The situation in Algiers in the years following the annulment of the 1991/2 elections did get international media attention, and no observer ever doubted that it was a civil war.

Islamic fundamentalism came into being slowly at the end of the nineteenth century, growing to adulthood in the twentieth. Only in the late 1970s did it become a generally recognised phenomenon; before the 1970s it was almost completely absent from Western reports. It is not mentioned at all in a book of 320 pages by William Polk, *The United States and the Arab World*, published in 1965. According to Senator Frank Church, this book was 'a valuable introduction to the Middle East' containing 'worthwhile ... information for any person involved in determining American policy'. The author, at the time of writing the book, was a member of the Policy Planning Council of the US Department of State, and professor of Near Eastern Languages and History at Harvard University. According to him, the 'greatest of the merits of Islam is that it has been able to retain the simplicity of its beginnings. [...] To be or to become a Muslim', he concludes, 'is easy.'[28]

The second example of the relative invisibility of Islamic fundamentalism dates from 1967, two years after Polk's book, the confident tone of which no scholar can fail to envy. Dr Arnold Hottinger (b. 1926) is an unusually well-informed scholar and journalist who was Middle East correspondent for the *Neue Zürcher Zeitung* from 1961 till 1991. In 1993 he published a well-documented study of Islamic fundamentalism. Nevertheless,

[27] Ruthven, *Islam*, 158.

[28] Polk, *Arab World*, 46.

in the general book about the region which he published in 1967 he discussed that subject in exactly one page, and concluded that it had been unsuccessful because 'important parts of the population' were no longer interested in 'purely Islamic slogans' and thought that 'religion should have as little as possible to do with politics'.[29]

The earliest report in a Western language on the coming of age of Islamic fundamentalism appears to be an article by Bernard Lewis[30] in the monthly *Commentary*, written in the fall of 1975. Its title, 'The Return of Islam', made it possible for those who had lacked prescience to point out that Islam had never been away. Islam, Professor Lewis pointed out,[31] 'is already very effective as a limiting factor and may yet become a powerful domestic political force if the right kind of leadership emerges.' The right kind of leadership soon emerged: Khomeini came to power early in 1979. Nevertheless several professional students of Islam could not believe that their favourite religion had given birth to something as unpopular as Islamic fundamentalism. Even at the end of 1979, almost a year after Khomeini's revolution, the Amsterdam scholar Rudolph Peters expressed the considered opinion that 'at present the political role of jihad seems to lie exclusively in the field of propaganda with regard to the Arab-Israeli conflict.'[32] As late as 1987 a professor in the Leiden theological faculty brought the imminent fall of the Iranian fundamentalist regime to the attention of two local newspapers.[33] The two papers solemnly printed these prophecies but other newspapers all over the world missed the scoop.

The late 1970s and the 1980s also saw an infertile discussion on the question whether it was proper to use the term 'fundamentalism' of developments taking place in the world of Islam. Was this term not much too simplistic to give adequate expression to such a complicated phenomenon? In a way the discussion on the word 'fundamentalism' echoes the discussion once caused by the invention of the telephone. Would not the

[29] Hottinger, *Fellachen*, 32-3.

[30] Bernard Lewis, 'The Return of Islam', *Commentary*, vol. 61, no. 1, January 1976, 39-49.

[31] Bernard Lewis, 'The Return of Islam' in Curtis, *Religion and Politics*, 28.

[32] Rudolph Peters, *Islam and Colonialism: The Doctrine of Jihad in Modern History*, The Hague: Mouton, 1979, 158.

[33] The Amsterdam daily *De Volkskrant*, October 24, 1987, and the Leiden daily *Leidsch Dagblad*, November 14, 1987.

term 'telephone' be much too simplistic? Would it do justice to the beauty and the many possibilities of the device? How about 'speaking telegraph' or 'electrical speaking telephone'?[34]

Both Muslims and friends of the Islamic world feared that the word 'fundamentalism' had too much of a Christian flavour. Did it not stem from a North American Christian milieu, and was it not actually coined around 1920, and then by a journalist?[35] Would not a term like 'revolutionary extremist neotraditionalist ultra-Islamic radicalism' be preferable?

When asked to define this beautiful alternative, scholars usually produced a description very similar to what others have called 'fundamentalism'.[36] In 1989 the American scholar Bruce B. Lawrence[37] published a justification of the use of the term 'fundamentalism' that must have convinced even the most stubborn. When, moreover, it became known that in Arabic the terms *uṣūlī* and *uṣūliyya* (meaning respectively 'fundamentalist' and 'fundamentalism', two derivatives from *uṣūl*, 'origins') had become commonplace, this scholarly debate on terminology came to a quiet end.

The theory of revitalisation movements proposed by the American Anthony F.C. Wallace[38] in 1956 suggests that a variety of threats to a society can produce greatly increased stress on its members. 'Military defeat, political subordination and extreme pressure toward acculturation' may result in 'internal cultural conflict'. These words by Wallace read like an exact description of what has happened to the Arab world in the last two centuries. Could it be argued that modern Islamic fundamentalism is just another occurrence of a revitalisation movement of the type Wallace identified? Is it a special case of such a movement?

In describing revitalisation movements Wallace attached great value to the 'religious vision experience *per se*'. Does modern Islamic fundamentalism have such a dream? In the history of religion examples of such dream visions abound: a crucified Lord who has risen to appear to those who love him, an angel calling the unsuspecting Prophet, a table descending from heaven etc.

[34] See, e.g., Bill Bryson, *Made in America*, London (Minerva Paperback) 1995, 112.

[35] Lawrence, *Defenders*, 166.

[36] Marty and Appleby, *Fundamentalisms*, viii.

[37] His *Defenders of God*.

[38] Wallace, 'Revitalization', 269; cf. Stark and Bainbridge, *Future*, 177.

In Islamic fundamentalist statements we read that the world will be filled with 'fairness and justice after it has been filled with injustice and oppression', and that after 'the return of Islam' the Muslim world will have 'a brilliant future both economically and agriculturally'. These statements[39] may sound a little prosaic, but in the modern Middle East fairness, justice and prosperity are met with too often in dreams only. To hope for a better world 'both economically and agriculturally' may well be judged as a dream.

The revitalisation concept is less useful in analysing fundamentalism than one would wish, since in the revitalisation analysis proposed by Wallace little or no attention is paid to political power. This may reflect the circumstances in which Wallace did his research and his thinking – he conducted his investigations among American Indians who were much weaker than the United States which surrounded them and threatened their existence. In the 1940s and '50s no observer could have imagined that political or military force would in any way benefit the American Indians in their struggle with the United States.

One also has to assume that Wallace took it for granted that political or social change could be brought about without the application of force or violence. In the Middle East this cannot be assumed. The power of the state may hold back change, or work for change that is not deemed desirable; hence the question of the modern state and its power is central to all discussions of modern Islamic fundamentalism. This prevents the term 'revitalisation' from becoming the accepted term – although the analysis of religion which Wallace proposes together with his revitalisation concept is illuminating.

In the early 1940s the American Ralph Linton introduced the word 'nativism' to describe the amalgam of feelings experienced by someone who senses that his world, his culture and his way of life are being threatened by another culture, in which situation

> ...certain current or remembered elements of culture are selected for emphasis and given symbolic value. The more distinctive such elements are with respect to other culture...the greater their potential value as symbols of the society's unique character.

A 'nativistic' movement, in Linton's definition, is any 'conscious

39 Farağ, *Farīda*, 13 and 14.

organised attempt on the part of a society's members to revive or perpetuate selected aspects of its culture'.

Although the Islamic fundamentalism of the late 1970s was three and a half decades in the future when Linton wrote these lines, they apply almost miraculously. What better and more distinctive symbol of the unique character of Islamic society could one wish for than the Islamic sharīʿa? Linton's nativism concept suggests that the emphasis placed by modern Islam and modern Islamic fundamentalism on the sharīʿa is almost unavoidable. Moreover, what could be more distinctive than the special position which the 'Ulamā' and Ayatollahs hold in the world of Islam? Khomeini's vision of the universal supremacy of these functionaries is an excellent illustration of what Linton must have meant when proposing his nativism concept.

Nevertheless, the term 'nativism' is not likely to replace the by now familiar term fundamentalism, not only because it would be an unfamiliar or awkward term, but because of the limitations which Linton put on this concept. In the article describing the concept, he does not once use the word 'religion'. He is concerned with conflicts between cultures, and in his perspective religion is, one assumes, part of a culture. Whether this is wrong or not depends entirely on how one uses the words 'culture' and 'religion'. But a concept which, for whatever reason, does not take into account the religious nature of what we now call Islamic fundamentalism had, or has, little chance of becoming the accepted term for the phenomenon, no matter how much insight into its character it provides. It seems that for better or worse we are stuck with 'fundamentalism'.

We read in Koran 22:38–41: 'God will defend those who have believed, God does not love the false, the infidel.'[40] Nevertheless in the course of the nineteenth century the false and the infidel established their rule over the world of Islam, which by the end of the century was almost wholly occupied by Western, foreign rulers. What had happened to the Koranic promise? Could the Koran have been wrong – or misunderstood? Or had God decided to punish the believers for their neglect of His Word?

Many Muslims must have concluded that Islam and the Koran simply had been wrong, but of course the punishment which

[40] *Inna llāha yudāfiʿu ʿani lladhīna āmanū, Inna llāha lā yuḥibbu kulla khawānin kafūr.*

Islam prescribes for apostasy is an important reason why few Muslims have declared themselves to be ex-Muslims: only few are eager to be martyred for not believing in a reward for martyrdom. However, there is another reason why Muslims have hesitated to become ex-Muslims, namely that in the world of Islam ethics are firmly based on religion. In secularised Europe and America it is imaginable for humans to behave properly without finding or even looking for a justification for doing so in religion.[41] In the world of Islam, on the other hand, to declare that one has no religion might easily be understood as declaring that one has no ethics. Being perceived as unethical is not conducive to a healthy social life. And whereas people are perfectly able to live without religion, they are not able to live without a social life. Consequently, open apostasy from Islam has always been rare.

Reinterpretation, the second solution to the dilemma, assumed that the Muslims for centuries had misunderstood their own Islam and the Koran. Of course, such a prolonged misunderstanding is unlikely, and by its very nature this solution could never be popular. However, among intellectuals it did, all the same, have a certain appeal and in their circles led to a variety of reinterpretations of the Koran, Islam and Islamic law. However, such attempts at reaching a new understanding of Islam were not popular with the Ulema who, with the help of the authorities, often succeeded in suppressing such views. Muḥammad Abū Zayd[42] came into conflict with the established Ulema in 1930, Muḥammad Aḥmad Khalafallāh[43] did so in 1947, and there are many other examples up to the present.

Why did the authorities invariably condescend to do the 'Ulamā''s bidding? Did they themselves believe in the traditional interpretation (or rather, interpretations) of Islam, and think that the interests of law, order and stability would be served by opposing religious change? But whereas the 'Ulamā' need the authorities, if only to get their salaries paid, the authorities in their turn need the 'Ulamā': when they declare war or peace, nationalise or denationalise the economy, or are taking or considering great national decisions, the 'Ulamā' are called in to give their blessing to the proposed measures. Their approval serves socially almost

[41] A classic example is the hero of Albert Camus' novel *La Peste* (1947).

[42] J.J.G. Jansen, 'Muḥammad Abū Zayd'.

[43] Wielandt, *Offenbarung*, 134–52.

as a substitute for parliamentary approval. Governments in the Muslim world do not feel safe when their policies are not formally approved by the 'Ulamā'.

The 'Ulamā' give this approval on a condition. Whenever something is written or said, let alone preached, that touches upon what they regard as their own vital interests, the government is supposed to take vigorous action, and to use its powers of censorship and suppression. Since the substance of this type of dispute does not come within the sphere of what interests men in power, the authorities in these cases usually succumb to pressure from the 'Ulamā'. In the short run this is a wise policy that contributes to the general stability of society, but in the long run it prevents religious change and obstructs the adaptation of religion to its changing environment. This is dangerous and contributes to the general instability of the region.

The third, intellectually least problematic solution was that God had decided to punish His people for their neglect of the Islamic and Koranic duties which He had ordered believers to take upon themselves. This divine punishment consisted of their being militarily occupied by the false and the infidel. It followed that the false and the infidel would automatically be removed from their positions of power over the Muslim world once the Muslims returned to Islam and its laws. It was in this way that the Muslim world got bound up with the dream of the return to Islam with a Gordian knot of politics and religion.

The idea that failure in war and occupation by foreigners is a divine punishment dates back at least to ancient Israel. We meet with it in the Book of Judges[44] and in numerous other places:

> And the anger of the Lord was hot against Israel, and he delivered them into the hands of spoilers that spoiled them, and he sold them into the hands of their enemies round about, so that they could not any longer stand before their enemies. Whithersoever they went out, the hand of the Lord was against them for evil, as the Lord had said, and as the Lord had sworn unto them: and they were greatly distressed.
>
> ....
>
> And the anger of the Lord was hot against Israel; and he

[44] Judges 2:14 and 20-1, in the 'Authorized Version' (1611) of the Bible.

said, Because that this people hath transgressed my covenant which I commanded their fathers, and have not hearkened unto my voice; I will not henceforth drive out any from before them of the nations which Joshua left when he died: ....

In the Bible we see an endless alternation of injustice perpetrated by conquerors and injustice suffered by those who are conquered: the inevitable fluctuations of fortune in wars of conquest are not the random result of circumstances but the result of a divine reaction to the obedience or disobedience of the Elect. We are even asked to regard the cruel infidel Nebuchadnezzar as the instrument of God[45] when he robs God's own temple in Jerusalem.

In Koran 3:138(132)-175(169) we hear a not identical but very similar argument surrounding the battle of Uḥud, where in March 625 the Muslim army fought unsuccessfully against the pagans from Mecca, led by Abū Sufyān. According to the Koran, the success of the Meccan enemies of Islam was caused by God's wish 'that He might know the believers' (Koran 3:166). Here too the outcome was to the advantage of the enemies of God, but this was by God's own decisions. In his epoch-making article on nativism, Linton points out that when things do not gō well, leaders come forward who can explain the community's misfortune: if the community had respected its ancient values, things would not have gone wrong. Decline and disaster are caused by neglect of the old ways; the community has 'broken the covenant' and is thus being punished with defeat, occupation and humiliation.

The Biblical, Koranic and nativist model all give plausibility to the belief that the introduction or, perhaps, *re*introduction, of all details of the sharīʿa as the national system of law is sound policy. Once the sharīʿa is applied in its entirety, many think, Islam and the Muslims will return to their ancient glory and get the better of their enemies. This complete and total application of Islam can only be attained by a Muslim government, since the implementation of a system of law is not an individual matter: only strong governments can enforce it, and such governments can only be formed after struggle, *ǧihād*, against the existing regimes. Good Muslims, it is widely believed, should admonish their co-religionists to take part in these struggles. Again we are forced

45 Cf., e.g., Lodge, *Write On*, 163, and references.

to witness how religion and politics are being intertwined beyond hope of reversal.

In the Biblical and the nativist models, the chosen respectively show wilful neglect for the divine covenant and the ancient values of their community. Most Muslim thinkers have argued that the Muslims too have wilfully neglected the implementation of God's greatest gift to them: the sharī'a. With some, however, the theory takes an unexpected twist. It is no longer the religious laxity of the Muslims themselves that is to blame for the neglect of the sharī'a and the consequent decline of Islam; some have argued that the Muslims were forced by the overwhelming power of colonialism and imperialism to abandon their sharī'a, and that the decline this has caused is thus the fault not of the Muslims, but of those colonialists and imperialists, who after all are enemies of God and His religion.

If this is true, God has punished the Muslims for being forced to abandon the sharī'a under European and American, colonialist and imperialist pressure – punishment which, in human terms, is unjust. The doctrine that the sharī'a was neglected because of the wickedness and superior military force of the West has an obvious consequence. Some Islamic activists will argue that any anti-Western actions will weaken the West because the West has to respond. They now even have reason to believe that any weakening of the West may contribute to the reinstatement of the sharī'a. As a matter of course, effective anti-Western action is best, but many will welcome any anti-Western action since any weakening of the West contributes directly or indirectly to the implementation of the sharī'a.

The West, many fundamentalist activists believe, has forced the Muslim community to betray the sharī'a, but it now fears the Islamic movements. The pious are convinced that the West is afraid of what will happen to the world when the sharī'a is again implemented. This is only true if it means that a number of Western leaders profess to be worried that Islamist governments might support terrorism, for instance by allowing their diplomats to misuse diplomatic privileges. But it goes without saying that 'the West', *al-Gharb*, has no interest in the application or non-application of Islamic law. To Islamists this is difficult to believe, especially when they read in their newspapers that someone as influential as the former Secretary-General of NATO, the Belgian politician Willy Claes, warned that Islamic fundamentalism is as dangerous as communism. 'Do not underestimate the risk,' Mr Claes said *ex cathedra* in 1995,[46] only weeks before a corruption affair brought about his downfall.

Is there anyone who believes that the forces of NATO – the forces of Europe and the United States – would consider military intervention in the Middle East if a thief's hand is amputated or an adulterer is stoned? Law, and certainly penal law, is an internal affair, and states do not interfere in each other's internal affairs.[47] There is no reason to fear or expect that this principle would not continue to be respected when an Islamist government decides that the law should be the sharī'a. This does not mean that the West would not have a problem if a number of countries in the Muslim world were taken over by Islamic revolutionary fundamentalist regimes. In the long run, a chain of fundamentalist states 'from Morocco to Malaysia' would inevitably get its own international political sphere of influence. Changes in the international equilibrium, whatever their nature, are never welcome.

Does Islamic fundamentalism want to overrun the West? Is it expansionist? Since fundamentalists are intellectually in flight from the West, this is unlikely. Why would Islamic fundamentalism want to incorporate still more of the West and its civilisation within the religious frontiers of Islam?[48] But it does want to radicalise its own people. Islamic fundamentalists represent a serious danger, but to their own compatriots and coreligionists. Except in Palestine and Israel, fundamentalism propagates the concept of an Islamic struggle against an internal enemy.

In the short run, fundamentalist revolutions create first of all a refugee problem in the neighbouring countries. Thousands of Muslims fear an Islamist government, and the repeated purges in Iran in the 1970s and '80s and the ruthlessness of the Algerian Armed Islamic Groups in the early 1990s show that such fears are not irrational. The West might no longer be willing to accept

[46] *Süddeutsche Zeitung*, February 2, 1995. In the following days most other papers gave the matter their attention. A few days later the Iranian government reacted, saying that Mr Claes was wrong.

[47] NATO also did not interfere in the internal affairs of its own member states, although some believed there was some reason for doing so, e.g., in Salazarist Portugal (*ca.* 1930-74) and the Colonels' Greece (1967-74).

[48] So Pfaff, *Wrath*, 130.

political refugees if there were a mass exodus of Muslims in fear of their new Islamist rulers.

Islamic fundamentalists inspire fear in mainstream Muslims because of their belief that they have the right to take life. In this they are not alone, since Jewish and Christian fundamentalists also believe that they have this right. In 1994 a Christian fundamentalist and former preacher in the United States, Paul Hill, killed two people who worked for an abortion clinic in Florida. He shot his victims, the physician John Britton and his assistant James Barreth, when they arrived at the clinic. In 1995 he was sentenced to death for murder, but automatic appeals may take years. In December 1994 another fundamentalist Christian, John Salvi, was arrested in Virginia for attempting to shoot abortionists. It turned out that he was responsible for two earlier murders of abortionists, and in March 1996 he was sentenced to life imprisonment in Massachusetts. These two assassins had apparently narrowed the teachings of Christianity down to 'End abortion'.

In February 1994 Baruch Goldstein, a Jewish fundamentalist born and educated in the United States, killed a number of Palestinians in the mosque erected at the Cave of Machpelah in Hebron, the burial place of Abraham, Sarah and Jacob;[49] he did not survive the massacre he unleashed. Then in November 1995 Israel's Prime Minister Yitzhak Rabin was killed by an Israeli Jewish fundamentalist who was sentenced to life imprisonment in March 1996, and pointedly expressed no remorse for his deed. Both these assassins had narrowed down the elaborate teachings of Judaism to 'No Arab shall remain within the Biblical land of Israel'.

Islamic fundamentalists derive the right to kill from the traditional Islamic rules concerning apostasy from Islam. Here too it has to be remembered that Christianity and Judaism also once prescribed the death penalty for apostasy,[50] but in both religions this lost its practical importance several centuries ago. However, in the formative period of Islam it was not irrelevant to insist on the death penalty for apostasy. The Arab Muslim armies that occupied the present Islamic world from Morocco to Pakistan in the seventh

[49] In 1986, years before this incident, Harkabi already discussed the religious and ideological views that lie behind this Jewish 'counter ğihād', *Hakhra'ot*, 213.

[50] In Christianity and Judaism apostasy, bloodshed and adultery were regarded as capital offences. See, e.g., W.H.C. Frend, *The Rise of Christianity*, London, 1984, 409; Sanhedrin, YA, A-W; Cf. Deuteronomy 18:20 and Acts 3:23: 'Anyone who does not obey...shall be...destroyed.'

century AD were very small. If the soldiers in these occupation forces had gone native, the security of the Muslim state would have been under a direct threat. Thus in the social, political and religious context of the early Muslim empire it made sense to equate apostasy from Islam with desertion in time of war. In the twentieth century it makes little sense to hold on to capital punishment for apostasy, especially when apostasy is no longer sharply defined and may include a wide variety of acts that are common among certain groups of modern Muslims but bring down the wrath of the fundamentalists, like drinking beer or writing novels.

Despite all this, popular support for Islamic fundamentalism grows stronger. Since conversion to the tenets of a new movement, whether political or religious, usually takes place through pre-existing social networks,[51] and since in totalitarian societies in the Middle East the only permitted social network (apart from family ties) is the mosque, the possibilities of new intellectual, political or social movements that are not mosque-related growing up are extremely small. Hence the only movement with the capacity to grow is the Islamist movement.

In a way this success prevents the fundamentalist leaders from participating in government. Their support is simply too strong. In a genuine coalition the partners should all be roughly as weak as each other. Regimes that have no popular support and rule by force of arms naturally hesitate to let in the fundamentalists who have huge popular support and who – at least for the time being – rule by force of persuasion.

The Islamists' propaganda cannot fail to be successful because the public to whom it is addressed love to hear it. In the past profane opposition movements of liberal, Marxist or bourgeois inspiration have been ruthlessly exterminated, and therefore the only context in which citizens of the Arab world can hear criticism of their governments, which they usually detest, is that of Islamism. The humour with which the popular Egyptian preacher Sheikh Kishk (b. 1933) ridiculed his government gained more souls for Islamic fundamentalism than his prayers ever could. The language of Islamic fundamentalism is the only language of political opposition left, and it simply no longer occurs to most people that there could be any other alternative form of opposition.

Islamist propaganda is effective because to the public at large

[51] Stark, *Future*, 186, 292, 307–24, etc.

it sounds like propaganda for Islam. The cultures and societies within the Islamic world are not homogeneous. Morocco differs from Indonesia. But in the whole Islamic world it is widely believed that apart from the local Arabic dialects a higher, uniform variety of pure Arabic is the real language of scholarly communication. It is also believed that apart from the local form of Islam a higher, uniform variety of pure Islam is the real religion of God and His Apostle. Likewise, Islamic law is supposed to shine far higher than the local laws. Similar beliefs are held in other fields, and this permanent tension between the higher ideal and its imperfect local reflection is at the basis of Islamic thought. Nothing could be simpler and more effective than to present Islamic fundamentalism to a Muslim audience as a new and determined attempt to implement Islam finally in all its purity. Cries from liberal, westernised or traditional Muslims that this is merely a power struggle which exploits the traditions of Islam are rarely taken seriously even by the Muslim audience to whom they are addressed.

It has been suggested that Christian fundamentalism in the United States is the religious continuation of the Southern Confederacy that lost the civil war in the 1860s. After a political and military defeat the South nevertheless wanted to teach the modern North a lesson. The modern North had to learn about God's intentions for the universe – if not for the United States.[52] Islamic fundamentalism can be interpreted in a similar way. The colonial powers left the Middle East under pressure from 'the masses', but they did not hand over their power to these 'masses' but to military élites. After the decolonisation process, the populations were almost completely prevented from playing the game of politics: no effective political parties were allowed to exist, and no elections that mattered were held. In such a perspective, Islamic fundamentalism is an unprecedented attempt by the masses to re-enter the game, if necessary by force, and indeed it can be seen as a creation of the West, coming into being because of the way in which the Arab Islamic world was decolonised by its Western occupying powers in the first half of the twentieth century.

52 Harold Bloom, *American Religion*, 197.

2

THE CENTURY OF AL-AFGHĀNĪ AND IBN TAYMIYYA

Two figures have dominated the history of Islam in the twentieth century: Ǧamāl al-Dīn Al-Afghānī and Taqī al-Dīn Aḥmad Ibn Taymiyya, who lived respectively in the nineteenth and the thirteenth centuries.

The history of fundamentalism in modern Islam starts with Al-Afghānī's activities in Cairo during his stay there in 1871-9.[1] This was a significant period in the history of Egypt. The Suez Canal was opened in a blaze of glory in November 1869, and in 1876 Britain and France formed a commission to take over the Egyptian economy until the debts incurred by Egypt in the process were repaid. In 1882 there was a failed military rebellion led by Colonel Aḥmad 'Urābī.[2] Much of what Ǧamāl al-Dīn Al-Afghānī (1838-97) said and did in this period has been deliberately kept secret. Hence explanations and interpretations differ. Nevertheless, there is no reason to doubt that his teachings in this period did indeed consist of a combination of Islamic philosophy, reformism and powerful xenophobia.[3] And xenophobia especially, however reasonable it may have appeared within the political context of the region at the time, foreshadowed later fundamentalist convictions.

It is not only Al-Afghānī's teachings during his Cairo period which are subject to controversy. His ethnic and religious identities have also been disputed by scholars: was he a Sunnī Muslim from Afghanistan or a Shī'ī? After the detective work undertaken by Nikki Keddie[4] in 1972 there can be no doubt that he was of

[1] Keddie, *'al-Afghānī'*, esp. 81-127.

[2] Cf. Artemis Cooper's eloquent summary of the history of the period, in *Cairo*, 10-11.

[3] Keddie, *op. cit.*, 129.

[4] *Ibid.*, 427-33.

Iranian Shīʿī descent. According to contemporary reports, he spoke Persian like an Iranian and Turkish like a Azerbaijani. This and the documentary evidence indicate that he was born in northwestern Iran.[5] However, in his contacts with Arab Sunnī Muslims Al-Afghānī assumed an Afghan identity. The Afghans, as is well known, are Sunnī Muslims. Of course, this assumption of a false identity should not be judged from the point of view of modern morality. But, even from that point of view it can be argued that beside the struggle at the end of the nineteenth century between Islam and the West, the differences between Sunnī and Shīʿī Islam paled into insignificance.

Al-Afghānī lived at a time when the West was at the height of its power, and almost the whole Muslim world was occupied by its military forces. Since Napoleon Bonaparte's invasion of Egypt in 1798, the European powers took for granted the availability of Muslim lands as both a theatre for their rivalries and as the resulting prize. When Al-Afghānī was in Egypt, Arabic-speaking Muslims had been in direct contact with post-Enlightenment Europe for almost a century.[6] Pressure to westernise was relentless.

Al-Afghānī's response to the Western challenge was both political and religious. According to a contemporary account,[7] he identified two causes for the decline of the world of Islam. The first was *ta'aṣṣub*, 'fanaticism', by which he meant the misuse and misinterpretation of religion with the intention of legitimising the existing religious and social order. The second was *istibdād*, 'tyranny', which Al-Afghānī believed could only be ended by the institution of a parliamentary regime, i.e. by the removal of the present governments. All later Islamist political and fundamentalist programs, whatever their phraseology, are minor offshoots from these two themes.

Reflecting Linton's theory of nativism, Al-Afghānī recreated a glorious past for the Muslim world that had been under such strong Western pressure since the beginning of the century during which the British completed the conquest of India, the Dutch of Indonesia and the Russians of the Caucasus and Turkestan. The British also established themselves in Aden and the Gulf,

5 *Ibid.*, 432. According to Rashīd Riḍā, Al-Afghānī spoke Arabic with an Iranian accent: Adams, *Islam and Modernism*, 4, fn. 1.

6 See, e.g., Mortimer, *Faith*, 84.

7 A report in *Miṣr* on May 24, 1879. Keddie, 108.

and Afghanistan and Persia were invaded repeatedly. France seized Algeria in 1830, and proceeded to subdue most of Muslim Africa.[8]

In the light of later developments it is interesting that, giving a public speech in Alexandria in May 1879, Al-Afghānī took his examples of the ancient glory that was to be restored not from the history of Islam but from the ancient Egyptians, the Chaldeans and the Phoenicians 'who taught the Greeks the art of writing'.[9] A century later few Muslims could think of non-Muslim prehistory other than in pejorative terms: the coming of Islam, so many emphasise at the present time, was preceded by a period of immorality, lawlessness, barbarism and ignorance: the period of *ǧāhiliyya*.

Like most of the fundamentalist leaders active in the second half of the twentieth century, Al-Afghānī had immediate political plans which probably involved a leading role for himself, but these did not materialise. Nevertheless, he was able to inspire young Egyptian intellectuals because he provided a bridge between their traditional culture and the acceptance of various modern approaches.[10]

> Jamāl ad-Dīn's wedding of Islamic and Iranian philosophical and esoteric traditions to practical political goals thus provided something that could be given neither by the true traditionalist nor the pure skeptic and Westernizer.[11]

Together with Muḥammad 'Abduh, he wrote a great number of articles in their journal *Al-'Urwa al-Wuthqā*, which argued repeatedly that the West was not as strong as it looked and could be defeated. The language of these articles is sometimes not difficult, but it is not always easy to be sure what they are trying to say. Their contents are sometimes obscure, at least to a reader who does not already know what Al-Afghānī seeks to prove. Implicit in these writings is the dilemma which, according to Al-Afghānī, necessarily springs from the decline of the world of Islam in the

[8] See, e.g., the survey in Mortimer, *Islam and Power*, 82-6; or the map which portrays the numerous Western attacks on the Muslim world in the nineteenth century in Lewis, *The Arabs in History*, 169.

[9] Keddie, *op. cit.*, 109.

[10] *Ibid.*, 124-5.

[11] *Ibid.*, 87.

nineteenth century: was Islam to be reinterpreted or was it to be re-applied?

This decline of the Islamic world was no doubt a divine punishment for not having lived in accordance with Islam. But did the modern Muslims have to rediscover the true precepts of Islam by reinterpretation, or did they have to try to apply and implement its traditional rules as codified and enshrined in the traditional handbooks?

In the century after Al-Afghānī, the emphasis has gradually changed from reinterpretation to application. This change approximately reflects the success of the respective decolonisation movements. Muslims under colonial rule tended to believe that they had to reinterpret Islam. After the eclipse of colonial rule, on the other hand, Muslims tended to believe that the divine order of things demanded straight application and implementation of the rules in the traditional handbooks.

However, these handbooks drove at least one of Al-Afghānī's later associates, Muḥammad 'Abduh (*ca.* 1850-1905), to despair. Biographies of religious leaders usually mention a period of despair, but in the case of Abduh there is little reason to doubt the historical character of the crisis. In his autobiography he tells of his early education:[12]

> I spent a year and a half...without understanding a single thing. [...] the teachers were accustomed to use technical terms of grammar or jurisprudence which we did not understand, nor did they take any pains to explain their meaning to those who did not know it.

'Abduh fled, but many others remained, finished their studies and became religious leaders and functionaries who, in 'Abduh's words,[13] were a 'calamity upon the public'.

This description dating from 1862-5 is still easily recognisable to anyone who has ever studied in the Middle East. The very same complaint can be heard today from Muslim students who study Islam or classical Arabic, whether in Indonesia or Morocco. It would be valuable to know whether this type of training strengthens or weakens the Muslim communities that provide and receive it. Does it prevent critical minds from becoming

12 Adams, *Islam and Modernism*, 22, quoting from *Al-Manār*, VIII, 381.

13 *Ibid.*.

religious leaders? Does this system protect Muslim communities from revolutions and reformations which, to be successful, would have to start from within the traditional religious leadership? How does failure in this type of training influence an individual's faith? Does success in it ensure an unshakable, fully traditional, unquestioned faith? Did Islam survive intact into the twentieth century in spite of this brand of teaching, or because of it?

Whatever the answers to these questions, 'Abduh (who eventually went back to Al-Azhar and got his *'ālimiyya* degree in 1877) did not think that this type of education served any purpose. Nevertheless, education later played a large role in his thought and activities. According to 'Abduh, the ancient glory of Islam would return only when Muslim higher education and the administration of Muslim justice[14] were modernised. It is probably this general emphasis on the importance of education in 'Abduh's writings that, in the years following the First World War, misled the great Hungarian scholar Ignaz Goldziher into thinking that 'Abduh had been rector of Al-Azhar University, the educational pinnacle of Islam.

Although a number of lesser scholars have repeatedly corrected this unimportant error,[15] it has occurred yet again in a history of 'Muslim theology from the beginning till the present' published as recently as 1994. The author, a leading orientalist from Germany, supposedly re-read 'Abduh's writings when preparing this work and, in spite of what the secondary sources have to say, he again assumed that 'Abduh did indeed fulfill an important function at Al-Azhar University, and, no doubt on the basis of Goldziher, states that he was its Rector.[16] In reality 'Abduh's association with Al-Azhar was less formal: he suggested a number of reforms for the institution to Khedive 'Abbās, part of which were carried out.[17] This, no doubt, counted as a success, and in the careers of Al-Afghānī and 'Abduh successes were rare. It was only many years later that they were to be seen as important figures within the history of modern Islam.

[14] Adams, *Islam and Modernism*, 81; 'Abduh, *Taqrīr fī Iṣlāḥ al-Maḥākim al-Shar'iyya*, Cairo 1300.

[15] Goldziher, *Richtungen*, 321; Adams, *Islam and Modernism*, 72; Jansen, *Interpretation*, 18; etc.

[16] Tilman Nagel, *Geschichte der islamischen Theologie. Von Mohammed bis zur Gegenwart*, Munich: C.H. Beck 1994, 253: *'Mohammed Abduh...als Rektor der al-Azhar Hochschule...'*

[17] Adams, *Islam and Modernism*, 70–8.

Whereas Al-Afghānī's ideological stance can easily be recognised as foreshadowing modern Muslim fundamentalism, this is less obvious with 'Abduh, whose lack of anti-Western sentiment, insistence on intelligibility and aversion to naïve faith in miracles[18] make him an improbable ancestor of modern Muslim fundamentalism.

Nevertheless he is among its founding fathers, if only because of his close association with Al-Afghānī and his criticism of the superficiality of the traditional religious functionaries. In traditional Islamic political literature it is a time-honoured assumption that just rule is assured by knowledge of the law and consultation with the 'Ulamā' on the part of the ruler. 'Abduh gave a modern, Mediterranean version of this assumption when he argued that only a just dictator, *mustabidd 'ādil*, could modernise the Muslim East.[19] Moreover, since 'Abduh is the author of a Koran commentary which is nowadays widely read, his reputation established the Sunnī credentials of what was to become modern Islamic fundamentalism.

Without 'Abduh's reformulations, the claim of the movement fathered by Al-Afghānī to be identical to true Sunnī Islam would have been laughable. 'Abduh may not have been a great theorist, but he was the Grand Muftī of Egypt, and as such a worthy founding father of modern Muslim fundamentalism. Muslims, Al-Afghānī and 'Abduh wrote[20] in *Al-'Urwa al-Wuthqā*, know no nationality apart from their religion and their faith. Taken seriously, such a statement undermines the legitimacy of secular national governments in the Arab Muslim world, and taken literally it foreshadows modern fundamentalism and its bloody battle against the national modern regimes in that world.

In 1897 a certain Muḥammad Rashīd Riḍā (1865-1935),[21] born and educated in Syria, left for Egypt to join 'Abduh. Attracted especially by the contents of the periodical *Al-'Urwa al-Wuthqā*. He soon became one of 'Abduh's closest associates, and with him the Afghānī movement again came one step closer to mainstream Sunnī Islam. Riḍā was certainly no mere spectator, and participated with enthusiasm in contemporary debates on the return of the

[18] E.g. Jansen, *Interpretation*, 26-7.

[19] Malcolm H. Kerr, *Islamic Reform*, 135.

[20] Muṣṭafā 'Abd al-Rāziq, ed., *Al-'Urwa al-Wuthqā*, 85.

[21] Brockelmann, *Geschichte*, III, 321-3; to be supplemented by Jomier, *Manār*, 23-43.

glory of Islam. He is reported to have had great influence on 'Abduh who, under pressure from Riḍā, embarked reluctantly upon the composition of a Koran commentary now known as *Tafsīr al-Manār*. Approximately the last half of it was written by Riḍā alone.[22]

Riḍā's fame is inseparably connected with the periodical *Al-Manār* which he founded as a weekly in 1898, and which continued to appear as a monthly till his death in 1935. *Al-Manār* is the first sustained attempt to use the modern media systematically as a vehicle for the progress of Islam. In it a variety of subjects were discussed, reflecting the history of Islam in the first three decades of the twentieth century. In Riḍā's lifetime it became commonplace to use the press for the cause of Islam, and the Afghānī movement became irreversibly identified with Sunnī Islam.

In 1923 Riḍā published *Al-Khilāfa aw al-Imāma al-'Uẓmā*, the Caliphate or the Supreme Leadership of Islam. It is difficult to do justice to the wide learning and the good intentions of this book. It has been widely studied,[23] and translated into French by the scholar Henri Laoust.[24] Malcolm H. Kerr wrote of it in 1965: 'For modernist reformers [like Rashīd Riḍā] the Caliphate is only a means to an end. That end is the application of the Sharī'a...'[25] In the mid-1960s the demand for application of the sharī'a was still regarded as an innocent, distant religious dream. In the mean time the rise of fundamentalism has created a situation in which every Western journalist sees the demand for application of the sharī'a as the shibboleth of Islamic fundamentalism.

It is not only the desire to see the sharī'a applied that connects Rashīd Riḍā to modern Islamic fundamentalism. He is also the Muslim thinker who rediscovered Ibn Taymiyya (1263-1328), whose works he started to re-edit in 1925.[26] Rashīd Riḍā made Ibn Taymiyya into the central medieval figure of the debate on politics and religion within modern Islam, and no other Muslim authority is quoted so often and so extensively in recent fundamentalist writings.[27] Of all the 'fathers' of classical Islam he

22 Jomier, *Manār*, 50.

23 See, e.g., E.E. Shahin, 'Rashīd Riḍā', in *Oxf. EMIW*, III, 410.

24 H. Laoust, *Le Califat dans la doctrine de R.R.*, Beirut: Institut Français de Damas, 1938.

25 Kerr, *Islamic Reform*, 55.

26 *Ibid.*, 208.

27 See, e.g., Sivan, *Radical Islam*, 94-113; and Farağ, *Farīḍa,* in Jansen, *Neglected Duty*.

became the dominant authority in the modern debate on Islam and politics.

This state of affairs raises several problems, some unexpected. First, Ibn Taymiyya appears to have condemned tyrannicide[28] whereas the modern fundamentalists see it as a religious obligation. At the end of his famous *Al-Siyāsa al-Shar'iyya*, he writes:

> It is said [*yuqāl*]: The *sulṭān* is God's shadow on the earth; sixty years of an unjust ruler [*imām ǧā'ir*] is better than one night without *sulṭān*.

To attach 'it is said' as a prefix to such a statement is clearly not the same as an ardent appeal to the Koran or the Traditions to bolster its truth. Of course, the authority of 'what is said' can never equal the authority of the Koran or the Prophet, but the statement does not help to establish the reputation of Ibn Taymiyya as the spiritual father or modern Muslim terrorism.

Secondly, many authoritative modern Muslim scholars, among them Shaykh Ǧād al-Ḥaqq 'Alī Ǧād al-Ḥaqq,[29] Muftī of Egypt, have equated the modern fundamentalists with the ancient, early Islamic movement of the *khawāriǧ*. The most striking parallel between the modern fundamentalists and the ancient *khawāriǧ* is the belief of both groups that whoever does not live by God's laws is an unbeliever and thus excluded from the community. Exclusion from the Islamic *umma*, in both these cases, implies being sentenced to death. According to some sources, both groups even quote the same verses of the Koran to justify their violent aspirations.

It is ironic that this seventh-century movement of the *khawāriǧ* is the very object of the wrath of Ibn Taymiyya whom the present-day fundamentalists quote so extensively. Ibn Taymiyya writes about the *khawāriǧ* on several occasions, e.g.[30]

> [A multitude of] reliable Traditions from the Prophet reports how Muḥammad said: 'Some of you will be displeased to pray together with these people, or to fast with them, or to recite the Koran together with them, because these people read the

[28] Ibn Taymiyya, *Al-Siyāsa al-Shar'iyya*, 185.

[29] See, e.g., his *Al-Fatāwā*, 3742; and cf. already Mitchell, *Muslim Brothers*, 320, esp. fn. 63-5.

[30] *Maǧmū' Fatāwā*, XXVIII, 512; *Al-Siyāsa al-Shar'iyya*, 146-8.

> Koran but it does not enter their hearts, and they leave Islam like an arrow leaves the bow. 'Wherever you find them, fight them.'[31] At the Day of Resurrection God will reward those who killed them...

He continues:

> Caliph 'Alī b. Abū Ṭālib and the Prophet's Companions who were in 'Alī's camp all waged war[32] against the *khawāriğ*, and a wide and general consensus existed among the early exemplary Muslims that these *khawāriğ* had to be fought. [In the two earlier civil wars[33]] the Prophet's Companions had been divided into three groups: some fought on 'Alī's side, others on the other side, and some remained neutral. But as far as the *khawāriğ* are concerned, no Companion of the Prophet can be found among their number, and no Companion ever forbade to fight them...

When Ibn Taymiyya spelled out his condemnation of the seventh-century *khawāriğ*, it was his explicit aim to convince his readers that their Mongol contemporaries 'who invade Syria again and again'[34] were even worse than these *khawāriğ*. Every good Muslim, he taught, has always been convinced that it is a religious obligation to fight the *khawāriğ*; consequently, every good Muslim should be equally convinced that it is a religious obligation to fight against the Mongols, since the Mongols represent an even greater evil than the *khawāriğ*.

Ibn Taymiyya's teachings concerning the Mongols are a clear case of a 'war theology'. He was part of the resistance movement against the Mongol invasion of Syria and Egypt. This movement was led by the Mamlūk Sunnī Muslims who ruled Egypt and Syria, like Al-Malik al-Manṣūr Lāğīn (r. 1297–9). The Mamlūks fought a war against the Mongols and their king Ghāzān (1217-1304), a direct descendant of Genghis Khān (1126-1227) through his grandson Hulagu (1217-65) who seized and sacked Baghdad in 1258 and overthrew the Abbasid Caliphate. However, Ghāzān

[31] 'Wherever...them' from Koran 9:5.

[32] The battle of Ḥarūrā, 658.

[33] The battle of the Camel in 656 between 'Alī and his opponents Ṭalḥa and Zubayr, who were supported by Muḥammad's widow 'Ā'isha; and the battle of Ṣiffīn in 657 between 'Alī and the later Ummayad Caliph Mu'āwiya.

[34] *Mağmū' Fatāwā*, XXVIII, 509.

converted to Islam in 1295. He was supported not only by the Muslim and non-Muslim tribes that fought in his army, but also by Muslim scholars who served in his camp and at his court, e.g. the Persian historiographer Rashīd al-Dīn. In a hagiography compiled in the seventeenth century[35] we read a perhaps largely historical account of a meeting between the Mongol king Ghāzān and the Mamlūk war propagandist Ibn Taymiyya:

> I was present at a meeting between Ibn Taymiyya and the Mongol King Ghāzān. Ibn Taymiyya started to talk to the King about the word of God and His Apostle, on Justice and on other things. Ibn Taymiyya raised his voice loudly to the King and, while talking to him he came closer and closer to him until their knees touched each other; nevertheless the King took both his hands and listened attentively to what he had to say. [...]
>
> Ibn Taymiyya said to the interpreter: 'Say to Ghāzān: You allege [*taz'um*] that you are a Muslim; you have a qāḍī, an imām, and a [Ṣūfī] shaykh in your camp, and there are muezzins as well... Yet you fight against the Muslims. Your father and your grandfather were both pagans [*kāfirayn*] but they did not act like you do; when they concluded a treaty, they kept it...' Then Ibn Taymiyya left Ghāzān while the latter honoured him for his good intentions in exerting himself in order to safeguard the Muslims from bloodshed.

Ibn Taymiyya's reference to the presence of muezzins in the Mongol camp is of particular interest, since it goes against a famous statement preserved in one of his fatwās:[36]

> We saw the camp of these [Mongols] and we noticed that most of them do not pray. We saw no muezzin in their camp, nor an imām..

It is difficult to imagine that a spurious text would so blatantly contradict a well-known authentic text. The contradiction may thus be seen as an argument for the historicity of the report on the meeting between Ghāzān and Ibn Taymiyya. There can also be little doubt that the Mongols did have muezzins in their camp if only for their Muslim non-Mongol allies.

[35] Mar'ī, *Kawākib*, 162.

[36] *Mağmū Fatāwā*, XXVIII, 520.

It is actually easier to imagine that in his fatwās, which served the purpose of preparing people to fight the Mongol invasion, Ibn Taymiyya went a little further than the facts properly allowed, a not infrequent phenomenon in propaganda wars. In an actual conversation with a Mongol king displaying such zeal would have shown a lack of urbanity.

The hagiography continues by reporting how in 700/1300 Ibn Taymiyya went to Cairo, capital of the Mamlūks, where he

> ....incited people to wage *ǧihād*, and recited to them verses from the Koran as well as Traditions from the Prophet, and told them about the rewards which God has prepared for those who go to war against unbelievers.

By what standards could Ghāzān be regarded as an unbeliever after his conversion to Islam in 1295? At this point Ibn Taymiyya's legal genius comes into play. The Mamluk-Mongol war dictated that the Mongol enemies should be depicted as evil, and who, in the theory of Islam, is more evil than an apostate from God's own religion? In order to portray the Mongols as apostates from Islam, Ibn Taymiyya, with great ingenuity and vehemence, constructed a theory by which the Mongols, despite their conversion to Islam, could still be portrayed as apostates: Ibn Taymiyya repeatedly emphasised that they did not apply Muslim sharīʿa law but followed their own customary laws, known as *Yāsā* or *Yāsiq*. Muslim sharīʿa law differs from the laws and customs of the peoples of the Middle East. These discrepancies have been widely studied and discussed, but they pale into insignificance when Muslim law is compared with, say, the customary law of the Papuans in New Guinea – or the customary law of the Mongols of Central Asia in the thirteenth century AD. Ibn Taymiyya was on safe ground: if the Muslim Mongols were really to abolish their customary law and adopt the sharīʿa, this would mean a total disruption of their social life which in turn would certainly have consequences for their military effectiveness. The more traditional teachers of Islam recognise the disruptive effect of rejecting existing customs, and consequently treat recent converts to Islam, *qarīb al-ʿahd bi-'l-islām*, leniently.

Leniency, however, was not what Ibn Taymiyya looked for. He wanted to characterise the Mongols of his day as subhuman enemies of all Muslims in a credible way:

> A consensus [*iǧmā*'] exists that someone who makes it possible to follow another religion than the religion of Islam, or to follow another law than the law of Muhammad, is an infidel [*kāfir*]. His unbelief is even explicitly mentioned in the Koran:[37] [it] is like the unbelief of whosoever believes in part of the book and does not believe in other parts.[38]

In other words Ghāzān, who perforce 'made it possible' for his soldiers to follow Mongol customary law, by this very fact committed the crime of apostasy, and was henceforth to be regarded as the arch-enemy of all good Muslims. Thus by ruling a partly Muslim population by laws other than those of Islam he had become an apostate from Islam by converting to it. Without even mentioning the Mongols Ibn Taymiyya continues:

> It is well-established rule of Islamic law that the punishment of an apostate will be heavier than the punishment of someone who has never been a Muslim....[39]

> Any group of people that rebels against any single prescript of the clear and reliably transmitted prescripts of Islam has to be fought, according to all leading scholars of Islam, even if the members of this group publicly make a formal confession of the Islamic faith by pronouncing the *shahāda*....[40]

> The forefathers and the leading authoritative imams have always agreed that such people have to be fought. The first one who did so was Caliph Alī b. Abū Ṭālib, may God be pleased with him. All through the Umayyad and Abbasid Caliphates, Muslim army commanders have continued to do so, even when they themselves were unjust[41] [and not good Muslims]. Al-Ḥaǧǧāǧ and his lieutenants were among those who fought them. All Muslim Imams command to fight them.[42]

Finally the Mongols are mentioned:

37 Koran 2:85: *takfurūn^a bi-ba'ḍ^in*.

38 *Maǧmū 'at Fatāwā*, IV, 288.

39 *Ibid.*, 293.

40 *Ibid.*, 281.

41 This phrase may well be a chaste reference to the way the Mamlūk rulers applied the Sharī'a.

42 *Maǧmū 'at Fatāwā*, IV, 299.

> The Mongols and their like are even more rebellious against the laws of Islam than these *khawāriǧ* [or any other group]. Whosoever doubts whether they should be fought is most ignorant of the religion of Islam. Since fighting them is obligatory they have to be fought, even though there are among them some who have been forced to join their ranks.[43]

Although Ibn Taymiyya had his Mongol enemies in mind when he wrote those lines in the thirteenth century, his words must sound strangely relevant to Muslims in the twentieth century who want to see the sharīʿa applied. Modern Muslims in Egypt and Syria also live under rulers who make it possible to live by other laws than the laws of Islam.

Ibn Taymiyya put his anti-Mongol theology in such general and abstract terms that present-day rulers in the Arab world can equally be regarded as apostates according to the norms which he created for the Mongols. Although Ibn Taymiyya's condemnation of the Mongols was dictated by the particular military circumstances of the Mamlūk-Mongol wars of his time, many modern Muslims prefer to regard this condemnation as generally applicable and valid for all places and all times.

Ibn Taymiyya's anti-Mongol war theology has been firmly tied by Ibn Kathīr (*ca.* 1300-83), in his Koran commentary, to a fragment from a verse (5:44) from the Koran:

Whosoever do not judge	*man lam yaḥkum*
by what God has sent down	*bi-mā anzala 'llāh*[u]
they are	*fa-ūlā'ika*
the unbelievers	*humu 'l-kāfirūn*[a]

In the twentieth century this fragment is recited daily, from Indonesia to Morocco, to affirm one's lack of faith in present-day secular rulers and their regimes. Those who quote it understand 'to judge' as 'to rule', connecting the Koranic Arabic verb *yaḥkum*, 'to form an opinion', with the modern standard Arabic noun *ḥākim*, 'ruler'. 'What God has sent down' is identified with the prescripts of the Islamic sharīʿa, and 'unbelievers' is understood as 'apostates'. The full translation of the fragment then becomes: 'Certain political leaders are born as Muslims but rule by their

[43] *Ibid.*

own laws. Such leaders have committed apostasy from Islam and have to be assassinated.'

The verse is already used in this way by Rashīd Riḍā himself.[44] According to him, this fragment from Koran 5:44 applies to

> ....whomsoever thinks it is distasteful to rule in accordance with the just rules which God sent down, and does not rule by them because he holds different views, or because he has worldly interests. According to these verses, they are the [apostate] unbelievers; because true faith requires obedience. Obedience requires deeds, and is not consistent with dislike [of the rules of the sharī'a] and omitting [to apply them].

The Israeli scholar Emmanuel Sivan interprets the passage as follows:

> [Koran 5:44 applies to] those Muslim [rulers] who introduce novel laws today and forsake the Sharī'a enjoined upon them by God.[...] They thus abolish supposedly distasteful penalties such as cutting off the hands of thieves or stoning adulterers and prostitutes. They replace them by man-made laws and penalties. He who does that has undeniably become an infidel.[45]

Although Sivan makes Riḍā's meaning quite clear, his paraphrase it not a translation in the traditional sense. But his explicit language correctly reproduces what Rashīd Riḍā wanted to emphasise: that 'Koranic punishments' or *ḥudūd* cannot be abolished by governments which feel that they do not belong in the twentieth century. *Ḥudūd* is the Islamic technical term for a number of fixed punishments for five acts. The acts are unlawful sexual intercourse, false accusation of unlawful sexual intercourse, drinking wine, theft and highway robbery, and the punishments are death, flogging or amputation.[46] Public opinion in the modern Muslim world attaches importance to these Koranic punishments. Although lawyers all over the world make their living mostly from the practice of civil law, lay people all over the world tend to identify the law in general and its practitioners with penal law and crime. Muslims are no exception. When the Koranic punishments are carried out, and especially when the authorities take care that

44 Riḍā, *Tafsīr al-Manār*, VI, 330.

45 Sivan, *Radical Islam*, 101.

46 See, e.g., Schacht, *Islamic Law*, 175-87.

they are carried out in public, many Muslims see this as a sure sign that Islam finally has its way. No government that calls itself Islamic can afford not to exploit this mechanism.

In retrospect it is evident that Riḍā shared these popular feelings about the Koranic punishments. Moreover, he appears to have subscribed to the radical view that condemns modern heads of state in the Arab world as apostates from Islam, and it is difficult today to see why an earlier generation of orientalists regarded Al-Afghānī, 'Abduh and Riḍā as modernising, westernising liberals. The desire for the return of the glory of Islam which these three reformers felt so strongly, and the particular socio-political circumstances in which they lived, made them *not* into liberal modernisers but into the founding fathers of Islamic fundamentalism.

In October 1941 the Egyptian government suppressed *Al-Manār*, which a certain Hasan al-Bannā had recently taken over from the heirs of Rashīd Riḍā.[47] It is with Ḥasan al-Bannā that professional violence became part and parcel of the movement we now call Islamic fundamentalism. He and his followers not only committed professional violence but they also suffered from it. Seen in today's perspective, it may all seem on a small scale: a certain Judge Ahmad al-Khāzindār was killed in Cairo in March 1948 because he sentenced one of Al-Bannā's followers to prison. On 28 December 1948 the Egyptian Prime Minister Al-Nuqrāshī was murdered by a veterinary student called 'Abd al-Mağīd Hasan who was a member of the Muslim Brotherhood, the organisation founded by Hasan al-Bannā probably as early as the late 1920s. On 12 February 1949 Ḥasan al-Bannā himself was shot. These assassinations were, of course, just the tip of the iceberg. In 1969 Richard P. Mitchell published his classic study of the by then notorious organization which was the 'iceberg' itself: *The Society of the Muslim Brothers.*

Hasan al-Bannā was born in October 1906 in a small village, Mahmūdiyya, about 90 miles north-west of Cairo. At the age of twenty he was appointed as a teacher of Arabic in a state primary school in Ismā'īliyya. In September 1927 he left Cairo for his new home and his new job.[48] In the last week of May 1929 he read newspaper reports of an important religious and political event that had taken place in Italy earlier that

47 Mitchell, *Muslim Brothers*, 23.

48 Mitchell, *Muslim Brothers*, 6.

month.[49] The Italian parliament had ratified the Lateran Accords between Mussolini and the Pope. The discussion in the parliament in the second week of May 1929[50] preceding this ratification received little or no attention in the Egyptian press. However, on May 13 Mussolini delivered an important address on the subject which was extensively reported, e.g. in *Al-Muqaṭṭam* on May 16, under the heading 'Mussolini's Great Speech', *Khuṭbat Mussolini al-kubrā*.

Parts of the speech, and parts of the Lateran Accords, made a great impression on Ḥasan al-Bannā and some of his friends.[51] Did not these Accords win back for Christianity much of its old glory and power? Moreover, did they not put the whole Italian educational system at the service of the propagation of the Catholic faith? The position of the Italian men of religion had been enormously strengthened, or so it appeared. Surely Islam was in need of the same medicine?

According to Ḥasan al-Bannā's autobiography, the Muslim Brotherhood was founded either in March 1928 or in the Muslim month Dhū al-Qa'da 1347,[52] which ended on May 10, 1929, a few days before Mussolini's parliamentary speech on the Lateran Accords. A pamphlet by Al-Bannā and his friends entitled 'A Memorandum on Religious Education' mentioned and indeed quoted Mussolini's speech which certainly means that it dates from after May 16, 1929. Nevertheless it contains not even the slightest allusion to the existence of something like the Muslim Brotherhood. Should it not have done so if the Brotherhood had been in existence for over a year when the pamphlet was written? This makes March 1928 a less probable date for the founding of the Brotherhood than its alternative, May 1929. If, on the other hand, Ḥasan al-Bannā correctly remembered Dhū al-Qa'da 1347 (ending May 10, 1929) as the month when the Brotherhood was founded, this event may almost have coincided with Mussolini's 'Great Speech' on the Lateran Accords (May 13).

The 'Memorandum' contains a second reference to current affairs, which also points to a preference for May 1929 over

[49] Jansen, 'Earliest Pamphlet', 254–5.

[50] Binchy, *Church and State*, 428; Webster, *Cross and Fasces*, 110.

[51] Al-Bannā, *Mudhakkira*, 13.

[52] Mitchell, *Muslim Brothers*, 8, fn. 19.

March 1928 (if these are the only alternatives) as the date when the Muslim Brotherhood was founded. The 'Memorandum' opens:

> With great concern we have awaited the [Government's] new plan for education.... The newspapers have now reported on this new plan, and it is everything we feared....

On Friday, May 3, 1929, the newspaper *Al-Muqaṭṭam* briefly mentioned the plan for the first time, and used a turn of phrase which implies that before that date the Egyptian press had not known about or mentioned the new educational plan. On May 5, the front page of *Al-Muqaṭṭam* carried a long article headed 'The New Plan for Compulsory Education'. Both dates fall in the last week of the Muslim month of Dhū al-Qa'da 1347, in which Ḥasan al-Bannā remembered the Muslim Brotherhood being founded.

To Al-Bannā and his friends it must have seemed absurd that in the very week that the parliament of Christian Italy approved an arrangement to give more space, time and money to religious education, the authorities in Muslim Egypt decided to give *less* space, time and money to this noble aim. As soon as they knew the details of the new Egyptian plan, Al-Bannā and his friends in Ismā'īliyya must have decided to do something about it: to write a pamphlet and even launch a movement against it. Was this how the Muslim Brotherhood came into being?

The May 14 issue of *Al-Muqaṭṭam* (p. 5) printed the full text of the new decree. Now Ḥasan al-Bannā and his friends could start work on the actual composition of the pamphlet, which they dedicated not only to everyone with responsibility for the affairs of a Muslim child, *kull man yalī amr ṭifl*[in] *muslim*, but also to the King, his ministers, the members of parliament, the scholars of Al-Azhar, and the Ministry of Education. They claimed that the draft law which this Ministry had introduced contained nothing but 'useless, meaningless and ineffective changes'.

Such a judgement must sound familiar to anyone in the teaching profession today. However in the 1920s, the civil servants in the Egyptian Ministry of Education may not have reached the levels of equanimity now taken for granted, and would have resented these words, especially coming from a twenty-two-year-old provincial schoolteacher with less than two years' practical teaching experience.

It seems only reasonable to suppose that this pamphlet is the cause of the mysterious investigation (*taḥqīq*) carried out, according to Ḥasan al-Bannā's autobiography, by the Ministry of Education in 1930. The autobiography is ambiguous about the accusations which caused the investigation.[53] Five are mentioned. Was Ḥasan al-Bannā accused of being a communist, an anarchist or a republican working against the King? Was he accused under rules governing the civil service against the raising of funds or of being a member of the Wafd party that opposed the then Prime Minister Ṣidqī? According to the autobiography, all these possibilities were laughed out of court by the investigators, one of whom, we are told, even became a member of the Muslim Brotherhood once he had understood the real nature of Ḥasan al-Bannā's activities. Regrettably the autobiography does not identify this convert, of whom his descendants might well be proud. Or is it in reality not an autobiography but a hagiography compiled from autobiographical fragments which Ḥasan al-Bannā published during his short life-time?

Whatever the truth of the matter, it is strange that Ḥasan al-Bannā's account of the 1930 investigation does not mention the May/June 1929 pamphlet, which after all explicitly dealt with a draft law originating from the Ministry of Education – the very ministry that had instigated the 1930 investigation. If the latter had simply concerned Ḥasan al-Bannā's political reliability, why would it be the Ministry of Education that requested it? No doubt several branches of the Egyptian security services might have noticed and decided to investigate Al-Bannā's activities in Ismā'īliyya in 1929 and 1930. The account given in the autobiography represents these activities as exclusively local.

Even if the May/June 1929 pamphlet solves the mystery of the 1930 investigation into Ḥasan al-Bannā's behaviour, it creates another mystery: why is it not mentioned in his autobiography *Mudhakkirāt Al-Da'wa wa-'l-Dā'iya*? It may, of course, simply have been lost, but there are other possible explanations.

One of the co-authors of the pamphlet, Aḥmad Muḥammad al-Sukkarī, came into open conflict with Ḥasan al-Bannā in the spring of 1947, and was even dismissed from the Society of the Muslim Brothers.[54] Al-Sukkarī had played an important role in

[53] Al-Bannā, *Mudhakkirāt al-Da'wa*, 89: 'Ḍidd al-Niẓām al-Qā'im'.

[54] Mitchell, *op. cit.*, 54.

the Brotherhood. He had been Ḥasan al-Bannā's deputy, and held secret meetings with Egyptian politicians on behalf of the Brotherhood.[55] In 1945-7 he saw himself as the political leader of the Muslim Brothers and Ḥasan al-Bannā as their spiritual guide. At that time, in Mitchell's words, he decided to challenge Al-Bannā's role as leader of the Brotherhood.[56]

The conflict with Al-Sukkarī was still recent in 1948 when a Syrian sympathiser compiled Ḥasan al-Bannā's biography from autobiographical material he had written in the Society's newspapers,[57] but in such a procedure omissions and errors are inevitable. The May/June 1929 pamphlet and the role of Al-Sukkarī in the early history of the Brotherhood may even have been omitted by chance. Secondly, unlike the tracts by Ḥasan al-Bannā that were collected in the official compilation of his publications,[58] the May/June 1929 pamphlet does not quote the Koran or Tradition, but refers exclusively to Western sources and to various Western examples including Friedrich Froebel, Victor Hugo, Frederick the Great and Mussolini. It admonished the reader to follow these non-Muslim examples in religious primary education. However, in retrospect such deference to Western examples may have appeared in a different light; the later 'canonical' tracts describe the West as the source of all evil.[59] The 1929 pamphlet appears to represent a stage in Al-Bannā's thinking preceding his rejection of Western values. Its content simply is not compatible with later Brotherhood methods, views and opinions.

Already in January 1929 the daily newspaper *Al-Ahrām* had published a photograph of twelve 'founders' of a religious association devoted to the promotion of good and rooting-out of evil, which it referred to as the 'Muslim Brotherhood'. However, the association was regarded as one of the many religious associations which have always abounded in Egypt. Officially it appeared to be a branch of the Ḥaṣāfiyya, one of the many Muslim mystical fraternities active in Egypt. In February 1929 the Muslim Brotherhood was reported to have branches in Cairo, Nag Hammadi, Asyut and Benha.[60] Its

55 *Ibid.*, 49.

56 *Ibid.*, 9 and 54.

57 *Ibid.*, 1.

58 *Mağmū'at Rasā'il al-Imām al-Shahīd Ḥasan al-Bannā*, Beirut n.d., 382 pp.

59 Al-Bannā, *Mağmū'at Rasā'il*, e.g. 136-40.

60 Carré and Michaud, *Frères Musulmans*, 17; Carré, 'Bannā', in *Oxf. EMIW*, I, 195.

rapid growth 'within the full light of history' is reported for 1932 and 1933. It is tempting to suppose that the events of May–June 1929 are the watershed between the Brotherhood as an insignificant provincial branch of a ṣufī fraternity and the disciplined mass movement it later became.

Europe meanwhile was passing through a rather turbulent phase due to the activities of disciplined mass movements in Germany and Italy. When the Second World War broke out, the Arab world, especially Egypt, quickly became an area of exceptional strategic importance. Representatives of the Allied powers which fought the Axis did not take it lightly when Egyptians and others in the region considered themselves in need of reinsurance in case the Allies lost the war. Moreover, Egypt's disciplined mass movement, the Muslim Brotherhood, followed the principle that 'the enemy of my enemy is my friend', and consequently displayed considerable sympathy for the Germans and Italians who were expected to liberate them from foreign, i.e. British, occupation. Of course the Brotherhood was not alone in its pro-Axis sympathies. Two notable examples were King Fārūq (reigned 1936-52) and Anwar al-Sādāt, who was president from 1970 till his assassination in 1981. Some of their activities indicated considerable pro-Axis sympathies.[61] They, of course, have left the scene, but the radical Islamic movement still exists.

In the spring of 1941 Al-Bannā was deemed important enough to be banished for a few weeks from the capital to Qena in Upper Egypt;[62] British Military Intelligence had discovered that he was preparing to sabotage British communication lines to coincide with the next German offensive.[63] Next October he was arrested again with a number of his followers after a mass meeting denouncing the British.[64] It was on this occasion that *Al-Manār* and the other Muslim Brotherhood periodicals were suppressed by the government. Although Al-Bannā was soon released from prison, it must have been obvious to him that matters could not continue like this: in future resistance against the British would have to be professionalised. Consequently in late 1942 or early in 1943 the Muslim Brotherhood set up a secret apparatus to

[61] E.g. Cooper, *Cairo*, 103-5 (on Sadat); 134 (on Fārūq).

[62] Cooper, *op. cit.*, 161; Mitchell, *op. cit.*, 22-3.

[63] Cooper, *Cairo*, 161.

[64] Mitchell, *op. cit.*, 22; Cooper, *op. cit*, 161.

carry out extra-legal action against the existing order.[65] In 1943 this organisation (*al-ǧihāz al-sirrī* or *al-niẓām al-khāṣṣ*) began to play the part of defender of the Muslim Brotherhood movement against the police and successive Egyptian governments. At about the same time, the Brotherhood as such was reorganised in 'families', *usar* – cells whose members were limited to five. The Brotherhood kept this structure until its formal dissolution by the Nasser government.[66] In the light of all this it is not surprising that Al-Bannā and Al-Sukkarī were among the usual suspects rounded up when the Egyptian Prime Minister Aḥmad Māhir Pāshā was assassinated on February 24, 1945, as he read out the declaration of war against the Axis in the chamber of deputies.[67]

Even if some observers and participants have exaggerated the speed with which the Muslim Brotherhood grew, it is undeniable that the number of its members increased with amazing speed. Could the Brotherhood have had half a million members in 1945?[68] In the history of religions high growth percentages do occur but they are rare. The Unification Church, popularly known as the Moonies, must have maintained an annual growth-rate of 40% in the United States over a period of about seventeen years from 1962, when they were first observed, till 1980.[69] No matter how one looks at such arithmetic, it can only mean that the availability of converts to the Brotherhood must, for a variety of reasons, have been high. The readiness of Egyptian Muslims in this period to become Brotherhood members can only mean that in its existing form their religion served them inadequately.[70]

Moreover, in a stable and prosperous society a crisis cult[71] – if the Muslim Brotherhood of the early 1940s can be so designated – has only limited possibilities. However, Muslim Egyptians saw the presence of large numbers of non-Muslim foreigners in their country at that time as the cause of the instability and poverty from which they suffered. Members of the Muslim Brotherhood

[65] Mitchell, *op. cit.*, 30-1.

[66] *Ibid.*, 32.

[67] The assassination was not carried out by a Brotherhood member but by a member of the National Party. Mitchell, *op. cit.*, 33.

[68] Carré, *Frères Musulmans*, 21. The numbers imply an annual growth-rate of 100%.

[69] Stark and Bainbridge, *Religion*, 346-65, esp. 352.

[70] *Ibid.*, 360.

[71] *Ibid.*, 177.

obviously knew what they were doing when they argued that the British presence was the cause of shortage of food and fuel.[72] They were preaching to the converted. Fast growth, xenophobia, secrecy, extra-legal activities, assassinations, mass political meetings – being a member of the Muslim Brotherhood in the 1940s must have been exciting. Still, after the assassination of Al-Bannā the Brotherhood started to decline. Did the leadership lose its hold on the sections of the organisation that were prone to use violence? Certainly after the purge of 1954 things did not go well. On 26 October of that year, a certain Maḥmūd al-Laṭīf tried unsuccessfully to assassinate Nasser, and on 9 December six leaders of the Muslim Brotherhood were hanged for this assassination attempt. However, it was widely believed that the Egyptian government had staged the event in order to rid itself of the Society.[73]

The event became known as the Manshiyya incident, after Manshiyya Square in Alexandria where it took place. The revolutionary trial that followed proved, if anything, that the Brotherhood had been shaken by mutual distrust and lack of loyalty.[74] In this period the Muslim Brotherhood seemed to have lost much of its appeal, and it could be questioned whether it was still a dangerous competitor for power and popularity, as the government obviously once feared. Without Ḥasan al-Bannā's charisma, the Brotherhood had changed. It was no longer a disciplined mass movement that could boast of secret branches; as irreverent diplomats now dared to say, being a member of the Muslim Brotherhood had become 'a state of mind'.

At the Manshiyya trials, in 1955 a certain Sayyid Quṭb was sentenced to fifteen years in prison. He had been arrested for the first time early in 1954, together with the whole leadership of the Brotherhood. Just before his arrest he became editor of the Brothers' newspaper – an important and responsible position in an organisation that was quickly losing its coherence. It seemed to be developing into something of an audience cult,[75] proclaiming that all things are possible, but not able to do more than proclaim diffuse hope for a better and more Islamic world.

[72] See, e.g., Cooper, *Cairo*, 163.

[73] Mitchell, *op. cit.*, 151.

[74] *Ibid.*, 156.

[75] Stark and Bainbridge, *op. cit.*, 208-33.

Sayyid Quṭb was to become the main ideologue of modern Muslim fundamentalism. Out of the ruins of the Afghānī movement and with the help of Ibn Taymiyya's war theology, he created a coherent ideology which has shown itself able to inspire many people to face their own death calmly for the sake of Islam, and to kill in its name.

3

ONWARD MUSLIM SOLDIERS

Contemporary Islamic fundamentalists want Islamic law, known as the *sharī'a*, to be applied. This is the centre of their existence. However, the laws of Islam are important in more than one way. The fundamentalists are at times obliged to resort to violence against the enemies of Islam, and for this a knowledge of Islamic law is essential because it can give the zealots confidence that the use of violence is just. It is especially the ideology developed by the Egyptian writer Sayyid Quṭb in the 1950s and '60s that makes the killings which fundamentalist groups have committed seem reasonable and necessary within the terms of Islamic law. Quṭb's writings transformed the fundamentalist Muslims from pious civilians into self-conscious conscript soldiers having no choice but to make war against the enemies of Islam.

Ibrāhīm Ḥusayn Shādhilī Sayyid Quṭb,[1] the main ideologue of modern Muslim Sunnī fundamentalism, was born on October 9, 1906, in Mūshā, a village near Asyūṭ in Upper Egypt; he received the death sentence on August 21, 1966, which was executed without delay – eight days later on August 29, 1966, in a Cairo prison.

In 1920 Sayyid Quṭb moved from his native village for his secondary education to Cairo, where from 1929 till 1933 he studied at Dār al-'Ulūm. He worked as a teacher for about six years, then became a functionary in the Ministry of Education. This ministry sent him on an educational mission to the United States, where he spent almost two years – from November 1948, when he went to New York by boat from Alexandria,[2] till August 1950, when he returned by plane.[3]

[1] Jansen, 'Sayyid Kutb', in *EI* (2nd edn); and references in Al-Khālidī, *Sayyid Quṭb*. Much has been written about Quṭb, but see especially Kepel, *Prophet and Pharaoh*, 36-67, and Sivan, *Radical Islam*.

[2] Al-Khālidī, *op. cit.*, 194.

[3] *Ibid.*, 210.

It is usually assumed that Sayyid Quṭb joined the Muslim Brotherhood in 1951, on the eve of the Naguib/Nasser revolution. Up till then, nothing in his career or his writings had indicated that he was destined to become the most prominent martyr for Islamic fundamentalism yet seen. Before 1950 he had published only literary works: a volume of literary criticism in 1933, a volume of poetry in 1935, a novel in 1946, and two largely autobiographical novels in 1946 and 1947. A collection of his contributions to the prestigious literary periodicals of the time had been published, also in 1946.

When the July 1952 revolution took place, Sayyid Quṭb was in close contact with the Free Officers, and he served as the cultural adviser to the leaders of the new regime. There is no reason why we should not believe that in the early phase of the revolution he had a place in the innermost councils of the Free Officers. Still, he soon parted from the new leaders because of ideological differences. We now know he believed that Islam should be the basis for the new Egyptian regime. In October 1952 he left the Ministry of Education.

His first arrest was in early 1954, when he had become editor of the Brotherhood's newspaper. He remained behind bars for three months. The second followed on October 26, 1954, in the wake of the Manshiyya incident, supposedly an attempt to assassinate President Ǧamāl 'Abd al-Nāṣir in Alexandria's Manshiyya Square. In 1955 he was sentenced to fifteen years in prison. Mediation by the Iraqi president 'Abd al-Salām 'Ārif during a state visit resulted in Sayyid Quṭb's release from prison in 1964, but now his troubles started in earnest. On August 9, 1965, he was arrested again, accused of attempting to assassinate the President, of treason, and of planning a *coup d'état*. His trial was presided over by the notorious military judge Fu'ād al-Diǧwī[4] who, in the words of the French scholar Gilles Kepel, 'offered the accused all the guarantees of fairness characteristic of a military court in a dictatorial state trying defendants broken by torture'.[5] The trial ended, predictably, with a death sentence being pronounced on August 21, 1966. Sayyid Quṭb was hanged before the month was out.

It can be argued that Quṭb was executed to demonstrate the futility of resisting the government. Perhaps a Western court would

[4] See especially Shawkat al-Tūnī, *Muḥākamāt al-Diǧwī*.

[5] Kepel, *op. cit.*, 34.

have found him guilty of little more than professing eccentric beliefs. Perhaps the Egyptian government decided on his execution mainly to demonstrate its own omnipotence, and not because it feared the Muslim Brotherhood and its theologies. But these theologies and ideologies in the mean time managed to recruit so many supporters that nowadays they are perceived as being extremely dangerous. There may not be a Muslim fundamentalist army on the march, but there are certainly a great number of soldiers and officers.

Sayyid Quṭb published his most influential book *Ma'ālim fī al-Ṭarīq*, 'Landmarks', in November 1964. In it he accused contemporary Muslim societies of not being Islamic but *ğāhilī*. It is well-known that this adjective originally refers to the state the Arabs were in before the advent of Islam.[6] It does not occur in the Koran, but its derivative, the noun *ğāhiliyya*, occurs four times. In the writings of Sayyid Quṭb and his spiritual heirs the latter word is definitely not the designation of a historical period which ended with the advent of Islam in the sixth/seventh century AD. In the new context, its connotations are disturbingly vague and general: first 'pre-Islamic', 'pagan' and 'barbaric', but also 'anti-Islamic', 'vicious', 'stupid', 'lawless', 'chaotic' and 'wicked'. Moreover, the accusation of being *ğāhilī* implies apostasy from Islam, one of the consequences of which is the death penalty.

Sayyid Quṭb's most widely distributed book is undoubtedly his commentary on the Koran, *Fī Ẓilāl al-Qur'ān al-Karīm*, literally 'In the Shadow of the Koran', in thirty volumes; it may actually be the most widely translated and distributed Islamic book of all time. When Quṭb was arrested in 1954, sixteen volumes had appeared, and the remaining ones were written from prison, with Sheikh Muḥammad al-Ghazālī acting as a government-appointed censor. In 1960 a revised edition of this commentary started to appear. Volume 13 of the revised edition, up to Sūra 14, appeared in 1964. Arrest and execution prevented the revised edition, often characterised as *tafsīr ḥarakī*, 'activist exegesis', from being completed.

The contents of the commentary often testify to Sayyid Quṭb's preoccupation with politics. When, in Sūra 12, the Koran tells of Joseph becoming the viceroy of Egypt, Sayyid Quṭb points out that the rule of Pharaoh had been *ğāhilī*, but Joseph was a

[6] *Mağma', Mu'ğam: al-ḥāla allatī takūn 'alayhā al-umma qabl an yağī'ahā al-hudā wa-'l-nubuwwa.*

Prophet. Islam teaches that prophets are protected by God from committing sins and are thus infallible, *ma'ṣūm*. This has an important consequence: Joseph must have ruled in accordance with the laws of God.

When the Pakistani writer and ideologue Al-Mawdūdī made the same point, he received a critical letter arguing:

> The text of the Koran leaves no doubt at all that [the Prophet] Joseph, Peace Be Upon Him, became a member of an un-Islamic government, and that the system of government and the law of the land remained un-Islamic.... [In the text of the Koran] God does not censure [Joseph] for this, but, on the contrary, praises him.. This is [only] one of the indications that it is fully allowed for Muslims, even Prophets, to participate in non-Islamic government.[7]

This, of course, is not the lesson a fundamentalist would want to draw from the Koranic story of Joseph. On the contrary, according to the fundamentalist ideology, a Muslim should not work for or cooperate with a non-Muslim government.[8] The long refutation (*radd*) which Al-Mawdūdī devotes to the letter is not easy to understand, and perhaps not always fully to the point. Al-Mawdūdī, surprisingly, concludes that 'perhaps the way of thinking [of the writer of this critical letter] has a long and painful history of moral decay.'[9]

In the general introduction to his Koran commentary, the layman Sayyid Quṭb carefully explains that he had 'heard God speaking to [him] in this Qur'ān' – an important remark. Sayyid Quṭb did not have a traditional Al-Azhar-type training and was no *'Ālim*, but he had a secular, literary, education. Did he, nevertheless, have the right to interpret the Koran independently? His right to do so, we are to understand, was not based on human diplomas but on the very voice of God addressing him.

Like so many reformers Quṭb was not a professional 'man of religion'. None the less, he had heard the voice of God through the Koran, and had to transmit what he had heard to his fellow

[7] Al-Mawdūdī, *Ḥukūma*, 48-50.

[8] E.g. Muḥ. 'Abd al-Salām Farağ, *Al-Farīḍa al-Ghā'iba*, 52 and 53, in Jansen, *Neglected Duty*, 184.

[9] Al-Mawdūdī, *Ḥukūma*, 57.

Muslims. His authority was sealed by his martyrdom. A widespread story reports that he smiled on his way to the gallows.[10]

Sayyid Quṭb may have had good news for Muslims, but for others the news was less good:

> The role of the white man came to an end.. his role ended whether he was Russian or American, English or French, Swiss or Swedish....[11] Every way of life...is the religion of that life. Consequently those who follow a certain way of life...take that way of life as their religion. If they follow God's way of life, then they are within God's religion. If they follow another way of life, they do not follow God's religion.[12] When immoral men or women feel the whip on their tender and soft skin, or when they feel the stones upon their delicate bodies, they will defend themselves by speaking in high-sounding terms about the laws of civilisation, and accuse Islam of barbarism. However, they themselves are the barbarians who [with their sexual license] are sinking back into an animal-like primitive state.[13]

However, important problems of political philosophy have been solved:

> In Islam the individual and the group are not enemies... an individual does not prescribe for the group how to act, and the group does not prescribe for the individual how to act. They are both subject to the law of God that takes care of both of them.[14]

Sayyid Quṭb's writings abound with similar passages that proclaim his intense preoccupation with the law of God. Sociologists often argue that religion supplies compensations for anything of which one painfully feels the lack, e.g. love of one's neighbour in a competitive society. When one accepts this, the fundamentalist preoccupation with the unchanging laws that the Muslims received from an unchanging God, who can be known from an unchanging book, is more easily understood.

10 Al-Khālidī, *op. cit.*, 476-7.

11 Quṭb, *Mustaqbal*, 56.

12 *Ibid.*, 15.

13 Quṭb, *Salām 'Ālamī*, 81.

14 Quṭb, *Salām Ālamī*, 131.

Legal security is rare in the Middle East.[15] Either the law is not applied at all, or it is in a state of constant change, flux and amendment. In such a situation it is inescapable that the dominant religion should preach that there is a higher and better world that possesses divine, stable, unchanging, just and perfect laws. Modern Muslims, especially, who have undergone substantial westernisation are bound to be distressed when they see the many ills from which their society suffers through not being regulated by law. Close contact with the Western world, e.g. during an 'educational mission' to the United States like that which Sayyid Quṭb undertook in 1948-50, may make these feelings more intense and acute. Would Islamic fundamentalism have looked any different if Sayyid Quṭb had been sent on a mission to the Soviet Union or China, instead of the United States?

However, the desire of concerned Muslims to make their world a safer and more stable place has had disastrous consequences for public safety. Since the 1960s, primitive rebellion has repeatedly broken out among small groups of Muslims who allowed themselves to be inspired by the theories of Sayyid Quṭb. The Arabic word for 'groups', *ǧamā'āt*, even became a familiar term in the Western press.

However, there are different sorts of Islamic militant *ǧamā'āt* in the region. According to the Egyptian expert Dr Faraǧ Fōda,[16] born in 1945 and assassinated by a fundamentalist gunman in Cairo on June 8, 1992, we have to discern three main tendencies within modern Islamic fundamentalism: the traditional, the revolutionary and the affluent. The wordplay linking 'revolutionary', in Arabic *thawrī*, and 'affluent', *tharwī*, should be noted, but the pun does not imply that Faraǧ Fōda was not serious when he proposed this threefold division.

The first group that he wants to identify, the traditional Islamists, is generally moderate, even though it may have radical wings or occasionally produce secret terrorist cells. This group of traditional Islamists, *al-ittiǧāh al-islāmī al-taqlīdī*, is the organisational remnant

[15] See, e.g., Ḥasan Ḥanafī, *Ḥukūma*,16: *Ḥukūmāt al-yawm allatī ya'īsh fīhā al-insān khā'if^{an} 'alā ḥayātihi wa-rizqihi....*, 'the present governments under which man has to fear for his life and his daily bread....', or the insistence with which media commercials assure a prospective buyer that the advertised product will bring him *rāḥa* and *amān*, 'repose' and 'security'.

[16] Fōda, *Suqūṭ*, 159-66.

of Ḥasan al-Bannā's Muslim Brotherhood. In Farağ Fōda's own words:[17]

> They always keep a delicate balance between their claim to be an organisation that does not attempt to take power and their preoccupation with political activities that have the taking of power as their only goal.

However, the leadership of the Muslim Brotherhood had a number of good reasons for not wanting the organisation to try to take power in the way adopted by political parties. In the first half of the twentieth century political parties in Egypt were ineffective; power was in the hands of the British and the Palace. In other Arab countries political parties hardly did any better. Real power was exercised not by political parties but by the military, the colonial or occupying power, etc. Thus in Egypt the Muslim Brotherhood could not develop into a political party in the period before the July 1952 revolution. After the revolution the possibility of legally becoming a political party no longer existed. In other Arab countries similar sets of circumstances produced similar results.[18]

In Egypt, memories of the bitter struggle between the regime and the Brotherhood in the 1960s poisoned the atmosphere during the next decade. This precluded the perhaps natural development of the Muslim Brotherhood into a political party within the Sadat empire. Nevertheless, in the Mubarak era representatives of the Muslim Brotherhood entered the Egyptian parliament after the elections of 1984 for the first time.[19] By 1985 Farağ Fōda believed that this would have a positive effect in enabling the traditional Islamists, the former Brotherhood, to develop gradually into a political party.

However, this has not happened for two reasons. The old Brotherhood élite has slowly disappeared from the scene and no longer plays an important role. The hardened cadres, tempered in battle, look down upon the world from heaven. Furthermore, by being metamorphosed into a political party the Brotherhood loses its special, unique character and cannot any longer claim

17 *Ibid.*, 159.

18 Kedourie, *Democracy*, 25-62, discusses why this should be true for Iraq, Syria and Lebanon.

19 See Muḥammad al-Ṭawīl, *Al-Ikhwān fī al-Barlamān*, Cairo 1992.

that it has no rivals, no equals and no competitors: political parties were invented to compete with each other. The more, in the late 1980s, the Brotherhood discussed the concept of *ḥizbiyya*[20] or 'partyism', the more it lost its dangerous magic.

Farağ Fōda calls the second tendency *thawrī*, revolutionary. The main ideological characteristic of the groups that make up this tendency is their belief that modern societies in countries usually thought of as Muslim are in reality *ğāhilī*, 'un-Islamic'. This was also how Sayyid Quṭb perceived them. These groups consequently believe that true Muslims should fight the world in the way the early Muslims fought the Meccans in 622-30 AD. These groups have fascinating names like *Al-Nāğūn min al-Nār*, 'those who are to be saved from hell fire', or *Al-Shawqiyyūn* – after their founder Shawqī al-Shaykh[21] and not from Arabic *shawq*, 'love'.

According to the Egyptian political scientist Dr Hāla Muṣṭafā,[22] these revolutionary organisations themselves can again be roughly divided into three. The most important division, usually referred to as *Al-Ğamā'a al-Islāmiyya*, has its basis in Upper Egypt and in the poorer parts of Cairo, especially Maṭariyya and Embāba.

In the second division of organisations, usually referred to as *Tanẓīm al-Ğihād*, a few subgroups with names such as *Al-Wāthiqūn min al-Naṣr*, 'Those who are certain of victory', and *Al-Qiṣāṣ al-Islāmī*, 'Islamic Revenge', became notorious. It was from among these that Sadat's assassins were recruited in the second half of September 1981.

The remnants of the movement of Shukrī Muṣṭafā are considered to form the third group. Some of these may be continuations of groups and cells that Shukrī founded when he was imprisoned in the early 1970s.

Often the press refers loosely to such groups as 'the *ğihād* movement', or 'the *ğamā'āt*'. Quṭb's concept of *takfīr* is central to their thoughts and aspirations. Members sincerely believe that God wants them to have power, and in order to obey God's special command to them they do not hesitate to use force. They do not fear death and martyrdom but, on the contrary, see martyrdom as the key to Paradise. The Egyptian government has been ready to oblige them: for instance, between 1992 and the

20 See, e.g., Freysen, *Banier*, 66-8.

21 Hāla Muṣṭafā, *Dawla*, 378.

22 *Ibid.*, 377-8.

summer of 1995 approximately seventy fundamentalists were sentenced to death.

These revolutionaries, Farağ Fōda explains, are above all dangerous; their partisans, who are all aged between fifteen and thirty-five, have ample opportunity to meet and organise; they have no responsibilities, no hope that even the most modest material ambitions can be realised in the present state of society, and no interest in discussing or analysing the details of a society they regard as totally corrupt. Only armed struggle, they believe, can put things right and make the world more Islamic. Farağ Fōda called them weak, but by the very nature of their methods and aspirations it is impossible to assess their real strength.

Almost a decade after Farağ Fōda published this analysis, most observers readily agree, at least in principle, with his assessment of these two component parts of contemporary Islamic fundamentalism in Egypt. But in the mean time it has become clear that similar groups exists among Muslim communities all over the world. Some are very small and insignificant, but the Oklahoma bombing of April 1995 showed once again that a group does not have to be large to do serious harm.

Farağ Fōda's description of the third tendency within Egyptian contemporary Islamic fundamentalism whose existence he assumes – the affluent tendency, *al-ittiğāh al-tharwī* – will be less readily accepted, yet it may be accurate. He suggests that it is led by people who amassed their fortunes in the 1980s in Saudi Arabia or in post-Sadat Egypt during the happy times of the *infitāḥ*, or economic 'open door' policy, when economic possibilities were unlimited. The people in this group believe that it is possible to establish a Saudi-style regime in Egypt. Being good Muslims they reject man-made laws, and are therefore strongly in favour of free trade and strenuously object to government price-fixing or *tas'īr*, one of the few instruments the Egyptian government possesses for protecting the poor from the economically powerful.[23] Because of their rejection of man-made laws, they want to limit all taxation to the Islamic *zakāt*-tax. They represent Islam, so they regard all opposition to their own views as an un-Islamic activity that has to be punished commensurately.

They think they can keep the populace amused with the spectacles provided when the *ḥadd* punishments are carried out in

[23] It is not certain that *tas'īr*, even if wisely used, is an effective instrument.

public: flagellations and stonings for sexual offences and amputations for theft. Under such a system the poor should concentrate on the blessing they will receive in the hereafter. As this faction sees it, it is an important duty of the modern state to distribute small gifts of sweets and dried fruits to the poor on religious holidays. To the adherents of this tendency, Farağ Fōda writes, the Islamic state is nothing more than an efficient instrument to increase their wealth. Moreover, it is an instrument that is well equipped to guarantee political stability in the Arab world. Its Islamic ideology puts it in a position where it will have a popular base, *qā'ida sha'biyya,* from which it can confidently attempt to quell any form of political opposition. The populace, Muslims and non-Muslims alike, would no doubt understand and accept its religious despotism.[24] Political stability is much sought after in this region, and it would be interesting to know whether or not the intelligence agencies that analyse such questions hold the same or similar views.

According to Farağ Fōda, the strength of this third tendency is its low visibility. The militants of this faction are strong, and they work according to modern techniques. At present, 'Fōda asserted, they are the only effective lobby within Egyptian society. They are not troubled by the activities of the old Brotherhood traditionalists, which can only be helpful to their aims. They regard Islamic revolutionary activities with suspicion and hostility. The militants of the affluent faction do not fear the traditional financial institutions; on the contrary, the traditional financial institutions fear these pious and affluent activists who engage in a wide variety of pursuits in publishing, printing, investment and banking. The pious Islamic projects they undertake usually receive much favourable publicity. Their Islamic investment companies may suffer temporary setbacks, but they provide a solid basis for a financial empire that cannot fail to make its magnetism felt throughout the region.

Farağ Fōda was engaged in professional international consultancy concerning agricultural development projects. Hence he did not hesitate to give a sober evaluation of the strength and methods of each of the three tendencies which he assumed to be present within modern Islamic fundamentalism in Egypt. A theologian

[24] Cf. Kedourie, *Democracy*, 105.

or an orientalist is trained to postpone giving value judgements, but such a luxury was alien to a professional consultant like Fōda.

Whereas it may be possible to divide what we nowadays want to call 'Islamic fundamentalism' into three, it is also possible to see three aspects to modern Islam as such. Apart from the fundamentalists, (1) the quietist, mystical Ṣūfī element and (2) the orthodox legalist influence of the 'Ulamā', represented in Egypt by Al-Azhar and its graduates, have to be recognised. The state usually supports and encourages its own mixture of these two factors, and is therefore responsible for what many call (3) 'official Islam'. It is the impression of many outsiders that in the mid-1990s the 'Ulamā' tend in many parts of the Arab world to have considerable sympathy for what Farağ Fōda called the 'affluent' faction within the fundamentalist movement.

One of the most prominent 'Ulamā' is Shaykh Muḥammad Mutawallī Al-Sha'rāwī,[25] born in 1911, a well-known guest and preacher in television programs on Islam all over the Arab world. He has published thousands of pages, granted hundreds of interviews, delivered innumerable sermons and fulfilled a great number of important functions, the most prominent being as Cabinet Minister for Awqāf (pious benevolent foundations) and Al-Azhar affairs in Egypt from November 1976 till October 1978. Although he is Egyptian, he worked for years in Algeria and Saudi Arabia. Although he definitely does not advocate violence, many observers feel that his declarations encourage militancy.[26]

Within the spectrum of Islamic religious politics it is not easy to pin Sheikh Al-Sha'rāwī down. This is amazing in itself: the Sheikh's output is enormous. How can one write and preach so much without revealing one's innermost convictions? Despite the abundance of the material, evidence has to be almost exclusively circumstantial; yet it does all point in the same directions. First, the Sheikh's biography: he spent many years in Saudi Arabia. He came back to Egypt during Sadat's *Infitāḥ* period, when he even became the Cabinet Minister for Religious Affairs, retaining the portfolio from November 1976 to October 1978. These two circumstances both point to his being closest to *al-ittiğāh al-tharwī*, the affluent tendency.

Sheikh Al-Sha'rāwī cannot be close to the traditionalist or

[25] Jansen, *Neglected Duty*, 121-50.

[26] *The Economist*, 21 May 1988, 60.

revolutionary tendencies. He was attacked several times in the magazines and books published by the traditionalists in the Muslim Brotherhood. For example, the monthly *Al-Da'wa* attacked him in 1978 when he was still a cabinet minister, and Dr Yûsuf al-Qarḍāwī, a prominent Muslim Brother traditionalist, did so – though without mentioning his name – in a book published in 1984.[27] Such attacks are reliable circumstantial evidence that the Muslim Brother traditionalists do not think of Sheikh Al- Sha'rāwī as one of them.

Sheikh Al-Sha'rāwī in turn attacked representatives of the revolutionary tendency. In a long interview he gave to *Al-Ahrām* concerning Sadat's assassination in November 1981, he said of the assassins who at that time were awaiting trial and execution in a Cairo prison: 'If these people had been real *anṣār*, helpers, of Islam, nothing could have stopped them....' Since nothing *did* stop these people from killing Sadat, what does the Sheikh mean? In his own words, 'Their aim was not only to assassinate [Sadat]. Wasn't the real aim of [their] whole operation to seize power in Egypt?' The general tone of this interview suggests that the Sheikh feels himself to be very much above these revolutionaries who use such primitive and ineffective methods to serve the cause of Islam. These are no more than circumstantial indications that the Sheikh does not belong to the traditionalist or revolutionary factions. But can he be connected to the affluent faction by other, more direct evidence? There may be much better material in the thousands of printed pages he has published, but a letter written by the Egyptian novelist Tawfīq al-Ḥakīm to the weekly *Al-Liwā' al-Islāmī*[28] contains a surprising juxtaposition of Sheikh Al-Sha'rāwī and one of the ideological shibboleths of the affluent faction, namely the much-neglected Islamic duty of paying *zakāt*.

In the letter Tawfīq al-Ḥakīm complains that contemporary Muslim activists often talk of *ǧihād* and the application of the Islamic *ḥadd* punishments: should they not, he asks, pay more attention to the possibility that paying *zakāt*, this strangely neglected Islamic duty, may automatically put things right in this world? Where did Tawfīq al-Ḥakīm suddenly get this idea? In his earlier writings on the rigidity of Islam he did not discuss *zakāt*.[29] Was

[27] Jansen, *Neglected Duty*, 128, 145.

[28] April 25, 1987 (170), 3.

[29] Jansen, 'Tawfīq....', *Bibliotheca Orientalis*, 38 (1980), 13-16.

he prompted by Sheikh Al-Sha'rāwī? At the end of the *zakāt* letter the Sheikh is abundantly present: when Tawfīq al-Ḥakīm was in hospital, the letter informs us, the Sheikh visited him and prayed in his room, and Tawfīq was cured – in Arabic, *zāranī fī l-mustashfā wa-ṣallā fī ḥuğratī fa-shafānī Allāh.* Tawfīq thanks God for the existence of men of religion like Sheikh Al-Sha'rāwī – and then at once rambles on about the duty of the state to establish *zakāt* committees to take care of the poor.

Finally, Sheikh Al-Sha'rāwī's name crops up every now and then in the newspaper reports on Islamic banking, a profitable sideline of what Farağ Fōda called the affluent faction of truly modern militant Muslims. In February 1986 he was reported to have been elected president of a consultative committee appointed by the Governor of the Egyptian Central Bank to solve the problems existing within a financial institution called Al-Maṣraf al-Islāmī al-Duwalī.[30] According to the fundamentalist periodical *Al-Nūr*[31] Sheikh Al-Sha'rāwī's duties in this committee involved mediating in a conflict within the institution's board of directors and supervising the Islamic character of its future dealings. Furthermore, the Sheikh was reported to have founded an Islamic Bank in Austria at an unspecified date.[32] Finally, the Secretary-General of the International Union of Islamic Banks, Dr Aḥmad 'Abd al-'Azīz al-Naǧǧār, declared in early 1987 that 'without Sheikh Al-Sha'rāwī the Islamic Fayṣal Bank in Egypt [*Bank Fayṣal al-Islāmī fī Miṣr*] could not have been founded in the days when [Sheikh Al-Sha'rāwī] was Cabinet Minister for Religious Affairs....'[33]

It is difficult not to conclude from these slightly contradictory rumours and reports that Sheikh Al-Sha'rāwī is connected with the 'affluent faction' and a representative of it. However, the precise nature of his role within the faction can not be established without access to a great variety of archives that are either inaccessible or disappearing. Does Sheikh Al-Sha'rāwī favour the establishment, by force if necessary, of an Islamic state to replace the regime of Nasser, Sadat and Mubarak? Or does he prefer gradual, peaceful change that will have the same result? Does he accept the world as it is, or is he a soldier in the army that fights

30 *Al-Ğumhūriyya*, February 17, 1986.

31 February 19, 1986.

32 *Al-Ğumhūriyya*, April 1, 1986.

33 *Shabāb Bilādī* (Cairo), January 3, 1987.

for the return of the glory of Islam? The enigma of Sheikh Al-Sha'rāwī may never be solved.

By contrast, the secrets of the world of the Lebanese Sheikh Muḥammad Ḥusayn Faḍlallāh[34] have been partly revealed. In the early 1980s Faḍlallāh (b. 1935) and his followers believed that a Shī'ī, Islamic republic could save Lebanon from the ongoing civil war and interventions by un-Islamic foreign powers. He was educated in the Shī'ī centres in Naǧaf, and has been in close personal contact with most leading Shī'ī Ayatollahs. Like Sayyid Quṭb, he denies the Islamic character (and hence the legitimacy) of the existing regimes in the Muslim world. Since 1985 he has been president of the Lebanese council of the *Ḥizbᵘ Allāh*[35] or *Ḥizbollah,* and vice-president of the Teheran-based central council of that organisation. He has been active in Lebanon since 1966, in Nab'a, an impoverished part of Beirut that was devastated in 1976 by extremist Maronites.

April 18, 1983, sixty-three people, seventeen of them Americans, were killed when a truck filled with explosives detonated, for all practical purposes within the lobby of the United States embassy on the seafront in Beirut. September 20, 1984, a van pulled into the US embassy annex in East Beirut and killed twenty-four people when it exploded. On October 23, 1984, the French military headquarters in Beirut was bombed, and more than seventy people were killed. Almost simultaneously more than 200 American marines died when their four-storeys-high headquarters was blown up.[36] Having investigated these remarkable events, the world's intelligence services concluded that Sheikh Faḍlallāh had been connected with all four of them.[37] Faḍlallāh, it was decided, had to go and meet his Maker. On March 8, 1985, in a concerted effort by the secret world of Beirut, the apartment building where he lived was blown up. About eighty people were killed in the blast and some 200 wounded, but Faḍlallāh remained unhurt. Things had to be done differently, the professionals now realised, and they are reported to have approached him with the suggestion

[34] See O. Carré, 'Faḍlallāh' in *Oxf. EMIW*, i, 453-6.

[35] Literally 'the party of God', from Koran 5:56(61): 'the party of God, they are the victors (Arberry's translation).

[36] See the press for those weeks, and Bob Woodward, *Veil*, 245 and 379. Different sources give slightly different numbers.

[37] Woodward, *Veil*, 396.

that, in exchange for $2 million cash, 'he would act as [an] early-warning system for terrorist attacks on Saudi and American facilities.'[38] Apparently things now worked out according to plan, since no more terrorist suicide attacks ascribed to him have taken place.

Nevertheless, these suicide attacks created a problem, if not for the foreign powers that adjusted their Lebanon policies to Lebanese realities and left, then certainly for pious orthoprax Muslims familiar with the dictates of Islamic law. Islam does not approve of suicide. But does it approve of suicide bombings that are successful? No clear answer to this question emerged, and late in 1985 Sheikh Faḍlallāh declared:

> Attacks that only inflict limited casualties...should not be encouraged if the price is the death of the person who carries them out.[39]

Attacks causing *unlimited* casualties, it might be inferred, should be encouraged. However this may be, the kidnappings of foreigners in Lebanon now began in earnest. Kidnappings are, of course, less bloody than suicide bombings; they generate perhaps even more, and longer-lasting, publicity, and on several earlier occasions had already proved effective. Hostage-taking, moreover, was not condemned by Khomeini[40] – such lack of condemnation is generally understood as approval. But again Islamic law complicates matters. What exactly are the hostages guilty of? Which precept of the sharīʿa demands or allows their imprisonment? In a community whose members are willing to die for the application of Islamic law these are important questions.

Rules of conduct which Islam prescribes may have had a mitigating influence on what happened in Lebanon. Or – the least one is allowed to think – they *should* have had such an influence. During the civil war in Algiers the contrary seems to have been the case. The Algerian coalition of Islamic fundamentalists is known as the Islamic Salvation Front or FIS.[41] In late 1991 and early 1992 it seemed that the FIS might take power peacefully by means of an election. Although during the 1980s the Algerian

[38] *Ibid.*, 397.

[39] Kramer, *Hizballah*, 16.

[40] *Ibid.*, 22.

[41] From the French *Front Islamique du Salut*, in Arabic *Ǧabhat al-Inqādh al-Islāmī*.

army generally kept itself in the background, it now took matters into its own hands. On 11 January 1992 it carried out a *coup d'état*, forced President Chadli Benjedid to resign, and cancelled the elections. Chadli had perhaps been guilty in the late 1980s of trying to use the Algerian Muslim fundamentalists to strengthen his own position against the ruling party, the *Front de Liberation National*, which had grown out of the war of independence against France in the 1950s and '60s. However this may be, in February 1992 the military rulers of Algeria imposed a state of emergency in the country, and invited a popular FLN veteran, Muhammad Boudiaf, to return from exile in Morocco and become Prime Minister. The new military rulers thus denied the fundamentalists an electoral route to power, and in the following month civil war broke out between them and the FIS.[42]

All this deeply affected the discussions within the fundamentalist movement. Some of its theoreticians, e.g. the Syrian 'Adnān Sa'd al-Dīn, had previously argued that 'when we do not succeed in convincing the majority [of the need to introduce the *sharī'a* and establish an Islamic state], we shall have failed, and will have to exercise self-criticism'.[43] This view, of course, implied rejection of the use of force. After the Algerian coup, which had forcibly excluded the fundamentalists from taking part in the democratic process, such theoreticians looked like fools, and their appeal to Koran 42:36-39 sounded hollow and unconvincing:

> Those who answer their Lord
> and perform the prayer
> their affair [should be] counsel between them.[44]

Many had argued before the events of 1991-2 in Algeria, that the Koranic *shūrā* or 'counsel' implied that Islam demanded democracy. Ḥasan al-Bannā's distaste for political parties and democracy, so his son Aḥmad Sayf al-Islām attested, had been exclusively determined by the state of Egyptian political parties and Egyptian democracy in the 1940s, not by political parties and democracy as such.[45]

The exegetical acrobatics that transubstantiated Koranic *shūrā*

42 S.T. Hunter, *The Algerian Crisis*, 50, 58-9, and the references given there.

43 'Adnān Sa'd al-Dīn, 'Min Uṣūl..", 283.

44 In Arabic: *wa-amruhum shūrā baynahum*.

45 'Adnān Sa'd al-Dīn, 'Min Uṣūl....', 291.

into Western 'democracy' became irrelevant after the Algiers coup in January 1992. Many radical Muslims now believed that 'the secularists' would never let them have a taste of legal power. Only armed struggle could put things right and give Islam and its laws the place they deserved. Armed struggle now broke out all over the country, and soon the Western public became familiar with a second Algerian acronym: the GIA, from the French *Groupes Islamiques Armées*, Islamic armed groups. (Fundamentalism in Iran, Egypt and Lebanon has enriched the languages of the West with a number of Arabic words, like *ǧamāʻāt, ǧihād, ḥizbollāh* and *āyatollāh*. Algiers has been westernised to such a degree that even its fundamentalist acronyms are derived from French, not Arabic.)

The war, however, was not about linguistic niceties. About 40,000 people were killed in the period up to July 1995 when the negotiations between the regime and the fundamentalists broke down once more because of the 'intransigence' of the rebels. The rebels, however, had not only been intransigent, they had also been creative. They had decided that the regime was *ǧāhilī*, 'un-Islamic', and so were its servants. Since these government servants, whether small functionaries in a government office or police, were born as Muslims, they had committed apostasy from Islam. This is more or less standard fundamentalist post-Quṭb ideology, and is known among the initiated as *takfīr al-ǧumhūr*, literally 'branding the masses as apostate pagans', and evidently represents a more radical view than *takfīr al-ḥākim*, 'branding the ruler as an apostate pagan'. The Algerians, however, came up with a refinement that would cost the lives of many people.

The fresh apostates not only deserved the death penalty for apostasy, but also had to accept that according to Islamic law their marriages had been dissolved since Islam does not permit a non-Muslim man to be married to a Muslim woman. The new ex-wives were warned: if they remained in the conjugal domicile and spent the night there, they would according to the fundamentalist interpretation of Islamic law be guilty of *zinā*, adultery. In the case of a woman who has previously been married, Islam prescribes the death penalty for *zinā*. To uphold what they regarded as Islamic morality, fundamentalist activists informally executed such death sentences – unarmed woman are an easier target for assassination than armed soldiers or policemen.

In Algeria and Egypt the Muslim fundamentalists perceive the ruling secularist élite as their prime enemy. They are a dangerous, internal enemy. When Algerian activists threaten to kill foreigners residing in their country, they do so to destabilise the regime. They have no quarrel with these foreigners themselves; however, the fundamentalists reason retrospectively that by their presence in the country the foreigners help the enemies of Islam, and thus it is seen as religiously permitted to kill them. The forces of imperialism, the United States and other outside non-Muslim supporters of the ruling élite are in principle as guilty as the local tyrants, but the representatives of outside enemies come second. They are, after all, far away, and they did not commit apostasy from Islam.

Palestinian Muslim fundamentalists, on the other hand, have two enemies. Like all their kind they have an internal enemy, but unlike other fundamentalist groups they also have an external enemy. Both enemies are almost equally close and equally devilish: the internal enemy are the secularist élite of the Palestine Liberation Organisation (PLO), and the external enemy are the Zionists. In Israel, in the (Israeli occupied) Territories on the West Bank of the river Jordan, and in the territories controlled by the Palestine National Authority, the fundamentalists have to confront both enemies: the Israelis and the Muslim-born nationalist secularists who are united in the PLO.

The fundamentalists in the region maintain that their outside enemy, Israel, is strong because the Jews adhere to Judaism. Such an assertion could not but fall on fertile ground among the Arab Muslims who suffer from the Israeli domination of their lives. Could Muslims not make even more progress than the Jews did, simply by adhering to their own Islam? After all, a Muslim must of necessity believe that Islam is a better religion than Judaism, so the blessings a Muslim receives from adherence to Islam will be greater than the blessings Jews receive from adherence to Judaism. The insight that the Israelis were victorious because of their devotion to Judaism could not but stimulate the growth of groups that promised total adherence to Islam once they were in a position of power.[46] These groups, in turn, could not but see the secularist Palestine Liberation Organisation as their natural (internal) enemy.

However, the PLO has been involved in real negotiations with

[46] Cf. e.g., Abu-Amr, *West Bank and Gaza*, 13.

a versatile, professional opponent who, in his own perception of things, had plenty at stake in these negotiations. At the same time, the PLO was dependent on support from a number of Arab states. This support, it is well known, was given in varying degrees and subject to conditions that might change weekly. The PLO represented the Palestinians, but its policies were largely determined by others.

Under such circumstances the political positions of the PLO have inevitably changed frequently in the years since its foundation in the 1960s. Especially at times of sensitive negotiations with Americans or Israelis, the average Palestinian must have had great difficulty in understanding the silences or the declarations of the PLO. Compared to the bureaucratic PLO, the fundamentalist Islamic Ǧihād (*Tanẓīm al-Ǧihād al-Islāmī*) must have looked like a rock of resolve and resolution. Not only the economic conditions have been favourable for the growth of fundamentalist movements among Muslim Palestinians in Israeli-dominated territories.

However, outsiders have a problem when they want to understand the ideologies involved. The struggle between the Palestinians and the Israelis is an almost classical example of a struggle between two groups, each defining itself as a people and fighting for the very same piece of land. (Some authorities deny that the Palestinians are a people, and similarly other authorities deny that the Israelis – or the Jews? – are a people.) But what the Israelis and the Palestinians say about each other is determined much more by the demands of the political and military struggle which these two parties have been conducting since the 1940s than by the general history of Jewish-Muslim relations. Likewise, the study of the relationship between Rome and the Reformation should preferably not be conducted in Northern Ireland, or be limited to sources from that part of the world.

However that may be, Sayyid Quṭb's ideology[47] and Khomeini's revolution[48] have powerfully influenced religiously-inspired Palestinian resistance. The mainstream Muslim Brotherhood has been active in Palestine since the 1940s, and it is against the background of its activities that Islamic Ǧihād was founded, officially in 1980, the year after Khomeini's revolution, by two men from the Gaza strip, Fatḥī al-Shaqāqī and 'Abd al-'Azīz 'Awda (the phonologies

[47] *Ibid.*, 97.

[48] Rekhess, 'Gaza Strip'.

of spoken Palestinian Arabic and Israeli Hebrew collude with each other to change this name into *Odeh*). 'Abd al-'Azīz 'Awda, like Ḥasan al-Bannā and Sayyid Quṭb, studied at Dār al-'Ulūm in Cairo. He spent about a year in an Israeli prison in 1986-7, and 1987-8 was deported to Lebanon.[49]

In 1979 Al-Shaqāqī (b. 1952) was twice arrested in Egypt. In 1983 he was imprisoned in Gaza, and in 1986 again jailed and sentenced to four years. He started his career as a Nasserite, but after the defeat of 1967 joined the Muslim Brotherhood. By 1979 he appears to have developed into a disciple of the Iranian Islamic Revolution: in that year he published his *Al-Khumaynī: Al-Hall al-Islāmī wa-'l-Badīl*, 'Khomeini: The Islamic Solution and the Alternative'. He became influential and important enough to merit assassination – on October 26, 1995, in Malta, and by Israelis, if the suspicions of most people are correct.

Prison has always been a favourable environment for the propagation of a faith. Someone who gets thrown into prison needs to make new social contacts quickly, and may be ready to accept the religious convictions of new prison friends without difficulty, especially when these convictions give meaning and purpose to his imprisonment. This has been true of the Muslim Brothers in Egypt,[50] and equally so for the Islamic Ğihād in Israeli prisons.[51] This may have been one of the reasons why every now and then the Israelis have attempted to deport religious activists rather than imprison them.

Khomeini and his 1979 Islamic revolution made a great impression on the fundamentalists in Palestine. The Shāh had, of course, been an ally of the Americans: could other allies of the Americans also be removed? Could even Israel perhaps be removed? Moreover, Khomeini knew about the Jews: already on the first page of his *Al-Ḥukūma al-Islāmiyya* he warns his readers against the Jews who, he explains, have always tried to harm the Islamic movement. Al-Shaqāqī and other Palestinian fundamentalists admired Khomeini for understanding

....the great culture clash in progress between the Islamic nation

[49] Abu-Amr, *West Bank*, 93-4; Rekhess, 'Gaza Strip', 202. The two scholars give different dates.

[50] See, e.g., Al-Qarḍāwī, *Ṣaḥwa*, 128.

[51] Abu-Amr, *West Bank*, 95.

with its historical tradition, its faith and exemplary civilisation, and the West with its crusading spirit.[...] This was a struggle between the divine and the satanic forces.[...] The spearhead of the satanic forces in Israel....[52]

However, by 1988 the Palestinian branch of the Muslim Brotherhood had also formed its own 'military arm': Ḥamas (an acronym derived from *Ḥarakat al-Muqāwama al-Islāmiyya*, the Islamic resistance movement). By now the Palestinians had the unusual privilege of possessing at least three organisations which had no other reason for their existence than the liberation of Palestine from the Zionist oppressors: the PLO, Islamic Ǧihād and Ḥamas. All three regularly made the international headlines. Two were religiously inspired, one was nationalist. What little trust existed between these three organisations was not encouraged by their common enemy.

Khomeini has undoubtedly been the greatest soldier for Islam in the twentieth century. It was not only Palestinians who were captivated by his triumphs in Teheran; the Egyptians were too. Early in 1979 Egyptian media described the overthrow of the Shāh's regime as essentially a victory for Islam, a victory which had ended the un-Islamic foreign domination over Iran exercised by the Americans. Khomeini, so the readers of the Egyptian press were made to understand, achieved a victory over Christian Western powers. The subject of Muslim victories over non-Muslims is, of course, non-controversial in the Muslim world, and the greatness of such victories can safely be lauded in all places and at all times. Yet in the spring of 1979 the Egyptian public (if interested) might not yet have appreciated one more detailed and specific feature of Khomeini's ideology.

Khomeini, it is now widely known, came to power advocating a system of Islamic government where the highest authority would be in the hands of the 'Ulamā', who in the Iranian Shīʿī vocabulary are called Ayatollahs. *Wilāyat al-Faqīh*, 'the rule of the scholar of Islamic law', was the slogan that encapsulated this ideology. *Faqīh*, 'scholar of Islamic law', is incidentally a word common to both the Sunnīs and the Shīʿīs. Islam, Khomeini made clear, demanded an Islamic state led by the men of God. Ever since the Crusades, he wrote,[53] missionaries, orientalists and journalists had been striving

[52] Rekhess, 'Gaza Strip', 195, 204.

[53] Khomeini, *Al-Ḥukūma al-Islāmiyya*, 8.

to distort Islam and to prevent Muslims from setting up such an Islamic state. The time had come to do something about putting this Islamic imperative into action. However, in the months following the Iranian Islamic revolution of 1979 this interesting historical vision had to compete for the interest of the Egyptian public with a bold project of legal reform introduced by President Sadat or perhaps, according to the rumours current at the time, rather by the President's wife Ğihan Sadat.

In May 1979 President Sadat promulgated Law 44/1979 on marriage, divorce etc. This law contained several articles that were at variance with the Islamic sharīʿa, and aroused widespread public discussion. In such discussion it was held to be particularly offensive that this law designated polygamy as *ḍarar*, 'something which harms'. Since Koran 4:3 ('Marry such of the women as seem good to you, double or treble or fourfold') is widely understood as Koranic evidence that God permits polygamy, many pious Muslims were severely shocked that the Egyptian government designated polygamy, which the Koran itself approved, as harmful.

In May 1985 this law of 1979 was declared invalid by the Egyptian Higher Constitutional Court (*Al-Ğarīda al-Rasmiyya*, May 16, 1985) on formal grounds. In July 1985 the Egyptian government reacted by proclaiming the new Law 100/1985 which annulled most of the changes introduced in 1979.

It goes without saying that these legal reforms, both in 1985 and in 1979, provoked elaborate public discussion, in which the Iranian revolutionary example played little or no role. However, it is quite possible that the decisions which the Egyptian authorities took on this matter in 1985 were influenced by their desire to lay to rest a controversy that could only be to the benefit of the fundamentalists' propaganda. This propaganda had gradually increased in strength after 1980, when in an attempt to appease the fundamentalists the Egyptian government amended article 2 of the constitution, which now proclaimed the Islamic sharīʿa to be the main source of legislation, *al-maṣdar al-ra'īsī li-'l-tashrī'*.[54]

However, since the fall of 1979 an Arab intellectual wishing to know exactly what Khomeini professed or advocated could turn to an Arabic version of his book entitled *Al-Ḥukūma al-Islāmiyya: Wilāyat al-Faqīh*. This edition was privately printed and distributed by Dr Ḥasan Ḥanafī, professor of Islamic philosophy

[54] Hāla Muṣṭafā, *Dawla*, 214. Also see Chapter 8.

in the University of Cairo in Gizeh. In his introduction to this basic text, Ḥanafī summarises Khomeini's views with great understanding, but feels that he has to make six critical comments. (1) Although, according to Ḥanafī, Khomeini relies on reason when presenting his political and religious ideology, he also often looks for support for his views in controversial chapters of Islamic history. Here Ḥanafī refers to Khomeini's allusions to the early wars between Sunna and Shī'a, and concludes his first critical comment as follows:

> The need for the formation of an Islamic government is an obvious necessity which does not need to be shown to be true with the help of quotations from the Tradition; neither does the doctrine of the supremacy of the *Faqīh* need such support or proof; both these theories are clearly and solidly found in the Koran [*thābit bi-'l-Qur'ān*]. It would be all too easy to claim that such supporting Traditions are weak, or to cast doubt on their authenticity.

One cannot fail to note that these words fully endorse the essence of Khomeini's political ideology. Ḥanafī appeals to high authority indeed when he teaches that it is the Koran itself which teaches the doctrine of the supremacy of the *Fuqahā'*. His first criticism is actually rather mild and only concerns the way in which Khomeini attempted to prove this doctrine, not the doctrine itself.

(2) The second comment concerns the metaphysical element in Khomeini's theory: not everyone, Ḥanafī suspects, may share Khomeini's metaphysical belief in the uncreatedness and pre-existence of the Imams. 'Here', he complains, 'the theory of the Supremacy of the *Faqīh* looks more like a myth than like a positive political order.'

(3) Ḥanafī writes that Khomeini concentrates too much on the top, neglecting to discuss the basis: social change cannot be affected before present political authority has been removed, and this can only be achieved through revolutionary activities, which are doomed to fail if they have no mass support. It would perhaps be better, Ḥanafī suggests, to concentrate on enlightening the masses, *tanwīr al-shu'ūb*, since this is a necessary prerequisite for success in the battle for an Islamic state. Many an old Calvinist will be pleased to read in this connection that man needs to be

subject to the rule of the *fuqahā* ', because 'human nature is evil, and man is evil by nature'.

(4) Ḥanafī regrets that Khomeini does not give 'detailed theories', *naẓariyyāt tafṣīliyya,* on such essentials of the social order as class structure, the ownership of the means of production, the relationship between farmers and the soil or between workers and the factory, the nationalisation of banks and insurance companies and so on. Such details, he concludes, are needed to transform the doctrine of the supremacy of the *fuqahā*' from being merely a slogan into practice, *min al-shi'ār ilā al-taṭbīq.*

(5) Ḥanafī has his doubts about certain measures taken by the Iranian revolution concerning chador and *ḥiğāb*, nightclubs, wine, the execution of prostitutes etc. In these measures, he thinks, traditional ethics play a large role. Have political Islam and the ethics of Islam, he wonders, kept pace with each other? Is Khomeini's revolution not essentially a revolution of the oppressed and the hungry, and should it not give priority to the war against poverty and unemployment?

Hanafī chooses his words with great care, and his remarks every now and then become rather obscure. He certainly does not want to say anything that could be construed as an attack on the alleged cruelty of some of Khomeini's measures – nor, at the same time, does he want to arouse the suspicion that he seeks to defend those reprehensible forms of human behaviour to which Khomeini's regime put an end. This dilemma muddies his clarity of expression.

(6) Hanafī agrees with Khomeini on the necessity to preserve an Islamic identity, but he feels that to reject all things Western goes too far: rationalism, parliamentarism, humanism, progressivism, and a host of other -isms may nowadays seem to be Western, but according to him, these doctrines, if properly understood and reconstructed in the Islamic way, are all Islamic trends (*ittiğāhāt islāmiyya*) which the West took over from Islam in the Middle Ages. The Great Islamic Revolution is not, he says, only a reaction against the West, or exclusively an anti-Western movement; to regard it as such would be to belittle it. It is a movement which in principle is capable of welding together (*yumkin al-talāḥum*) revolutionary movements all over the world, 'the revolution of the priests of Latin America' not excluded.

Hasan Hanafī's six remarks can only be called constructive criticism. It is a form of criticism that implies an endorsement of Khomeini's views. Furthermore, Ḥanafī teaches that the Koran itself already prescribed these views, and that textual support from the different collections of Prophetic Traditions is superfluous and needlessly controversial. By doing so Ḥanafī lifts Khomeini's doctrine – nowadays known as *Wilāyat al-Faqīh* – above the Sunnī-Shī'ī division: as far as Traditions are concerned, Sunnī and Shī'ī Muslims have their differences, but for true Muslims the text of the Koran is elevated above any denominational or sectarian difference.

However, ideological sympathy with Khomeinism was at times abundantly present on the pages of the Egyptian opposition newspaper *Al-Aḥrār* in the 1980s, even during the war between Iraq and Iran in which Egypt, like most Arab countries, took Iraq's side. A number of Egyptian newspapers have for some time closely identified themselves with Khomeini-type Islamic aspirations. Representatives of these newspapers visited Iran in 1986 at the invitation of the Iranian government, and enthusiastic reports on the visit can be found, for example, in *Al-Aḥrār* for October 13, 1986: 'The mosque...is the centre of the command', 'The Islamic republic does not want war', 'The Muslim armies show the greatest possible determination' etc., or in *Al-Sha'b* for June 24, 1986: 'The [new] rulers of Teheran live as simply as they did before....', 'The leaders walk [without bodyguard] amidst the masses....', '[Khomeini] takes no luxury foods....' etc.

However, the emphasis in this feat of propaganda falls on such well-known clichés as the simplicity of the new rulers, the enthusiasm of the masses for the New Order, and the hatred felt by the populace for the expelled oppressors, and not on the new ideology which the Iranian Islamic revolution stands for.

Among Muslims in the 1990s three militant ideologies have emerged that outsiders do not hesitate to call fundamentalist. The first is the *takfīr* fundamentalism that goes back to the musings of Sayyid Quṭb. It is typical of the naïvety of the ruling secular élite and its intellectuals that in their circles it is still assumed that *takfīr* means 'atonement',[55] whereas the use of that term implies death sentences upon them. The second is the movement of Islamic social engineering associated with Islamic banking. It has ample support among the well-to-do, and is publicly represented by people like Sheikh Al-Shar'āwī though perhaps not by him.

[55] E.g. even Abu-Amr, *West Bank*, xiv; and many others.

These people are thoroughly familiar with Islam, and will smile when they see that the secular élite assumes *takfīr* to mean atonement. The third is the Iranian form. At the time of writing it appears to be stronger than the other two, if only because it has managed to take power and to hold on to it for almost two decades. This form has been much more successful than the other two because it did not consist of individual soldiers or even individual platoons, but was led by a general who knew how to weld these into an effective modern army.

Only the vicissitudes of war and civil war, of rebellion and repression, of intrigue and counter-intrigue will decide the future of these three particular varieties of the human endeavour to live in accordance with the will of God.

4

THE CASE OF SHUKRĪ MUṢṬAFĀ

Sheikh Muḥammad Ḥusayn al-Dhahabī, former Cabinet Minister for Religious Affairs and hence a symbol of official Islam, was murdered in Cairo on July 3, 1977. According to the official version of the murder, the Sheikh was kidnapped by members of the Shukrī group, who announced that he would be freed when a number of members of this group had been released from prison. The group also demanded a ransom of 200,000 Egyptians pounds.[1] At the end of 1977, shortly after Sadat's historic visit to Jerusalem, Shukrī Aḥmad Muṣṭafā was sentenced to death for his involvement in this killing, and in March 1978 he was executed.

Shukrī, born in 1942, became a Brotherhood activist in Asyūṭ in 1964-5 while studying agriculture at the university there. He was one of the many Muslim Brothers imprisoned in 1965, and developed his ideas about the necessity for the reform of Islam and Islamic societies in prison. He was released in 1971 in the wake of Sadat's 'Rectification Revolution', *Thawrat al-Taṣḥīḥ*. When, for religious reasons, some of Shukrī's followers in September 1973 withdrew to the desert near a place called Markaz Abū Al-Raqqāṣ in the Governorate of Asyūṭ, the authorities intervened and arrested a number of them. Shukrī himself was arrested on October 26, 1973, and released in April 1974.[2] There is little doubt that some of the contemporary *ǧamā'āt* are continuations of groups founded by him when he was in prison for the first time in 1965-71.

The connection between the Shukrī group and Sheikh Al-Dhahabī is an article which the latter wrote against the group. After his killing, the Egyptian Ministry of *Awqāf* reprinted his

[1] Fāḍil, *Mudhakkirāt*, 74.

[2] Ḥasan Ṣādiq, *Firaq*, 333-5; Kepel, *Prophet and Pharaoh*, 70-8.

short study of the Shukrī group, and this unexciting pamphlet remained on offer in the Cairo bookstalls at least till October 1982. At that time, publications on a multitude of even more violent events pushed Al-Dhahabī's learned article aside. The most offensive phrases in the article are found on its pages 4 and 28, where Sheikh Al-Dhahabī called the members of the Shukrī group sick (*saqīm*) and their views outrageous (*ǧā'ir*). This was because of Shukrī's conviction that the majority of contemporary Muslims are in reality apostates.

When, in November 1977, the court[3] that had to judge Shukrī asked him to describe his own ideas and those of his group, he proudly replied that he had already written about 4,000 pages on the subject.[4] The first of these writings was a book of about 700 pages, divided over eleven notebooks[5] and containing a 'detailed refutation of Sunnī Islam'.[6] The authorities, he informed the court, confiscated this manuscript when they arrested him in 1973. Its title cannot now be ascertained, but it may have been *Kitāb al-Iğmā'*, the book about the consensus. The outstanding characteristic of Sunnī Islam is well known to be its appeal to *iğmā* or 'consensus' (of the Islamic community)' as a source of Islamic law, and it is generally accepted that the legitimacy of this appeal is based on a Tradition preserved in the Ibn Māğa collection. This Tradition upheld that the Apostle Mohammed once said: 'My community will not agree on an error', *lā tağtami' ummatī 'alā ḍalāla*.

Islam is not the only religion to hold such a belief: its absence would imply that God had left his elect without reliable guidance. A community that feels itself to be on the right path can give no better expression to this feeling than by adhering to such a belief. Religions which teach that the word of God has been among men during only a limited period of time have to possess a mechanism which guarantees the truth and divine origin of the multitude of tenets that took their final shape after this period. Without it God's elect cannot be sure that they are not unknowingly in error.

[3] *Maḥkamat Amn al-Dawla al-'Ulyā al-'Askariyya,* The High Military Court for the Security of the State.

[4] Shukrī, *I'tirāfāt*, 53.

[5] *Ibid.*; for *iṣrār* read *iğmā'*?

[6] *radd*[un] *tafṣīlī alā ta'wīlāt al-muntasibīn li-madhhab ahl al-sunna.*

Nevertheless, according to Shukrī[7] it is highly improbable that the Apostle Mohammed (d. 632) ever said that his community would 'never agree on an error'. Ibn Māǧa (d. 887), in whose collection the saying is preserved, already suspected that Mohammed had not said it. Mohammed, Shukrī thought, did not teach that the community's agreement on the Islamic character of a prescript automatically implied its divine origin. Ibn Māǧa only preserved the Tradition because no good Muslim specialist of the Traditions would take the risk that through his own mistake a possibly authentic Tradition might get lost for ever. However, he did not vouch for its authenticity. Moreover, Ibn Māǧa's collection of Traditions about Mohammed is the *last* collection of the six canonical ones, and the *only* one that contains this disputed saying.[8]

In Shukrī's worldview, the saying was not disqualified only by these literary and historical circumstances. He believed that the decline of Islam started in the fourth century of the Islamic era (912-1009), shortly after the lifetime of Ibn Māǧa, when Muslims began to believe that their lives should be directed not by the Koran but by the opinions of the leaders of the great schools of Islamic law (*madhāhib*). Since then, Shukrī preached, Islam had degenerated into imitating (*taqlīd*) these men. God's own word, the Koran, 'had...been placed in a museum', *wuḍi'a fī mathaf.*[9]

Shukrī added that his second book, called *Al-Tabayyun*, 'The inquiry', and its manuscript too had been taken from him in 1973, the year of the October war against Israel. This book, of about 200 pages, had 'talked about how to rule over individuals and the society'. The third book, of 500-600 pages, was apologetic: it contained not only an elaborate defence of the group's thinking but also an analysis and refutation of the objections raised against them. Finally, this third book discussed the exegetical methods by which the views of the group were derived from the Koran. Despite its voluminous size, it was still unfinished. Its title is unknown.

He declared that the fourth book, which was small and unfinished, explained why reliance on the leaders of the great schools of Islamic law, *taqlīd*, was forbidden, and why the effort of using

[7] Shukrī, *I'tirāfāt*, 57.

[8] Wensinck, *Concordance*, I, 367, gives only one occurrence: Ibn Māǧa, Fitan, 8.

[9] Shukrī, *I'tirāfāt*, 56.

individual legal reasoning, *iğtihād*, was an obligation on good Muslims. The fifth book, of 150 pages, 'speaks of the positive[10] side of Islam, and its critics, and is regarded as an objective summary of the subject'. Furthermore, Shukrī added,

> we have books written by other members: Māhir 'Abd al-'Azīz wrote on local and international political problems, and on the legal status of our group. 'Alā' al-Dīn 'Alī Riḍā wrote *Kitāb al-Ḥukm*, a book on how to rule according to what God sent down,[11] as well as *Kitāb al-Hiğra*, a book on the duty of emigration from un-Islamic societies. We also have other pamphlets, the latest and the most important being my own *Kitāb al-Khilāfa*, the Book of the Caliphate.

Shukrī probably knew that he was doomed and took the opportunity to speak for history. His bibliographical introduction only whet the appetite of students of Islam and of millenarian[12] movements, who can only read the report of Shukrī's interrogation. Needless to say, none of the books mentioned is available except for (parts of) *Kitāb al-Khilāfa*, published in Arabic in London in 1991 by Dr R.S. Aḥmad with Riad El-Rayyes Books Ltd. If a successful fundamentalist revolution ever occurs in Egypt, it is unlikely that the Shukrī texts will be brought back into the open from the archives of the Egyptian security services. The view of the fundamentalist movements on *taqlīd* and their reliance on the great leaders of the Islamic legal schools differ fundamentally from the views of the Shukrī group. These books will consequently have to remain a quarry for specialists in the distant future.

Shukrī subsequently demanded the right to present to the court a general introduction, in three parts, to the thought of his group before he would answer specific questions and present his defence in the Dhahabī case. The court agreed, but ordered him to be brief: *qālat al-maḥkama na'm, qul fa-awğiz*. The first part, Shukrī explained, would prove that Muslims should only accept guidance and knowledge (*hudā* and *'ilm*) from God. The second part would

[10] This word is not fully legible in the original.

[11] 'Ruling by what God sent down' occurs three times in Sūra 5, at the end of the verses 44, 45, and 47. The Koran here calls whoever does not rule by what God sent down an unbeliever (*kāfir*), a wrong-doer (*ẓālim*) and a reprobate (*fāsiq*).

[12] E.g. Shukrī, *Khilāfa*, 119: *inna 'l-arḍ qad awshakat 'alā al-nihāya*, 'the world is about to end'.

inquire into the character of such guidance, after he had made clear what its sources ought to be. The third part would try to define what aims Islam should try to achieve, and how to reach them.

Although this may sound pious, such words can not be understood in the context of a Muslim society other than as a criticism of the Ulema and their trade. The Ulema teach, study, preserve, develop and continue the work of the traditional schools of Islamic law; hence Shukrī's formula 'accepting guidance only from God' can only be understood as an outright renunciation of the Ulema and a rejection of what they specialised in: the traditional rules of Islamic law as enshrined in the traditional handbooks. Criticism of the Ulema, however, also implies criticism of the state which supports them. Arab states in particular take no pleasure in being criticised and have macabre ways of showing their displeasure.

Shukrī phrases his statements rejecting the traditional system of Islamic law on his own behalf and that of his group in rather precise Islamic theological jargon. The rejection is obviously not the sudden impulse of an amateur who simply wants to rid himself of the burdens of the past without knowing what or whom he is talking about.

Continuing his lecture to the judges, Shukrī asked a number of rhetorical questions about the four founding imāms of the schools of Islamic law[13] from the eighth and ninth centuries:[14] Do Muslims have to believe that these jurists were infallible? Were they omniscient? Did they know both the past and the future? Is it possible that one day supplements may have to be added to their opinions? Are their writings part of God's revelation? Do Muslims really believe that the views of these early founding fathers of Islamic law supply something that was lacking in God's revelation? Are the words of these lawyers clearer than God's own word? Since their books are written in plain Arabic, why do we need so many commentaries on them?

Years later, one of Shukrī's ex-followers, 'Abd al-Raḥmān Abū al-Khayr, showed that he understood perfectly what Shukrī meant:

[13] Traditionally the four schools of law (*madhāhib*) are believed to go back to Abū Ḥanīfa (Iraq, d. 150/767), Mālik b. Anas (Medina, d. 179/75), Al-Shafi'ī (Cairo, d. 204/820) and Aḥmad b. Ḥanbal (Baghdad, d. 241/855). All reference works on Islam mention and discuss these four imāms and their significance.

[14] Shukrī, *I'tirāfāt*, 56.

We do not accept the words ascribed to the Apostle's contemporaries, or the opinions of those versed in Islamic law, the *fuqahā'*.[15] We do not accept the opinions of the early jurists, or their consensus, *iğmā'*, or the other idols, *aṣnām*, like analogy, *qiyās*.[16] How can words of mere humans be a source of divine guidance?[17]

If 'Abd al-Raḥmān Abū al-Khayr understood Shukrī's meaning, others must also have done. If so, Shukrī was a danger to the Ulema since his worldview implied an almost complete rejection of their world, of Islamic law and its handbooks, its commentaries on commentaries, and the canonical Traditions of Islam. It implied a rejection of Islam as we know it, with the exception of the Koran.

Even about the Koran itself Shukrī admitted, in his own writings[18] and under questioning by the court,[19] that he was not absolutely certain about the historicity of the Koranic stories or about the infallibility of the process of its transmission. In the words of 'Abd al-Raḥmān Abū al-Khayr, what is known of Islamic history is regarded as *waqā'i' ghayr thābitat al-ṣiḥḥa*,[20] 'stories of dubious authenticity'. The mere possibility that this might be true caused commotion in some Western university departments. How much more courageous Shukrī Muṣṭafā was than many Western academics! With his life and not merely his academic reputation at stake, he continued to defend publicly the ideas he suspected to be true.

One would not expect the Muslim Brotherhood, the Al-Azhar apparatus and the religious Islamic establishment in general to take kindly to Shukrī's views, yet surprisingly little public condemnation was to be heard from those sources. However, the editor of his texts, Dr R.S. Ahmed, writes[21] that his views generated much hostility against him among 'all Islamist movements, both the secret and the public ones'. He goes on that 'these detailed

[15] 'Abd al-Raḥmān Abū al-Khayr, *Dhikrayātī*, 93.

[16] *Ibid.*, 9.

[17] *Ibid.*, 139: *kalām al-bashar...maṣdar al-hudā*..

[18] Shukrī, *Khilāfa*, 116: *Fa'inna l-Qur'ān lā yusağğil at-ta'rīkh li-dhāt al-ta'rīkh.*

[19] Ḥāmid Ḥassān, *Muwāğaha*, 68-72, quoting p. 1350 of the proceedings of Shukrī's questioning (*maḥḍar al-ğalsa*) during his trial; also Shukrī, *I'tirāfāt*, 85.

[20] Abd al-Raḥmān Abū al-Khayr, *Dhikrayātī*, 35.

[21] Aḥmad, *Nabiyy Musallaḥ*, I, 104, fn. 25 and I, 105, fn. 46.

views held by Shukrī' made many people very angry, 'especially within the Al-Azhar organisation and within the Society of the Muslim Brothers'. When these two statements are combined, it almost appears as if Dr Aḥmad is implying that he sees the Azhar as the public wing of the Islamic movement and the Brotherhood as its secret wing. In the light of recent developments, such a suggestion is far-fatched but not to be completely rejected.

The fundamentalist monthly *Mağallat al-Tawḥīd* points out that it makes little sense to follow the example of the Shukrī group and to take only the Koran as a source of guidance, to the exclusion of the other generally recognised sources of Islamic law and behaviour. What, the monthly asks, is to be done with the multitude of points not raised in the Koran that are nevertheless regarded by Muslims as forming an integral part of Islam? As examples it cites the call to prayer, the times of prayer, certain marriage impediments, certain dietary laws etc.[22] It is unlikely that such points would have escaped the notice of the scholars in the Brotherhood or at Al-Azhar.

The Brotherhood monthly *Al-Da'wa*, which is always as close as it is possible to be to the government, quotes[23] the Egyptian journalist Muṣṭafā Amīn, who definitely does not sympathise with Brotherhood causes. In connection with the Shukrī trial this influential and authoritative writer of high prestige remarked that some Egyptian journalists were *ḥukūmiyyīn akthar min al-ḥukūma nafs'hā*, 'more governmental than the government itself'. According to Muṣṭafā Amīn, the Egyptian press had lost all objectivity, and had not checked the bizarre facts which the prosecutors gave to them. One of these 'facts' was that Shukrī claimed to be of higher rank than a Prophet – a claim Muslims will think blasphemous or ridiculous. The accusation might remind Christians of Matthew 26.65: 'What further need have we of witnesses?'

Among other accusations which *Al-Da'wa* mentioned as being reported by the Egyptian press were that leaders of the group denied the obligatory character of the pilgrimage to the Ka'ba in Mecca; that members were making profits from lending money against interest; and that the leaders forbade the use of tap water, urged the members of the group to emigrate to Europe because

[22] *Al-Tawḥīd: Mağalla Islāmiyya Thaqāfiyya Shahriyya*, V, 10 (Shawwāl 1397 AH 'Cairo, September 1977 AD, 14.)

[23] *Al-Da'wa*, XXVI, 16 (September 1977), 47-9.

Egypt could no longer be regarded as an Islamic country, declared that stealing from non-members was legal, and prayed not at the appointed times but two hours before the public call to prayer. The list[24] published by *Al-Da'wa* concludes with the charge that there was 'enough dynamite under the bed of the leader of the group *li-nasf mīdān al-Taḥrīr*, to blow up Tahrīr Square [the largest in Cairo]' – although it is difficult, even for explosives experts, to blow up a square; such experts usually attempt to blow up buildings or people. This list only contained items that for religious and other reasons touched sensitive nerves with the Egyptian public.

The second Brotherhood monthly, *Al-I'tiṣām*, wrote in a relatively positive way of Shukrī and his group in its very first issue that was allowed to appear in the Sadat era.[25] This was in the opening article of that issue by Ğābir Rizq, the prestigious chronicler of the Muslim Brotherhood's ordeals under Nasser. He wrote, among other things, that Shukrī and his group did not get a fair deal from the Egyptian press, *al-ṣiḥāfa al-miṣriyya lam taltazim bi-mīthāq al-sharaf*. He was particularly disturbed by attempts in the press to present the group as emotionally disturbed, criminally insane crackpots who ought to have been taken into custody long before. However, it is common in all times and places to portray members of sects or cults as lunatics or criminals. After all, founders of the three monotheist world religions have been so regarded: according to the Bible, Moses was a murderer who fled from justice; Jesus was executed like a common criminal, although the Bible leaves the reader some freedom to speculate what his crime actually was; and the Koran mentions repeatedly that Mohammed was called a madman, *mağnūn*, by his Meccan enemies.

Strategies of religious distancing[26] regularly use these same two qualifications. For example, lunacy and criminality were cited in press comments to explain the Jonestown mass suicides on November 18, 1977. In the eyes of an outsider, joining a religious movement comes close to being sent to prison or to a mental hospital, and it is an easily attested, cross-culturally held belief that anyone who joins or founds a religious group must be sick or a criminal.

[24] *Al-Da'wa*, September 1977, 48.

[25] September 1977.

[26] Chidester, *Salvation*, 15-50.

At this time, in the fall of 1977, the limits set on *Al-I'tiṣām*'s freedom of expression must have been considerable. As is so often the case, the relationship between the government, the judicial system and the press in matters of state security closely resembled that which pious Christians traditionally assume to exist between the Father, the Son and the Holy Spirit. Nevertheless, the opening article in that issue of *Al-I'tiṣām* showed little enmity towards the Shukrī group, whereas the tension between it and the government at that time was extremely high. Furthermore, criticising the press as Ǧābir Rizq did, especially in the midst of such a crisis, is widely regarded as the equivalent of criticising the government.

Al-Azhar, like the two Brotherhood monthlies, condemned 'as a matter of course' the murder committed by members of the group, but insisted on differentiating between the crimes it had committed and its thoughts, *al-tafriqa...bayn qaḍiyyat al-qatl wa-qaḍiyyat al-fikr*. The communiqué of March 1978 in which Al-Azhar expressed its views on the matter 'received wide coverage in the Arab press, though not in Egypt itself'.[27] Nevertheless, it was again the monthly *Al-I'tiṣām* that printed the communiqué, on pages 17-18 of its issue of March 1978, almost simultaneously with the execution of Shukrī and four of his followers.

As far as we can understand, the attitude of Al-Azhar and the Academy of Islamic Studies over the Shukrī affair was not friendly or helpful to either the prosecution or the judges. The court charged with judging Shukrī and his group even publicly complained of this lack of enthusiasm from the official men of religion, and the press reported or implied that it even tended to regard the incompetence it imputed to Al-Azhar scholars as one of the reasons for the aberrations of the group. Nevertheless, the court did not allow the Al-Azhar 'Ulamā' to testify at the trial, although this had been requested by Shukrī's lawyer, Dr 'Abdallāh Rashwān.[28]

The Azhar's declaration of March 1978, signed by *Shaykh al-Azhar* 'Abd al-Ḥalīm Maḥmūd, gave several reasons for the institution's refusal to come forward with a condemnation of Shukrī and his group. Such a condemnation, it maintained, needed familiarity with the authoritative medieval Islamic scholarly texts

[27] Kepel, *Prophet*, 101.

[28] Shukrī, *I'tirāfāt*, 102.

that *tamla' al-aswāq*, 'filled the markets'. Mere familiarity was not enough: actual knowledge of the opinions of previous generations of 'Ulamā' 'of which our culture boasts' was needed. Al-Azhar's communiqué argued, perhaps not without irony, that the expert members of the court did not need the Al-Azhar 'Ulamā' to help them fulfill this aspect of their duty as judges and scholars; moreover, it would also be necessary to have direct access to the writings and persons of the accused.

The court would not grant the Al-Azhar 'Ulamā' access to the prisoners, perhaps because it was not eager to have 'the markets filled' with leaked copies of writings 'of which our culture boasts' – not this time from the Middle Ages but from the Shukrī group. The communiqué also demanded to know *kāffat al-ẓurūf*, 'all the circumstances' surrounding the assassination of Sheikh Al- Dhahabī. It was for this murder that Shukrī was tried and eventually sentenced and executed.

The demand to be made fully acquainted with all the circumstances of the murder must have been understood by the initiated as an allusion to rumours that in reality Sheikh Al- Dhahabī had been killed by the police or by agents of the Egyptian secret services posing as members of the group. This rumour was sufficiently persistent to be referred to even by Gilles Kepel, Fouad Ajami and Muḥammad Muṣṭafā.[29]

Others were more forthcoming than the Al-Azhar Ulema. In response to the widely publicised complaints of the court, four scholars[30] came forward and together wrote a book against the Shukrī group entitled 'Confronting Extremist Thought in Islam.'[31] Its third edition, with 162 pages, was published in 1980, but it is difficult to determine whether the first two editions really exist. Strangely the name of the publisher is not stated, but it may have been privately printed.

On page 91 of the book is a poorly reproduced photograph, obviously cut from a newspaper, of one of the authors, Dr Ḥāmid Ḥassān, holding a microphone. It is clearly visible that in the newspaper the caption below the photograph read 'Dr Ḥāmid Ḥassān addresses the court'. In the book, however, there is an

29 Kepel, *Prophet*, 97; Ajami, 'Pharaoh', 28; Muṣṭafā, *Wazīr*, 78.

30 Dr Ḥāmid Ḥassān, Dr Muḥ. 'Abd al-'Aẓīm 'Alī, 'Abd al-Fattāḥ Yaḥyā Kāmil Aḥmad and Yaḥyā Kāmil Aḥmad.

31 *Muwāğahat al-Fikr al-Mutaṭarrif fi-'l-Islām*.

additional caption reading 'A picture of Dr Ḥāmid Ḥassān having a discussion with Shukrī Aḥmad Muṣṭafā, the leader of the group'. Whatever the truth of the matter, the picture obviously represents someone fulfilling an important duty. It occupies the upper half of the page, while the lower half contains a photograph of about twelve people behind bars, in a cage inside the courtroom. Shukrī sits in the middle, dressed in white. The condemned men smile condescendingly but happily. The original captions reads: 'Shukrī Aḥmad Muṣṭafā and members of his group follow from within their cage in court with interest ... the discussions on the ideas of their group'. To this the book adds: 'Shukrī and the members of his group listening to Dr Ḥāmid Ḥassān'.

How important in reality was the role of Dr Ḥāmid Ḥassān and the co-authors? Did they act independently? Did Shukrī and his group take them seriously? Did the judges take them seriously? Everyone connected with the Shukrī drama must have had strong individual opinions on these questions.

Ḥāmid Ḥassān's book enumerates and refutes tenets held by the group. Shukrī declared at his trial that the war between the Arabs and the Jews could not be regarded as an Islamic struggle. Of course the whole world belongs to Islam, Shukrī admitted, but why conquer Palestine if it would not subsequently be ruled according to what God sent down? When asked, he admitted that he would not be pleased if Jews were to enter his house, but he was also not pleased when the Egyptian secret police entered it. Had the earliest Muslims not fled to Ethiopia when they were persecuted, and was this not a good example?[32] To all this Ḥāmid Ḥassān and his co-authors answered by way of refutation:[33] *Khiyāna*!! Treason to God and His Apostle! Treason to Islam and Egypt!

Shukrī obviously did not accept the way Muslims in Egypt classify people. He classified Egyptian detectives and Israeli soldiers by the same criteria: did they, or did they not, violate the space in which he lived? To such an affront his opponents reacted emotionally, almost with hysteria. This emotional reaction reminds an outsider of the way Muslims responded to infractions of the *dhimmī* status.[34] Dissent, as well as such infractions, is understood

[32] Shukrī, *I'tirāfāt*, 98.

[33] Ḥāmid Ḥassān, *Muwāğaha*, 63.

[34] See Nettler, *Past Trials*, 10, for a medieval example.

by many Muslims as a rejection of the Islamic way of classifying persons, in this case Egyptian Muslims and non-Muslim Israeli Jews. It is also understood as a renunciation of the Islamic orientation in space and time, and indeed of Islam as such. Only an enemy of God can commit such offences.

The other sections of the book of our three authors are on much the same intellectual and emotional level. They discuss the group's alleged views[35] on marriage, prayer, mosques, literacy (seen by them as useless in Egypt's social context), the reliability of the transmission of the text of the Koran, and the Caliphate. Finally, the book compares the group to the dreaded *Khawāriğ*, a group who were especially notorious in the eighth century AD for executing apostates from Islam, following their own loose definition of an apostate as anyone who was not a member of their group.

The mention of the *Khawāriğ* is relevant, because under questioning Shukrī had to answer the question whether he regarded Sheikh Al-Dhahabī as an apostate from Islam: *a-muslim huwa am kāfir?*[36] Shukrī answered in the affirmative, *huwa 'indī kāfir.* Like Caiaphas many centuries earlier, the judge then had no other questions, not even whether Shukrī perceived himself or his group as involved in, or guilty of, the Sheikh's murder.

When the court told Shukrī that this was the end of his testimony, he showed some surprise and pointed out that he had been allowed to talk about his ideas in general, but that he was not yet ready to present his defence in the Dhahabī case. Then he appeared to understand what had happened. He said a short prayer for all present in the courtroom, and said: 'I place my affair in the hands of God, *ufawwiḍ amrī ilā 'llāh.*' Four months later he was hanged.

Our three authors, however, were convinced that it was all a conspiracy against Islam: 'The enemies of Islam send their agents in secret.'[37] They set out publicly to help the court because, as we now know, the official representatives of the official religious organisations offered no such help.[38] The book confirms explicitly and implicitly that the religious establishment – Al-Azhar and parts of the Muslim Brotherhood – were unwilling, or at least hesitated,

35 Kepel, *Prophet*, 86-91, gives a good idea of what these ideas consisted of in practice.
36 Shukrī, *I'tirāfāt*, 103.
37 Ḥassān, *Muwāğaha*, 15.
38 *Ibid.*

to condemn the Shukrī group. Why this unwillingness and this hesitation? Was there a connection here with the general suppression in 1977 by the Egyptian authorities of the widest possible spectrum of Islamic religious activists? This suppression took place, according to several detached observers who suddenly did not see the familiar spectacle of bearded men in the streets of Cairo, in the wake of the Dhahabī assassination in the first half of July 1977. At that time the Egyptian authorities were perhaps more guilty of intimidation than of suppression, but the representatives of official Islam possibly thought that the government was using the Shukrī group as an excuse for a much more general suppression of Islamic activism in Egypt. Furthermore, a few representatives of the religious establishment might even have agreed, at least in part, to a view expressed[39] by one of the survivors of the Shukrī group: 'I felt that God had sent Shukrī to lead the Muslims out of their lowliness', *li-yukhriğa al-Muslimīn min kabwatihim.*

The influence of Ğamāl al-Dīn al-Afghānī's teachings led many Muslim thinkers to develop a straightforward theory on the return of the superiority of Islam. They argued that the Muslim community is under an obligation to implement the God-given laws of Islam and that to neglect that supreme duty to carry out God's will causes political misery. Whenever the Muslim community is dominated by non-Muslim powers, it no longer lives in accordance with God's law, either because of widespread religious laxity or because the set of rules that it regards as God's law is in reality at variance with God's law.

Al-Afghānī himself and some of his direct pupils may have been inclined to accept that the traditional system of Islamic law was not identical to God's real command, which explains why they wanted to reinterpret the Koran and the Apostolic example and thereby (re)discover that command. On the other hand, Ḥasan al-Bannā, the founder of the Muslim Brotherhood, as well as his numerous followers, seem not to have hesitated to identify Islamic law in its traditional form with the true will of God.

Shukrī Muṣṭafā, instead, dismissed traditional Islamic law as the work of men, and this may have been regarded by some representatives of the religious establishment as an attempt at religious renewal, in line with the pattern set by Ğamāl al-Dīn al-Afghānī at the end of the nineteenth century. Could it lead Islam to new

[39] 'Abd al-Raḥmān Abū al-Khayr, *Dhikrayātī*, 33.

glory? Could Shukrī's ascetic and radical new religious movement contribute to its purification and help to purge it of those who knowingly or unknowingly impeded the implementation of true Islam?

Did not Al-Afghānī's movement put an end to colonial rule? Could the Shukrī movement deal with regimes led by allegedly anti-Islamic elements like Sadat and Asad in the same way? Could the Shukrī group be the party of God, the *Ḥizb Allāh*, which the Koran predicts will be victorious? Has the hour come for the final struggle between the party of God and the party of Satan?

Secularisation may make progress in some parts of a society, e.g. among university professors in a theological faculty or the ruling élite in the Muslim world. At the same time, religion may be intensified in other parts of the same society[40] – since true believers demand vigorous otherworldliness from their faith. The reaction to the natural and inevitable process of secularisation is either revival of the existing religious organisations, sometimes by sect formation, or the appearance of novel religious movements, sometimes imported ones. For instance, the secularisation of mainstream Christianity in the West ensures that Western Christianity is slowly replaced by novel religious movements: the monks are replaced by the Moonies in their very monasteries.

In Islam, however, things are arranged somewhat differently. Since the affair of the *Satanic Verses* it has become common knowledge that Islamic legal theory punishes apostasy with death. This is true and important to know, but it is even more important that in daily life apostasy from Islam is punished with the severance of a variety of social bonds. Human beings desire and need interpersonal bonds, and will usually try to protect these from being broken even if this means accepting, or continuing to accept, a religion in the process.[41]

It follows that within the world of Islam the religious innovation which necessarily accompanies secularisation cannot take the form of any sort of religious renewal that will cross the boundaries of Islam. There can be no Hare Krishna or Baghwan, no Scientology, Mormonism or Transcendental Meditation in Mecca or Cairo. Within the world of Islam religious renewal has to steer clear of

[40] Stark and Bainbridge, *Future*, 2.
[41] *Ibid.*, 324.

anything that implies or suggests apostasy. The social consequences of apostasy make any other course out of the question. Shukrī might have expected to be successful while presenting himself as a better Muslim, but could not have had any realistic hope of success as a religious leader in Egypt had he presented himself as an ex-Muslim.

In the Western world secularisation leads to the gradual decline of existing religions and the rise of new ones, but in the world of Islam the rules concerning apostasy force back into Islam all energy that could otherwise have led to religious innovation. It appears that Shukrī's group represents an attempt at religious innovation that remained only just within the limits of Islam, if it did so at all. Shukrī rejected Egyptian society in its entirety. He dismissed Islamic law in its accepted and traditional form, had doubts about the reliability of the transmission of the Koran, did not accept the authority of the Muslim professional men of religion, and regarded Sufism as meaningless. How much further could one go and still remain a Muslim in any meaningful sense? An outside observer can only regard the Shukrī group as a novel religious movement that was somehow historically connected to the Koran and the Islamic tradition. In the terminology of Rodney Stark and William Sims Bainbridge, it would probably be called a borderline case between a cult and a sect. One is tempted to conclude that the only reason why Shukrī called himself a Muslim was the strong taboo against apostasy from Islam both in Shukrī's own mind and in the minds of his potential converts and followers. He may have condemned the whole of the Muslim world as he knew it, but still stated repeatedly that he believed Islam and the Muslims to be superior in all senses of that word.[42]

The Shukrī movement differed essentially from the other, more conventional, Islamic radical movements in the 1970s and '80s. Whereas mainstream Islamic fundamentalism wants to apply the sharī'a whatever the cost, the Shukrī movement wanted to do away with it. It is ironic that the movement was nevertheless used by the Egyptian authorities to organise a general suppression of fundamentalism and of the Islamic religious revival taking place in Egypt in the late 1970s. This surely is the true significance of Shukrī's movement. It could be used in this way by the security services because of a serious flaw in its strategy, namely that it

[42] E.g. Shukrī, *Khilāfa*, 124.

drove members who contemplated renouncing its ideas into the arms of the authorities. In the summer of 1977 the government must have been convinced that they had no alternative left but to crack down on the whole of mainstream Islamic fundamentalism, no matter how badly organised the movement was at that time, because by insisting on the application of Islamic law it challenged the authority of the government, propagated revolution and demanded the establishment of a non-secular Islamic state. The government wanted, on the one hand, to appease the pious and on the other to be perceived as infinitely stronger than any 'religious' movement. Consequently it did not enter into a direct confrontation with mainstream fundamentalism, but used the Shukrī group as a warning to the percipient.

Muslims have felt attracted to the fundamentalist Islamic movements because they liked their slogans. After all, what better rule could one wish for than God's rule?[43] The Islamic fundamentalist movement in the 1970s, '80s and '90s cannot be explained away as the movement of the poor and the powerless. Had it only been that, the number of its followers would have been even larger. It has, on the contrary, been a movement of Muslims yearning for the millennium of Islam. Islamic fundamentalism is the natural response to the secularisation of the ruling élite in the Muslim world, whose power it challenges with religious arguments. Whatever police measures the authorities may take against it, it will be impossible to eradicate. Mainstream Islamic fundamentalism wants to put the power of the seemingly omnipotent, omnipresent and omniscient modern state into the hands of the best possible Muslims. It wants to introduce the application of the laws which the traditional Muslim sharī'a prescribes, thus guaranteeing the best of all possible fates for man – in this world and the next.

Nobody can falsify or verify the promise of a new and better heaven or earth. It is an immensely attractive promise, and in the execution chamber of a Cairo prison, a little after five o'clock on the morning of March 29, 1978, five men died for it.[44] One of them, Anwar Ma'mūn Saqar, had been found guilty of kidnapping and abducting Sheikh Muḥammad Ḥusayn al-Dhahabī. The court

[43] Koran, 5:55.

[44] See the Cairo daily newspapers *Al-Ahrām*, *Al-Akhbār*, and *Al-Ǧumhūriyya* of March 30, 1978, and 'Abd al-Raḥmān Abū al-Khayr, *Dhikrayātī*, 201-8.

found him guilty of threatening the family of Sheikh al-Dhahabī with a machine-gun, leading the kidnapped Sheikh into a car, and driving him to an apartment in the neighbourhood of the Gizeh Pyramids, where he was murdered. The second man to be executed, Aḥmad Ṭāriq ʻAbd al-ʻAlīm, was found guilty of actually firing the shots that killed him, and the third, Muṣṭafā ʻAbd al-Maqṣūd Ghāzī, of first chaining the Sheikh to a bed with iron handcuffs.

The fourth man, Māhir ʻAbd al-ʻAzīz Bakrī, was as the court put it, the 'philosopher' of the group which committed these crimes, and the fifth was Shukrī Aḥmad Muṣṭafā himself. He was found guilty of being the true leader, *zaʻīm*, of this group, which in the mean time had become widely known as *Ǧamāʻat al-Takfīr wa-'l-Hiǧra*, the group which accused [other, nominal, Muslims] of Unbelief and urged [true Muslims] to emigrate, away from the paganism and wickedness of modern Egypt.

This strange name sounds very much like a slogan or a summary of the group's programme. However, it is not a name this group ever chose for itself, but one which was created for it by the Egyptian authorities and press.[45] It is a name which draws attention to the two tenets of the group that are bound to be the least attractive to the Egyptian public: that true Muslims should emigrate to Muslim political communities, away from the day-to-day paganism of secular Egypt, and that people who do not live completely in accordance with the directives of Islam are not Muslims but unbelievers. The group called itself *Ǧamāʻat al-Muslimīn*,[46] the community of Muslims, or *Al-Ǧamāʻa al-Muslima*,[47] the Muslim community. Both names suggest a certain zeal for religious exclusiveness. It appears that the Shukrī group regarded itself in a very special way as the real community of Muslims. Anyone who refused to become a member of their group or wanted to leave it was declaring himself an enemy of God, and was to be treated accordingly.[48]

One of the group's surviving ex-members reports how members who considered leaving it were threatened with death, the tradi-

[45] See publisher's preface to ʻAbd al-Raḥmān Abū al-Khayr, *Dhikrayātī*, 8, and *Al-Siyāsa*, 27.10.79, fn. 6.

[46] Shukrī, *Iʻtirāfāt*, 63; id., *Al-Siyāsa*, 27.10.79, esp. fn. 6.

[47] E.g. Shukrī, *Khilāfa*, 134, 135 (twice), 136, 140, etc.

[48] Shukrī, *Khilāfa*, 138: *taqtīluhum idhā lazima 'l-amr.*

tional punishment for apostasy and desertion from Islam.[49] Members who contemplated the possibility of getting away from this group, as the same survivor reports, came to fear their fellow-members and hence became easy prey to agents of the Egyptian secret services: sometimes those people wanted to leave the group but dared not. Soon these people found out that remaining in the group as informers or *agents provocateurs* for the security services could be profitable.[50] It follows that in this way the group became the centre of a complicated game of information and misinformation which the uninitiated cannot unravel. Every piece of information that ever became available on the group has to be suspected of being part of the misinformation game. Likewise, every crime ascribed to its members could have been committed by, or at the instigation of, government *provocateurs*.

There can be no doubt that the renaming of the group by the media was part of the misinformation game. Polemical articles on this group which were published in Egyptian newspapers and magazines before it became notorious in July 1977, and which do not use its media name, can therefore be taken as part of the more or less genuine non-government-inspired discussion on its principles and practices. In the article which Al-Dhahabī wrote on the subject,[51] the Shukrī group was still only called *Ğamā ʿat al-Hiğra*, literally 'the group of emigration', and *Ahl al-Kahf*, 'people of the cave', references to their voluntary separation from society. The reference to *takfīr*, accusing other Muslims of being doomed apostates from Islam, had not yet been added to the group's name. At the time of writing, only one article which does not use the full and threatening media name for the Shukrī group is available. This exceptional item dates from 1973, four years before the group suddenly became notorious and prominent; it was reprinted in the Egyptian monthly *Mağallat al-Tawḥīd* in September 1977. Its contents show, correctly, that leaving the group was seen as the equivalent to desertion from Islam. It was also made clear that emigration to, and the establishment of, an Islamic political community was necessary because, after the days of the first four Caliphs (632–61 AD), there was no real Islam, *lam yakun thamma islām ṣaḥīḥ*.[52]

49 Abū al-Khayr, *op. cit.*, 134.

50 *Ibid.*, 134–6.

51 Al-Dhahabī, *Mādhā* Qāl, 3.

52 *Ibid.*, 10.

The 1973 article[53] correctly suggests[54] that the most important theoretical principle of the group was the belief that there is only one source of divine guidance: the Koran. Furthermore, at his trial in November 1977 Shukrī Muṣṭafā in his testimony summarised his views that (1) all present societies are un-Islamic;[55] (2) only members of the Shukrī group are true Muslims; and (3) the classical system of Islamic law must be rejected.

The tenet that all present societies are un-Islamic needs little explanation; Muslim radicals before and after Shukrī have repeatedly taught the same thing. It is based on the belief that even those countries conventionally called Muslim are not ruled 'by what God sent down', *bi-mā anzala 'llāh*,[56] but by man-made laws. Consequently they cannot be regarded as real Muslim states. Hence emigration from such countries to a Muslim state is a religious duty. It seems that the Shukrī group is unique in modern times in attempting to establish at least one desert settlement that would qualify as a Muslim theocracy.

The second tenet mentioned, namely that only members of the Shukrī group are true Muslims, is logically connected to the first. Society as such is in the power of those who resist God's plans for humanity, and Shukrī and his disciples are committed to the struggle against the enemies of God who are in power. This implies that his group alone fights for the implementation of God's will, and it therefore follows that its members are the only true Muslims. These two tenets taken together imply that in the past all allegedly Muslim states and empires were un-Islamic, and by implication that all present governments of countries inhabited by Muslims lack legitimacy.

The third tenet, the rejection of traditional Islamic law in its classical form, received less publicity than the other two, the *takfīr* theme and the *hiğra* theme. Yet it is more interesting and more important. Does it represent an ambitious, far-reaching and fundamental attempt at Islamic religious renewal? Whatever is the case, it differentiates Shukrī's group from the fundamentalist movement.

[53] *Mağallat al-Tawḥīd*, V, 10 (September 1977) 13.

[54] At least according to the 1977 reprint.

[55] Shukrī, *I'tirāfāt*, 100.

[56] Koran 5:44, 45, 47. 'What God sent down' can be understood as the Koran, the Torah, Islam, the sharīa in its traditional form, or revelation and religion in general.

The accepted view among mainstream Islamic fundamentalists prescribes that the Islamic sharīʿa should be applied in its entirety in both public and private life since it is the command of God. However, laws are only obeyed when a government implements them and punishes offenders, so for God's laws to be executed an Islamic state and an Islamic government are necessary. States can only be established by force, hence its use is justified if it helps to bring about an Islamic state and an Islamic government. Only the power of the state and the government can guarantee the total application of Islamic law in its classical form.

This line of argument is followed by the Muslim Brotherhood, by Sadat's assassins, and by a great number of well-known or obscure Muslim thinkers and activists. However, it is not that which Shukrī followed. Still, it was Shukrī Aḥmad Muṣṭafā who was sacrificed, and hanged, together with a number of his followers, in order to legitimise the subsequent attempt to suppress a far more dangerous movement. It is impossible not to wonder whether a little religious freedom of the kind that has become commonplace in Europe and North America might have saved the lives of both Al-Dhahabī and Shukrī, and perhaps even have changed the history of modern Muslim fundamentalism.

5

THE FAILURE OF THE LIBERAL ALTERNATIVE

Why do the traditional power élite of the Arab world not have an answer to Islamic fundamentalism? Why are the aristocracies of the region unable to offer an alternative to what might turn out to be their doom?

The traditional élite are not very religious, and know little about Islam. Many representatives of the upper classes apparently even misunderstand the word *takfīr*, a central term in the vocabulary of the Islamic fundamentalists. When they look it up in their dictionaries, they seize on the wrong meaning, 'atonement', rather than the grim 'being condemned to death as an infidel ex-Muslim'. They are simply unable to grasp that they are being cast as the bad guys in the play which they feel *they* are directing. The élite seem not to live on the same planet as the fundamentalists. Their tastes – which they follow – in clothes, food, education, travel, entertainment and housing are different from those of the masses; it is a difference comparable to the cultural gap between rural China and urban California. The élite, to borrow an expression from the vocabulary of traditional Marxism, have become dangerously estranged from the masses.

On some points the élites, the masses and the fundamentalists nevertheless appear to agree. The fundamentalist Muslims were not unhappy over the fall of communism in 1989-90. They had never expected anything else to happen to the communists, and to the pious the downfall of the Soviet Union only confirmed that atheist enemies of God can never prosper. The Koran is full of lines assuring the believers that God's enemies will come to naught already in this world. Whether this happens sooner or later is almost a matter of indifference. The important thing is the establishment of the rule of Islam and the removal of the local tyrant.

In fundamentalist pamphlets and sermons, communism was often placed in the same category of threats as Darwinism, Freudianism, Freemasonry, Existentialism and a number of other -isms which, unlike communism, never controlled a standing army or a state. Moreover, communism was perceived as alien and geographically far removed from the Arab world. Finally, it was generally known to have only the flimsiest support within the Middle East itself. Although there was no Arab country that did not have a few thousand devoted communists, usually recruited from among the traditional élites, a communist take-over was never on the agenda anywhere. Whether Afghanistan counts as part of the region or not is a matter of definition, but the failure of Afghani communism to remain in power even with full Soviet support illustrates the point.

The traditional and intellectual élites of the region were equally delighted over the fall of communism, but they perceived its demise quite differently: they believed that a new era of civil liberties for the whole world had begun, and that the fall of the Ceausescus of the region might be at hand. The Arab Ceausescus themselves, even the most eminent, became rather worried[1] by all this, and are reported to have studied the videos of the fall and execution of the Romanian dictator with particular concern. Especially during the Kuwait war at the end of 1990 and beginning of 1991, Arab newspapers abounded with speculations about the beginning of an era of democracy and civil liberty in the Middle East. This optimism came to nothing, because the Kuwait war was not about the democratisation of the Arab world but about one of the traditional principles of the existing world order:[2] international law leaves governments free to maim, expel, kill or imprison their own subjects, but it forbids them to use military force in order to be able to treat the citizens of neighbouring countries as if they were their own.

Religion played little or no role in the optimistic speculations indulged in around 1990 over the democratisation of the Middle East. But already long before the Kuwait war, religious sentiment in books by many writers of the upper classes appeared to be limited to vague and superficial references to the vicissitudes of fate. Intellectuals who can be seen as reflecting the views held in these upper classes, like the journalists Ibrāhīm 'Abduh and

[1] Freedman and Karsh, *Gulf Conflict*, 31.

[2] *Ibid.*, 440.

Muṣṭafā Amīn, are very much interested in politics and democracy, and only marginally, if at all, in religion or Islam. Muṣṭafā Amīn has been a member of the Egyptian élite since the 1930s. He was educated in the home of his grandfather Sa'd Zaghlūl, the leader of Egypt's most successful political party ever, and studied at Georgetown University in Washington. He has known everybody who has ever been anybody in Egypt. One example: Nasser was introduced to him at a tea party in the house of the great singer Umm Kulthūm several years before the Nasser/Naguib *coup d'état* of 1952. He is the author of a great number of newspaper columns, memoirs and (partly autobiographical) novels. The actions and thoughts of the heroes of these novels fill thousands of pages. These pages nevertheless contain not the slightest reference to Islam apart from vague generalities about God determining the fate of the world, and even pious and almost empty generalities of this kind are rare.

Muṣṭafā Amīn is the author of the longest Arabic novel ever published. It has 927 pages. At the same time no Arabic novel ever published has a shorter title: *Lā*, 'No'. The adventures and misadventures of the hero are almost unbelievable, and often very funny, but literary critics do not take the book seriously, and regard it as soap. At the end the hero and his friends are waiting for the coming to power of a certain Sayf Allāh. This is an uncommon proper name, meaning 'the sword of God'. *Lā* is the only book by Muṣṭafā Amīn that has the Islamic formula 'In the Name of God, the Merciful, the Compassionate', the traditional solemn *Basmala*,[3] printed on its opening page. Apart from this, the proper name Sayf Allāh is the only thing Islamic about the book.

Lā has some autobiographical elements. Its story is set against a background of worsening corruption and incompetence among government officials. Its fictional heroes suffer from this corruption and incompetence, but they expect the Sword of God to put things right. However, at the last possible moment, five lines before the end of the book, just as the reader is about to take leave of his heroes, one of the old, corrupt politicians takes a grip of things and becomes the new head of government. Does the book illustrate that even the traditional élite see no other

[3] See 'Basmala' in *EI* (2nd edn), I, 1084a.

way out but an Islamic revolution – and realise at the same time that such a revolution will not occur?

Ambassador Ḥusayn Aḥmad Amīn, born in 1932, son of the eminent historian Aḥmad Amīn (1886-1954),[4] is an important representative of the Egyptian intellectual élite. He has written a number of books and articles as well as carving out a career as a diplomat, representing his country in Ottawa, Moscow, Bonn, Tunisia and elsewhere. Ḥusayn Aḥmad Amīn believes that the present crisis in the Middle East has multiple causes, but he singles out two groups whose members he blames especially: the ruling political party and the Islamic religious leaders, the Ulema. That he perceives these two groups as playing a special role shows his understanding of the dual nature of Islamic fundamentalism: it is both a political and religious problem.

In a brilliant parody of the Protocols of the Elders of Zion he mentions the 'ridiculous incapacity' of the ruling party to come up with ideas that can compete with those produced by the writers and ideologues of the Islamic movement.[5] The imaginary minute-taker at a meeting of the imaginary Elders of the Muslims notes with great satisfaction:

> It is clear to all that the programmes of the [ruling] party are devoid of any crystallised ideas.[...] Nor do they contain workable solutions to the alarming problems of our society.[6]

An ambassador can only write such words when he puts them in the mouth of a card-carrying enemy of his government. Elsewhere Ḥusayn Aḥmad Amīn writes more soberly that it is imperative for the ruling party to come up with an alternative ideology that will attract the masses.[7]

To the 'Ulamā' he dedicates a short piece of poetry:[8]

O ye Ulema
O salt of the earth

[4] 1886–1954, See, e.g., A.M.H. Mazyad, *Aḥmad Amīn*, Leiden 1963; Brockelmann, S III 305.

[5] Ḥusayn Aḥmad Amīn, *Fī Bayt Aḥmad Amīn*, 241-2.

[6] *Ibid.*, 242.

[7] Ḥusayn Aḥmad Amīn, *Al-Islām*, 249-50.

[8] *Yā ma'shar^a l-'Ulamā', Yā Milḥ^a l-balad, Mā Yuṣliḥ^u l-Milḥ^a idhā l-Milḥ^u fasad*? Cf. Matt. 5:13.

Wherewith shall the salt be restored
If it has lost its savour?

When he listens to a radio program in which a leading *'Ālim* is asked questions on the problem whether Islam permits or forbids the use of the telephone, he is taught that

> Islam permits the use of the telephone when it is used for whatever God has declared to be permissible, and Islam forbids the use of the telephone when it is used for whatever God has declared to be forbidden.

The *'Ālim*'s answers disturb him deeply. Such stupid questions and stupid answers, he writes, are all that occupy the minds of our backward peoples, *shu'ūbnā al-mutakhallifa*.[9] Coming home from a concert in Bonn, he hears about disturbances in Asyūṭ in which fundamentalist rioters have smashed musical instruments. This makes him unhappy, but when he hears from enlightened Ulema who seriously and solemnly discuss Traditions on the question of whether the Prophet Mohammed and His Companions (Peace be upon Them) approved of music, he gets extremely angry and exclaims: 'Did we then reach such a degree of backwardness?' Ḥusayn Aḥmad Amīn writes that it is not difficult to understand why the *enemies* of music should justify their enmity with an appeal to Prophetic Traditions from the seventh century AD, but why, he asks, should such Traditions be quoted *in defence* of music?[10]

The philosopher Fu'ād Zakariyyā teaches at the University of Cairo in Gizeh and has written extensively and with academic precision on the opinions of the Islamic fundamentalist movements. He is one of the few Middle Eastern academics who has examined them – for example, their views on human rights. The debate on human rights cannot fail to touch on a number of issues to which both the fundamentalists and their antagonists within their own culture attach great value. One of these concerns the limits of state power. Many inhabitants of the Middle East suffer under regimes that recognise no limits to their power, and for the subjects of such regimes one of the good and strong sides of the sharī'a is that it does limit the powers of the state.

[9] Ḥusayn Aḥmad Amīn, *Fī Bayt..*, 268.
[10] *Ibid.*, 262.

Application of the rules formulated in the 1948 declaration of human rights would also effectively limit the power of the state. Of course there can be no competition between two sets of rules one of which is as elevated as the Islamic sharīʿa and the other as secular as the United Nations declaration of human rights from 1948. The sharīʿa carefully describes once and for all which rights God has given to man, and there can be no question of other rights. In the eyes of a professional theologian of strict epistemological principles there is no sound basis whatever for the arrogation of other rights, not even by international bodies like the General Assembly of the United Nations. However, many Islamic thinkers felt that it is good when human rights as envisaged by the declaration of 1948 can be seen as already present in Islam and the Sharīʿa.

The literature in Arabic on this subject is immense, and repetitive. In this corpus of texts Fu'ād Zakariyyā detects four errors that are constantly repeated, and quotes as an example a short passage, twenty-four words in Arabic, containing all four of them. He came across the passage in an article entitled 'The development of the concept of human rights' written by a certain 'Uthmān Khalīl 'Uthmān.[11]

> Islam established a state ruled by law, a state that was subject to the sharīʿa and that protected the rights of man before the establishment of this principle, which only appeared in Europe after the French Revolution.

First, the supposed priority in time of Islam where human rights is concerned is given more attention than the actual contents of the rights granted. Is the Islamic understanding of human rights really superior to the Western perception, or is the author only concerned with priority in time? Secondly, the comparison is between religion (Islam) and a region (Europe), or perhaps between a creed and a culture. A proper comparison can only be drawn between entities that are comparable, e.g. the historical experience of Europe and the historical experience of the Arab world, or the principles of Christianity and the principles of Islam. Thirdly, the *theory* of Islam may have established such a state, but 'the slightest knowledge of the history of Islam after the period of the Prophet and the Rightly-Guided Caliphs', i.e. from about

[11] Fu'ād Zakariyyā, *Ṣaḥwa*, 107.

632 till 661 AD, would show that the principle of human rights was not recognised in practice. Fourthly, it is of course a mistake to think that such 'principles' are suddenly discovered, before or after the French Revolution. They arise gradually as does the consensus about them.

Fu'ād Zakariyyā here addresses a Muslim readership, to whom the distinction between the Golden Age, in which all was perfect, and the later period of distortions and transgressions is of course essential. However, it is not certain that a non-Muslim historian would agree that human rights were respected in any meaningful sense even during the Prophet's lifetime. Fu'ād Zakariyyā gently tries to make this point:

> If we would study the history of Islam looking for a society of pure faith that was free of worldly ambitions, we would have to go back further and further without finding it until we arrive at the age of the Rightly-Guided Caliphs, seeing that many imagine it as the society that is closest to what we are looking for. Historical realities, nevertheless, make it unavoidable for us to admit that the often bloody quarrels that characterise even this age show that it was not completely free of worldly ambitions and interests.[12]

Some writers, like Muḥammad Sa'īd Al-'Ashmāwī,[13] have tried to resolve the same difficulty by retreating to the period of the Prophet and his first two successors, Abū Bakr and 'Umar. Others have limited the Golden Age even further by only approving of the days of the Prophet in Mecca and Medina. Finally, it has been argued that only the Meccan period qualifies as a Golden Age since only then did Islam use no force at all.

Fu'ād Zakariyyā goes no deeper into this matter but he continues by making the well-known point that even if the law is divine and perfect, those who have to apply it are not simply because they are human. He concludes that there is an essential difference between a human regime admitting its humanity and one which is human too (since no other regimes are imaginable) but claims to be established on a divine, religious basis. Fu'ād Zakariyyā believes that the mistake of the intellectuals who represent the Islamic movement is that they seek to abolish history and the

12 Fu'ād Zakariyyā, *Ṣaḥwa*, 110.

13 Al-'Ashmāwī, *Ma'ālim*, 19.

course of history. In consequence, they overlook the well-documented realities of the past, giving more attention to the ideals of the Koran and the canonised Traditions ascribed to Mohammed. It may be excusable to take the unhistorical approach in human rights discussions, but it may be a much more general phenomenon. However, it is doubtful whether a historical, this-worldly view of one's own religion is compatible with the demands of a traditional, other-worldly faith.

Fu'ād Zakariyyā is pessimistic over the future of the Arab-Islamic world, which he thinks cannot be better than the present or the past. The different states in the Arab world, according to Fu'ād Zakariyyā, have three different types of government: half-liberal regimes that have gradually developed into harsh dictatorships; regimes built on the rule of a family; and military regimes. The Arab readers of Fu'ād Zakariyyā's books do not have to be told which regime falls in which category. Iraq and Syria are examples of liberal or at least non-religious, regimes that have developed into dictatorships. Kuwait and Saudi Arabia are ruled by families. Egypt's regime, in origin at least, is military. This is important, Fu'ād Zakariyyā teaches, because a regime without an institutional basis, *di'āma mu'assasiyya*, can never guarantee the preservation of human rights. He believes that only when the way in which people live, think and are ruled in the Arab world changes completely is progress possible; it is ironic that over the need for complete change he appears to be in agreement with Islamic fundamentalism.

Marxism in Egypt was never stronger than in the mid-1970s, when the Egyptian government decided to turn the Islamists loose on the Marxists, hoping that the two would devour each other. In the same period Dr Muṣṭafā Maḥmūd, who had started his intellectual career as what is often called a liberal, published a book against Marxism, *Al-Mārkisiyya wa-'l-Islām*, which had a great commercial success all over the Arab world.

Fu'ād Zakariyyā's review[14] of this book by Muṣṭafā Maḥmūd is devastating. It may well be that Muṣṭafā Maḥmūd is not the profoundest critic of Marxism the century has produced. Nevertheless his writings are important, because two of the fallacies we meet in them are common to almost all contemporary Arabic writing on Marxism, including fundamentalist writings. The first

[14] In *Rūz al-Yūsuf*, September 1976; repr. in Fu'ād Zakariyyā, *Ṣaḥwa*, 199-206.

is a mutation of a fallacy we met with in the discussion about human rights. Muṣṭafā Maḥmūd argues that Islam like Marxism rejects the class structure (*al-ṭabaqiyya*) and large differences in wealth, allowed the interference of the state in the national economy, and knew of dialectical logic, and used it, many centuries ago. In short, the main principles of Marxism are already to be found in Islam, so if this is true, why should Muslims want to attack Marxism, and why was it never recognised by Muslims in earlier generations? Why did Muslim scholars only read such things into their holy texts after Marxism had formulated them?

The second fallacy concerns the way the participants in the discussion on Marxism use the word 'materialism', *māddiyya.* It may not always be clear what Marx and Engels meant by this word, but they certainly did not mean what most modern Arab writers today think they meant, namely the unthinking pursuit of material benefits. However, in the Marxist utopia people were to be free to dedicate themselves to culture and intellectual pursuits, free from worries about their daily bread. In the Marxist view it is capitalism that only has eyes for profit and revenues only and is 'materialist' in the modern Arabic sense.

In the West Islamic fundamentalism (if not Islam itself) is seen as an oppressor of women. The West has come to hold the view that both genders are equal, although this is a comparatively recent development which is by no means general. Nevertheless, many Westerners apply their own recently-acquired standards to the world of Islam and therefore condemn what they regard as the social inferiority of women in Islamic societies. When a woman is seen not only to be Muslim but also to turn to fundamentalist Islam, she is believed to act against her own interests. However, it is easily observable that a great number of women have turned to fundamentalist Islam, which proves to many outsiders once again how oppressive Islam and Islamic fundamentalism really are by making women act even against their own interests. In particular the conspicuous Islamic garb, *al-ziyy al-sharʿī,* in which ever more women have dressed since the 1970s is widely seen as a symbol of the rejection of Western views and Western values, both by Muslims and by Westerners.

However, Islamic female dress, at least in the Arab world, is remarkably similar to the traditional outfit of Roman Catholic nuns, with colours added. There may be some irony in the fact that the decade in which the black and white habit worn by nuns in the West disappeared also saw their dress code reemerge – in full colour – in the Muslim world. To a true believer it must be difficult to believe that this is pure accident. Is this similarity in religious fashion yet another sign, like the rebuilding of some European churches into mosques, that Islam has come to replace Christianity? But there may also be a this-worldly explanation. Islamic female attire is seen by Muslim young women as attractive because it gives them a freedom that was not available to their mothers. Dressed in Islamic robes they can play a larger variety of social roles than previous generations. They can move with impunity, as the habit enabled nuns to do in the Roman Catholic church. Being dressed in robes like a nun's does not necessarily mean that a Muslim woman has turned to fundamentalist Islam. It may simply mean that she is pragmatic.

However this may be, Muslim antagonists of Islamic fundamentalism do not approve of 'Islamic dress' or *taḥağğub*. According to Fu'ād Zakariyyā, it is utterly wrong to regard hiding the body as the 'first entrance to the world of the spirit', *al-madkhal al-awwal ilā 'ālam al-rūh*. Islamic robes, he believes, emphasise the importance of the body in the same way as revealing clothes would do, and they proclaim that the body is a permanent object of desire; both a provocatively dressed woman and a woman hidden within Islamic robes suggest to the world that the most important thing about a woman is her body, and that the way in which men look at her is basic to her life.[15]

The similarity between the nun's habit and Islamic female attire gives Fu'ād Zakariyyā no satisfaction: a Muslim woman can never be a nun. He quotes with distaste a preacher who exclaimed 'O woman dressed the Islamic way, be a whore with your husband', *yā muḥağğaba, kūnī 'āhira ma'a zawğik*. Being obliged to be a part-time nun and a part-time whore, he believes, may create serious psychological difficulties.[16]

Women are admonished to hide themselves within Islamic robes because of the behaviour their bodies might provoke among men, but Fu'ād Zakariyyā thinks this is unjust. Why, he asks, should the burden of male misbehaviour be borne by women, and why do the fundamentalist leaders not propose measures against

15 Fu'ād Zakariyyā, *Ṣaḥwa*, 146.

16 *Ibid.*, 147.

'the wolves', *dhi'āb*, that men supposedly become when they see women? Why do they encourage women to remain unseen? Why should these 'wolves' eyes', '*uyūn al-dhi'āb* be a reason to force anyone other than the alleged wolves themselves to change their behaviour? How can it be fair to accuse all men indiscriminately of wrongful behaviour against women? But if one is going to suggest punishing the men who do misbehave, this will not happen 'because men set the rules of the game.'[17]

However, in the gender question it is not only dress that evokes spirited discussions. Islam punishes the crime of adultery with death. Fu'ād Zakariyyā is not certain that this proves Islamic law to be superior to man-made law: can a case of adultery, he asks, be seen in isolation without taking account of the general state of society where housing and similar factors are concerned? Doesn't emphasising the Islamic punishment for adultery ignore the social realities of the Middle East? A male audience may be glad to hear from the pulpit that Islamic law severely punishes the greatest imaginable sin, but does this help to solve the problems of women in the Muslim societies of the region?[18]

Fu'ād Zakariyyā does not like the way fundamentalist preachers talk about women. In their sermons they praise women profusely – on the surface. Women are called by untranslatable honorific titles like *al-ğawhara al-maṣūna*,'the well-preserved gem', or *rabbat al-ṣawn wa-'l-'afāf*,'queen of chastity and virtue'. But what does such praise mean? Fu'ād Zakarriyā here draws a remarkable comparison with the way dictators refer with great affection in their speeches and declarations to 'the people', *al-sha'b*. Nothing seems to be dearer to them, yet in reality they take measures that hurt the people and show contempt for them.[19] An Egyptian who reads such lines will understand them instantly and think of Nasser, whose media-proclaimed love of the Egyptian people, *al-sha'b al-miṣrī*, was equalled only by the unpopularity of the measures taken by his regime that affected the lives of Egyptians. Praise, Fu'ād Zakariyyā believes, is only flattery and hides hatred.

Both fundamentalist and mainstream Muslim preachers frequently explain that the position Islam gave to women in its first decades was a great advance compared to their position before

17 *Ibid.*, 148-9.

18 *Ibid.*, 141-2.

19 *Ibid.*, 142.

the advent of Islam. Should these people not ask, Fu'ād Zakariyyā writes, how such a comparison contributes to the solution of women's many problems in the world of Islam? *Mā lanā naḥnu wa-'l-Ǧāhiliyya*? What do we today have to do with the half-primitive age before Islam which ended more than ten centuries ago?[20] Fu'ād Zakariyyā's readers of course know well how relevant the *Ǧāhiliyya* period has become since the 1950s and '60s: Sayyid Quṭb and his like since then have accused them of being *ǧāhilī*, and hence apostates from Islam who must be killed. The 'half-primitive age that preceded Islam' became very relevant to their lives and their physical safety. The writer concludes with a question: 'When it is true that Islam gave women a position better than the one they held before, does this mean that Islam has really liberated women?'[21]

Judge Muḥammad Sa'īd Al-'Ashmāwī is in many ways a lonely man, and this is reflected in his career and his writings. He has written a number of polemical books and articles against the ideas and beliefs of fundamentalist Islam, and at the same time has carved out a career for himself within the judiciary: when he retired in 1993, he was president of the High Court for State Security, *Maḥkamat Amn al-Dawla al-'Ulyā*. Neither his writing nor his judicial functions can have made him many new friends in the feverish atmosphere of the fight against fundamentalism. In modern Arabic polemics the antagonists rarely mention each other by name, but in spite of the anonymity there can be little doubt that the following is directed at Al-'Ashmāwī:

> The roles of politician, scholar, judge and security officer should be kept separate... Books are published that people are at loss to understand. Do they read a message addressed to them, or a memorandum to the police?[22]

He is harsh when he looks back on the political and religious struggle that has taken place in the Arab world in recent decades:

> Mercy has been replaced by terrorism, moderation by extremism, scholarship by ignorance, refinement by primitivism, cosmopolitanism by provincialism, renewal by stagnation.[...] Con-

[20] *Ibid.*, 144.

[21] *Ibid.*, 144.

[22] Huwaydī, *Tadayyun*, 200.

> fusion reigns...people are unable to differentiate between the spheres of the sacred and the profane. People render unto man the things which are God's, and unto God the things which are man's.[23]

In its context the last sentence is a clear reference to the fusion of religion, politics and violence which takes place in the Middle East under fundamentalist pressure. The traditional strict separation in Islam between the human and the divine is not being preserved when politics and religion get intertwined as they do at present.[24]

Al-'Ashmāwī does not hesitate to call Islamic fundamentalism a form of *ǧāhiliyya*[25] – since Sayyid Quṭb it has usually been the fundamentalists who call everybody else *ǧāhilī*. Such an inversion can only be called courageous. The essence of the *ǧāhilī* mentality, Al-'Ashmāwī believes, is its inability to be moderate and to reach a compromise. This, he knows, inevitably leads to the use of violence, whereas in his view the essence of Islam is its demand on man to be moderate and just.

Whereas the sharī'a is divine, as Al-'Ashmāwī writes in several instances,[26] the jurisprudence of Islam, the *fiqh*, is the work of fallible men. And the conflict between fundamentalists and governments, he believes, has nothing to do with the sharī'a but is about the *fiqh*. In other words, it is about the (re-)introduction and (re-)application of traditional rules of the man-made jurisprudence of Islam and not about divine laws. The Koran, Al-'Ashmāwī points out,[27] does not mention, let alone prescribe, a punishment for many crimes which the Egyptian penal code punishes heavily: bribery, espionage, forgery, counterfeiting money, arson, negligence when erecting a building (not uncommon in Cairo!), endangering life on the road, the drug trade and much else, and some of these are also not covered by Islamic jurisprudence. Like all inhabitants of the Middle East, Al-'Ashmāwī lives in a world which in general believes that the Koran and the sharī'a are complete, perfect and valid for all times and places. This belief is repeated so often that to most Muslims it sounds like a

[23] Al-'Ashmāwī, *Ma'ālim*, 10-11.

[24] E.g. *ibid.*, 238-9.

[25] *Ibid.*, 17-20; 31-7, 48 etc.

[26] E.g. *ibid.*, 267.

[27] *Ibid.* 289.

truism. In such an atmosphere Al-'Ashmāwī's remarks about the incompleteness of Islamic law must sound impossibly eccentric.

A number of interviews with journalists[28] with Al-'Ashmāwī gives a clear picture of what the general reader regards as unusual in his thinking – the journalists, when they are doing their job properly, ask particularly for these unusual views. For instance, it is thought rather unusual that he pleads for the introduction of family courts competent to decide on all the consequences of divorce, and of course on divorce itself. He explains that at present divorce, alimony, guardianship and the multitude of other legal issues that might spring from divorce are all taken care of in different courts, and he fears that this makes it next to impossible for the average Egyptian citizen to get his rights.

The press regards Al-'Ashmāwī's views on alcohol and drugs as even more unusual. Alcohol was a serious problem in the early centuries of Islam, he says, but even today there are those who demand the prohibition of alcohol as if all Egyptian houses were filled to overflowing with wine, whereas in reality most Egyptians never touch it. The real problem today is drugs: in the 1970s and '80s, more than half of the capacity of the judicial system in which Al-'Ashmāwī worked was devoted to the war on drugs like cocaine and heroin. Apart from a small number of *fatāwā* that Al-'Ashmāwī says are full of fallacies, the fundamentalists have little to say about drugs or the drug trade – or any other of the real problems of modern Muslims in the modern world.

Al-'Ashmāwī's view of the interpretation of Koran 5:48, the verse on ruling 'by what God sent down',[29] is also thought to be remarkable, although he does little more than quote the traditional Muslim Koran commentaries. This verse, he says, has nothing to do with Muslims but is addressed to the Jews of Medina.[30] It is not directed at Muslim rulers or even about ruling, but is about mediating in controversies.[31] However, journalists, Al-'Ashmāwī's readers and Al-'Ashmāwī himself all know that the verse is now used to condemn non-fundamentalists to death for apostasy from Islam.

[28] Reprinted in his *Ma'ālim*.

[29] See above, pp. 38 and 93.

[30] In his Koran commentary Sheikh Kishk argues that if the Koran in 5:44 calls the Jews of Medina apostates because they do not live by their own Torah, what should we today call the Muslims when they do not want to be ruled by what God sent down to them?

[31] Al-'Ashmāwī, *Al-Islām al-Siyāsi*, 90; id., *Ma'ālim*, 273.

Al-'Ashmāwī thinks that interest and usury are not the same, and that Islam permits moderate interest: The journalists enjoy this. He expresses doubts on one of the most widespread myths of the Arabic-speaking world, the story of *al-ghazw al-fikrī*,[32] which wants the Arab world to believe that the West is launching a sustained intellectual attack on Muslim thought and on Islam itself, under the tutelage of Darwin, Freud and others. Al-'Ashmāwī explains that at the time when they entered the worldwide intellectual debate, the ideas of these thinkers attacked the accepted and established views of the West itself. But we have the sad spectacle of Al-'Ashmāwī's moderation and reasonableness treated by contemporary Arab media and their public as freakish despite his eminent position in society. He is not ashamed to admit that his contributions to newspapers are sometimes even turned down.[33]

The nostalgia Al-'Ashmāwī feels for a better and greater Arab world is obvious from the concluding remarks in one of his interviews in the late 1980s:[34]

> Where are the books by [Arab Muslim philosophers like] Avicenna, Averroes and Al-Fārābī, [or the classics of Arabic literature like] the *Books of Songs* and the *Ring of the Dove*? They have all disappeared from the markets. Their place has been taken by books that discuss the punishment of the grave, or the ideas of the *khawāriǧ* and the extremists.

The journalist, the diplomat, the academic and the judge quoted above all understand and write about what is happening to the Middle East. They take part in the debate from their own place within society, and they may exert influence on the world. However, they have not attempted to create a substantial following and, when approached, have declined positions of authority in organisations that could have contributed to politico-religious change. They are individuals without organised support for their views. They want to analyse and to warn, and their words may be prophetic but they have no weapons other than words. Their enemies, by contrast, did not rely on words and arguments but took stronger measures to things their way. In at least two prominent cases they succeeded.

32 *Ma'ālim*, 245 and 297.

33 E.g. *Ma'ālim*, 241 and 256.

34 Al-'Ashmāwī, *Ma'ālim*, 292.

Naṣr Ḥāmid Abū Zayd was professor of Koranic studies in the faculty of Arts of the University of Cairo in Gizeh. He possessed the most important quality for a successful religious reformer: he was in close contact with potential followers. Moreover, if things were to go wrong he had an emergency exit available. In his writings he referred several times explicitly to his students who over the years attended his seminars on Koranic studies; he did so in the very opening lines of the preface of his most notorious book, *Mafhūm al-Naṣṣ*, 'What can be understood from the text', published in 1993.

In Egyptian universities the departments of Arabic are large and even overcrowded. Since Naṣr Abū Zayd lectured in such a department, the number of his students must have been considerable, and these student audiences represented the potential followers needed by a religious reformer.[35] He was also in close contact with the Cairo community of expatriate scholars and Islam-watchers, and with diplomats. It was on the strength of these contacts that he put forward his ideas, which were a logical sequel to the ideas on the Koran and on Koran interpretation advanced by earlier Egyptian Muslim scholars, especially Muḥammad 'Abduh (d. 1905) and Amīn al-Khūlī (d. 1967).[36] Naṣr Abū Zayd taught that the Koran had to be studied in the way that texts are studied in the twentieth century; the Koranic studies of the revered medieval forefathers are useful, but they have to be seen in the context of their times. The existing *iǧmā'* or consensus had to be reviewed, and the Koran and its interpretation have to be studied in their own historical contexts.

This hardly sounds revolutionary, and a modern scholar might consider that Naṣr Abū Zayd was wrong in believing, for example, that the *asbāb al-nuzūl*[37] as handed down by tradition must be seen as the historical context of the revelation of the Koran.[38] In the light of modern research it is probable that it is rather a creation of Koran interpreters of the early centuries who were at a loss to understand the text of the Koran. Much of the *asbāb al-nuzūl* may even go back to the storytellers who assembled

[35] Stark and Bainbridge, *Religion*, 105.

[36] See, e.g., 'Uṣfūr, *Hawāmish*, 44; and Jansen, *Interpretation*, 18-35, 65-8.

[37] Literally 'the causes of the revelation'. Stories about the circumstances in which a verse or a group of verses were revealed.

[38] Naṣr Abū Zayd, *Mafhūm*, 109.

every night round the camp fires of the Muslim armies during the earliest wars of conquest.[39] The reader of Naṣr Abū Zayd's book has to stomach Arabic versions of French post-modernist jargon, and may be perplexed that it is not made clear whether the word 'text' in the book's title refers to the Koran or to something else, e.g. the Koranic studies of Al-Suyūṭī (d. 1505) and Al-Zarkashī (d. 1392), or perhaps even the texts of the Traditions ascribed to the Prophet?

The wrath of the fundamentalists is easily provoked, but Naṣr Abū Zayd made no effort to befriend them when he wrote:

> The demand for the application of the rules of the Islamic sharī'a, and regarding this [demand] as a primary issue in contemporary religious thought, together with acceptance of the soundness of its theoretical starting points, is an assault on reality and disregards [it], especially when [this demand] gets reduced to asking for the application of the Islamic fixed punishments, as happens to be the case with many groups [*ǧamā'āt*] that call themselves Islamic. To reduce the aims of religion to stoning adulterers and cutting off the hands of thieves and flogging someone who drank wine etc. does no justice to the sharī'a and the revelation.[40]

However relevant to the present situation in the Arab countries, this may not be everybody's idea of a scholarly introduction to the Koranic sciences. Perhaps a scholar more inclined to patient diplomacy might have postponed spelling out such practical consequences of a more rational approach to Koranic studies and Koran interpretation.

Neither the Egyptian authorities nor representatives of the old élites can have been pleased to read:

> In these times of ours, when religious thought is subject to the whims [*ahwā'*] of the rulers, and in which the role of the *faqīh* has changed from guarding the interests of the nation to justifying the ways of the rulers and guarding the interests of the ruling exploitative classes, it has become imperative to review our understanding of the *iǧmā'* [consensus].[41]

39 Crone, *Meccan Trade*, 215-26.
40 Naṣr Abū Zayd, *Mafhūm*, 17.
41 *Ibid.*, 273.

There follow clichés about the media being in the hands of the authorities and so on. Moreover, the idea that religion and its representatives are subject to the whims of the ruler and the wishes of the exploiting classes sounds like an echo of Khomeinism as taught before the 1979 Islamic revolution which overthrew the Shah and his exploitative entourage.

Nevertheless Naṣr Ḥāmid Abū Zayd must have expected things to work out. Scholarly disputes, after all, are not settled in court; however, a number of lawyers formally accused him of apostasy from Islam. The court in Gizeh ruled in his favour in 1994, but the Court of Appeal in Cairo ruled against him in the middle of June 1995, and he then quickly found shelter in Western Europe.

If Naṣr Ḥāmid Abū Zayd could have remained within the region, he would first of all have hurt the monopoly of the 'Ulamā' on religious and Koranic studies. Muḥammad 'Abduh and Amīn al-Khūlī had been bad enough, but at least they were Sheikhs, trained as 'Ulamā'. Not so Naṣr Ḥāmid Abū Zayd who was just another modern effendi infringing on the rights of the 'Ulamā' and abusing pious Muslims who simply asked for the application of Islam. The Ulema want to live in the certainty that they will retain the monopoly on religious studies that has been theirs for centuries. They feel that modernity has already taken much from them, but they have almost always loyally supported the modern governments to which they are subjected, often in delicate situations, because they trust that they will be allowed to keep this one monopoly. Now they expected the government to help them against Naṣr Ḥāmid Abū Zayd, but if it did this has been kept a secret.

It was, surprisingly, not a fundamentalist organisation but a private citizen, a lawyer called Muḥammad 'Abd al-Ṣamad, who with thirteen other lawyers took Naṣr Ḥāmid Abū Zayd to court. They demanded that the court dissolve his marriage on the ground of his apostasy from Islam. Apostasy, they argued, was implicit from the content of his writings. The action of Muḥammad 'Abd al-Samad was based on a chapter from Islamic law (*hisba*) that many supposed to have lost its force with the abolition of the Egyptian sharī'a courts in 1955. According to both Egyptian law and the Islamic sharī'a a non-Muslim male cannot conclude a marriage with, or remain married to, a Muslim woman. This meant that when the court decided that Naṣr was no longer a

Muslim, this amounted to a dissolution of his marriage. If the lawyers had asked for other legal consequences of apostasy being applied in Abū Zayd's case, their chances of success would have been small. The death penalty for apostasy may be part of Islamic law proper, but is not part of Egypt's present system of law; however, the prohibition on non-Muslim men marrying Muslim women is.

With the cooperation of judges whose piety cannot easily be surpassed, the patient diplomacy of the lawyers managed to create an impossible situation for Naṣr Ḥāmid Abū Zayd. Both he and his wife were now open to accusations of adultery since, though not married any longer, they lived together. There was also a real risk of individual fundamentalist Muslims applying what they saw as the law of God – the name of Naṣr Ḥāmid Abū Zayd must have been cursed in those circles in Egypt that are responsible for law and order. He and his wife left Egypt in the summer of 1995 and it is almost inconceivable that they could have done so without the silent cooperation and encouragement of the Egyptian authorities at a high level. His return will also need the same degree of determined high-level cooperation. Many young intellectuals in the Middle East must have found Abū Zayd's fate discouraging. On the other hand, many old liberal activists who have quietly worked for a more humane society will merely see him as a traitor, who made no serious attempt to help the causes of moderation and reason. If Muslim courts would dissolve the marriage of every academic found lacking in diplomatic skills or who had written a bad book, the prospects for the wives and children of academics would look bleak indeed.

The problem of the millionaire businessman and consultant Dr Farağ Fōda was solved in a more drastic way with his assassination on June 8, 1992. Farağ Fōda engaged in the debate on Islam and politics with unusual virtuosity. From late July 1991 till his death he wrote a column in the Egyptian weekly *Uktūbir* attacking Islamic fundamentalism, and his assassin declared under interrogation that he had killed Farağ Fōda because of his articles in *Uktūbir*. The man could hardly read or write. Farağ Fōda did not allow himself to be intimidated by his opponents, and early in the year of his death he refused professional protection.

His opponents often asked him why he needed to worry about application of the sharīʿa: why should someone care as long as he did not intend to steal, commit adultery, drink wine or perpetrate the crime of apostasy from Islam?[42] But he explained, patiently and repeatedly, that it was not that simple. Application of the Islamic fixed punishments would lead, gradually but certainly, to an Islamic state, in which everything connected with art would have to disappear. For instance, if the death penalty for adultery was reintroduced, how could we execute people for that crime while night clubs still flourished all along Cairo's Pyramid Road? The belly-dancing which takes place in these night clubs, Dr Fōda wrote, was permitted, and folk dancing, which is difficult to distinguish from belly-dancing, was recognised as an art. Would this not have to be changed as well? And what about ballet? What about soccer players who dress in shorts that permit the public to see a part of their body above the knee?[43] Then there were television programmes and the theatre. Application of the fixed Islamic punishment for adultery, Farağ Fōda argued, would inevitably lead on to many things which at first sight are unrelated to adultery. Theatre, film and television faced a bleak future, and would almost certainly be banned.

Farağ Fōda's words here may have been even more to the point than he could then realise. An article devoted to the Islamic policy on art and literature which Sayyid Quṭb wrote several decades earlier explicitly confirms Farağ Fōda's fears:

> Both literature and art will take part in the operation of purification and change. They do not differ from the other human activities that [will contribute] to the universal triumph of Islam.[44]

Such a passage suggests that Farağ Fōda was right to suspect that a fundamentalist Islamic government might have a special and intense interest in literature and art.

By now it must be evident that the list of wrongs attributed to Farağ Fōda by his enemies is a long one. One of these enemies is a certain Dr 'Abd al-Ghaffār 'Azīz, the chairman (*ra'īs*) of the Department of Propaganda (*da'wa*) of Al-Azhar University, the supreme academic authority on Muslim law within the world of Islam. According to this influential figure, Farağ Fōda had attacked Islam and rejected the application of the sharī'a. Nothing could be worse than this. He was, furthermore, accused by Dr Abd

42 Farağ Fōda, *Qabl al-Suqūṭ*, 52.
43 Farağ Fōda, *Suqūṭ*, 53 and 63.
44 Quṭb, *Ta'rīkh*, 29.

Al-Ghaffār of having objected to the broadcasting of religious television programmes. Among the other charges against Farağ Fōda are that he expressed the opinion that the production and sale of wine were permitted, encouraged Christians to be inimical to the Muslims, showed sympathy for the Israelis, unjustly attacked the 'Ulamā', showed disrespect for scholarly specialisation, and made fun of Traditions ascribed to the Prophet and verses from the Koran, which amounts to apostasy.[45] What other encouragement could an assassin need?

In the last article he published before his assassination, Farağ Fōda ridiculed 'Abd al-Fattāḥ Mūrū, a Tunisian fundamentalist leader and founder of a political party, and also

> ....hero of a videotape...in which he struggles bravely, in his own way, in his own library, together with an extremely beautiful Tunisian female comrade.[...] Some people blame the authorities for putting such things on tape but Mr Mūrū is to blame even more.... For what advantage is it to a man if he gain a political party and influence, and lose himself?[46]

In the same article Farağ Fōda expressed his belief that members of the Islamic fundamentalist movements are obsessed with sex and that their sexual phobia explains their proposed measures against women who do not behave and dress as they should:

> Why do we not demand the abolition of women? Why do the hungry not demand the abolition of food? Why do the thirsty not demand the abolition of water? The reason is simple. Man cannot live without food and drink. He can live without sex...but he will not let others live.[47]

Much has been written about the assassination. Farağ Fōda's assassin was put on trial, and executed in 1994. One of Fōda's enemies, shortly after the assassination, summarised the indictment against him as follows:

> Farağ Fōda distorted the image of Islam in a way that was unacceptable to a Muslim. He insulted the symbols of Islam

[45] 'Abd al-Gaffār 'Azīz, *Man Qatal..*, esp. p. 118.

[46] Reprinted in 'Abd al-Ghaffār, *Man Qatal*, 194, and Farağ Fōda, *Ḥatta lā..*, 237-8. Cf. Luke 9:25.

[47] Farağ Fōda, *Ḥattā lā..*, 245.

> in a way that was improper, and spoke to the Ulema of this nation [*'Ulamā' al-Umma*[48]] ridiculing and mocking them. He openly cast doubt on their honesty and their honour.[49]

It is striking how often the theme of making fun of the Ulema is repeated in the polemics against Farağ Fōda. Does this mean that the link between them and the fundamentalist terrorists is stronger than outsiders think? Or can this be simply explained by the fact that in the Muslim Middle East it is mainly the Ulema who do the writing? Whatever the truth of the matter, Farağ Fōda was the first martyr for many centuries to be killed for criticising the professional men of religion, if we forget about the senseless killing that went on in post-revolutionary Iran.

Here we see that a journalist, a diplomat, a philosopher, a judge, a Koran scholar and a businessman – all men of high distinction – have written books and articles, which are widely read and regularly reprinted within the Arab world itself. These writings are intensely appreciated by a great number of literate people. However, unlike their fundamentalist foes, they have not attracted large masses of followers. At best, their following can be described as what Stark and Bainbridge call an audience cult. Such an audience receives a diffused hope from reading the books and articles of its heroes. Its members find listening to these men (and sometimes women) to be of great importance, but at the same time no significant efforts are made to organise such an audience[50] – certainly not in a way that is comparable to what the fundamentalists have managed to do, and one has to admit that this is no more than what one would expect. It is not easy to enlist the moderate in an army that has to fight and die for moderation. Who wants to be martyred for being moderate and reasonable, and either to die or to kill in the attempt to reach compromises? Does moderate enlightened rationalism need a disciplined Islamic mass movement? The Middle East, as it has become, teaches us that perhaps it soon will.

48 *Umma*, in Modern Standard Arabic, means both 'nation' and '[religious] community'. In the present phrase it is difficult to decide which translation fits best.

49 'Abd al-Ghaffār 'Azīz, *Man Qatala Farağ Fōda*, 11-12.

50 Stark and Bainbridge, *Religion*, 27-30 and 208-33.

6

THE JEWS: BACK TO THE GOLDEN AGE

Christian theologians often believe that the Jews and Judaism should have a special place within the framework of any Christian theological system.[1] As with any other religious belief, there is no way of deciding if they are right or wrong to believe so.

Christianity is certainly not the only religion that has a special interest in Judaism, which also has a particular place in Islam. The Jews and Judaism are mentioned so often in the Koran that Muslims who know its text and believe that it is the literal and true word of God may feel that they hardly need additional sources of information in order to know all there is to know about the Jews.[2] Certainly they will feel they are treading on familiar ground when Judaism is mentioned.

In modern times, the Koranic perspective on the Jews is heavily re-emphasised. In the medieval classical period Muslims, Christians and Jews coexisted on the basis of Judeo-Christian surrender to Islamic superiority. These were the centuries of the *dhimma*, 'protection', when in theory at least the Muslim patrons protected their non-Muslim monotheist clients. However, the medieval *dhimma* and the relative harmony that it brought are nowadays largely forgotten. At the end of the twentieth century, the slogan of the day seems to be 'Back to the Koran as far as the Jews are concerned'.

The Koran does not only mention the Jews in connection with the well-known stories of Moses and Jesus, but it also directly addresses the Jews of Medina who were contemporary with Mohammed, and who for much of the time were his enemies.

[1] One example out of many: Karl Barth, *Dogmatics in Outline*, London (SCM), 13th edn 1979, 72–80.

[2] Dr Suha Taji-Farouki (University of Durham) points out in a paper to be published soon that the ideas of Muḥammad Sayyid Ṭanṭāwī, Muftī of Egypt, are a case in point. See the interview with the Muftī in *Al-Muṣṣawar*, 27 January 1995, and his book *Banū Isrā'īl fī al-Qur'ān wa-'l-Sunna*, Cairo, 3rd edn 1986, 704 pp.

They represented the competition. They used a religious vocabulary that was similar to that of Mohammed, but it looked as if either many of their claims or many of his were false. This enmity, naturally, is reflected in the text of the Koran:

> Assuredly thou [i.e. Mohammed] wilt find
> that the most violent of the people
> in enmity against those who have believed
> are the Jews and those who practice idolatry.[3]

On several occasions the enmity between Mohammed and the Jews of Medina led to war, expulsion, mass executions, assassinations and murder, and this chain of confrontations ended in complete victory for Mohammed. However, it is difficult if not impossible to judge his treatment of the Jews by present-day moral standards. The fate of the Jews of Medina 'may have been a bitter one, but it cannot have been unusual according to the harsh rules of war during that or any other period.'[4] However, in the classical period of Islam the Jews were to be shown tolerance once they had been subdued and made tribute-bearers. Much mythmaking surrounds the issue of Muslim tolerance and benevolence towards the Jews in this period. Both nineteenth-century orientalists, many of them Jews, and twentieth-century Arab nationalists had good reason to sketch a favourable contrast between Islamic behaviour towards the Jews in the classical period of Islam, and that of Europe in almost any period. Zionists, on the other hand, tended to draw attention to recurrent elements of intolerance and persecution[5] in the history of the Jews under Islam.

However this may be, the tolerance of Islam and the Muslims was always extended exclusively to Jews and Christians who took their superiority for granted and had no political ambitions or aspirations of their own. The continuation of the fragment from the Koran quoted above already makes this obvious:

> Thou wilt find those of them
> who are nearest in love
> to those who have believed
> to be those who say:

[3] Koran 5:82(85) in Richard Bell's translation.

[4] Norman A. Stillman, *The Jews....Source Book*, 16-18.

[5] See, e.g., B. Wasserstein, 'Writing on the Wall', 9.

'We are Naṣārā [Christians]'
that is because there are amongst them
priests and monks
and because they count not themselves great.[6]

If there were Christians in Medina, they were individuals without tribal (i.e. military and political) protection; hence they did not count themselves great and were humble. According to Koran 5:83 they even burst into tears when they heard the Koran recited – the reason for this is not stated.

In the exemplary days of Islam in Medina, we have to conclude, two phenomena that are of the greatest importance today were arranged differently from the way they were in the medieval, classical Muslim period. First, political and religious authority in Medina went hand in hand, and the Jews and Muslims were in fierce and often bloody competition. In the classical period, on the other hand, political and religious authority quietly became separate. Secondly, the Jews surrendered to Islamic superiority and usually lived quiet lives within the context of a society dominated by Islam. The Muslim-Jewish enmity that existed in the days of the Prophet was not taken as a model of behaviour for the classical period.

In the classical period the Jews had their place within the world of Islam, circumscribed by the rules of the protective *dhimma*[7] pact which regulated the lives of 'the people of the book' (i.e. Jews and Christians of various ethnic backgrounds) within Muslim society. The *dhimma* arrangement, as is well known, presupposed Islamic political supremacy. However, Islam gradually lost this supremacy at the end of the pre-colonial period. Furthermore, the rise of nationalist movements and the change in the idea of the state eventually reached all Muslim peoples. All this caused the concept of *dhimma* to lose its traditional content, and eventually the *dhimma* status itself was abolished.

In modern times, especially after the establishment of an independent Jewish state in Palestine, anti-Jewish enmity became commonplace in many circles in the Arab world. Suddenly the situation which had prevailed in Medina and is referred to so frequently in the Koran gained an unexpected relevance. The

[6] Koran 5:82, in Richard Bell's translation.

[7] See, e.g., Lewis, *Jews of Islam*, 21, and the article 'Dhimma' in *EI* (2nd edn).

utter unimportance of the Jews had ended, and they were back where they belonged. Not only was Christian, or rather post-Christian, Europe militarily superior to the world of Islam, but the same now seemed to be true even of the Jews. While Christianity had already been an increasingly troublesome problem for Islam since the beginning of the colonial period, the Jews and their state added insult to injury.

These developments and changes could not but leave traces in mainstream, day-to-day Islamic religious literature. However, the modern Islamic fundamentalist movement could not look at Israel and the Jews without seeing them within the context of the fundamentalist struggle against the existing governments. Whether the fundamentalists showed hostility or indifference towards the Jews and their Zionist state on Palestinian soil was determined by this greater internal political struggle.

In a Koran commentary dating from the height of the colonial period (1915) the Syrian reformer Rashīd Riḍā, who worked in Egypt, made the following remarks on the verse of the Koran mentioned above:

> At the times of the [great Islamic] conquests the Jews in Syria and Spain felt sympathy for the Muslims and wanted them to be victorious over the[ir] Byzantine and Gothic Christian [enemies].
>
> The Muslims and the Christians [in Spain and Syria] competed for kingdom in wars. Consequently, the hostility which arose between them was stronger than that which the Jews had felt for...[the first Muslims] in the earliest days of Islam.
>
> This may well be confirmed by the feelings which Christian missionary activities arouse today in the souls of the Muslims, and by the political tension and military aggression which exist today between Muslim and Christian states.
>
> However this may be, nothing like this [hostility] exists between the Jews and the Muslims.[8]

This calls for several observations. Going against the explicit text of Koran 5:82, Rashīd Riḍā identifies the Christians as the real enemies of Islam, and the Jews as, historically, the friends of Islam. When an influential Muslim reformer like Riḍā writes about Koran 5:82 and does not refer to an age-old enmity between

[8] Riḍā, *Tafsīr al-Manār*, VII, 6-7.

the Jews and the Muslims, it must be inferred that this was not very widespread in his time. Consequently, this enmity got its present dimensions only in the twentieth century, and certainly not before 1915, when Riḍā wrote the lines which openly state that no hostility between Jews and Muslims exists. If Riḍā had known of the existence of an ancient Jewish-Muslim feud, the exegesis of Koran 5:82 would have been a natural occasion to mention it. He could have done so simply by paraphrasing the text of the Koran. Riḍā also did not seem to be aware of a Zionist threat when he wrote these lines.[9]

The classical commentaries on this verse, 5:82, do not mention such an ancient Muslim-Jewish feud either, and hardly give any attention to the Jews who are the subject of the verse. The commentaries are mainly interested in the Christians, as is illustrated by Al-Wāḥidī (d. 1075) who, in his famous *Asbāb al-Nuzūl*,[10] simply writes: 'This verse came down concerning the Emperor of Ethiopia, the Negus and his companions.' This dignitary and the monks who surrounded him are reported to have wept when they heard the Koran being recited, and it is about them that the commentators write, very positively. Ibn Taymiyya (d. 1328) appears slightly disturbed by this generally positive purport of what the commentaries and the Koran itself say here about Christianity and the Christians, and feels he must utter a warning:[11]

> This verse does not praise the Christians for their belief in God, and does not contain a promise that they will be saved from eternal punishment.[...] It only argues that they are 'nearest in love'.

Riḍā remains completely in line with the classical, mainstream tradition, effortlessly contradicting the explicit text of the Koran and, in his commentary on verse 5:82, allowing a perfectly natural occasion to abuse the Jews to pass by.

Others would soon be less magnanimous. Half a century later things had changed greatly. In a Koran commentary[12] of the 1960s taken almost at random, the remarks on verse 5:82 have

[9] See also Jomier, *Commentaire*, 304-6.

[10] Al-Wāḥidī, *Asbāb*, 116-17.

[11] Ibn Taymiyya, *Daqā'iq al-Tafsīr*, III, 109.

[12] 'Abd al-Karīm Khaṭīb, *Al-Tafsīr al-Qur'ānī li-'l-Qur'ān*, Cairo (Dār al-Fikr al-'Arabī) n.d. (late or middle 1960s), IV, 4.

a distinctly paranoid flavour; its author, ʻAbd al-Karīm al-Khaṭīb, loosely represents Egyptian middle-class pro-regime opinion. The two most important crimes of which he accuses the Jews in this commentary are warmongering and creating religious doubt. No one will deny that warmongering is a serious crime, but it is one that can not easily be proved in a court of law, if only because the politicians who declare war will almost certainly deny that they are puppets of the Jews.

The passage every now and then sounds as if its author is familiar with the Protocols of the Elders of Zion,[13] but even so the accusations against the Jews are serious, although they are not very specific:

> Their path through life testifies eloquently that they are at war with the religions and the believers.[...] They are at war with all of humanity [even] before they are at war with the religions which people follow.
>
> But when religion is the foundation of human society and the point of departure of its spiritual and social life – it is [also] the field in which the Jews are active, to undermine societies and to hit these at their most vulnerable spot, viz. the field of religion. When people get loose from their religion, when the ties to their religion are cut, they change into ferocious animals who kill each other without thinking, without reason and without conscience. This is what the Jews do in all societies in which they live.
>
> The Jews are the *tuǧǧār*, traders, of these wars that go on in every region of the world, they harvest the fruits of these wars, they collect a great deal from what the dust of these wars leaves behind.
>
> First, they gratify their hunger for revenge on humanity by these rivers of blood that have been shed so abundantly by different races and nationalities. Secondly, they break the ties of love and brotherhood that exist between people by these wars that will certainly never end.
>
> Thirdly, they buy protection; they buy people's consciences – readily for sale anyhow in these stormy days, which encompass the whole of humanity. They get hold of their minds and

[13] On this spurious document and its genesis see Norman Cohn, *Warrant for Genocide*, London: Pelican Books 1970; Lewis, *Semites*, 208-17.

hearts.[...] Conscience has no value, because it does not exist. Honour is not taken into account because death is rampant, attempting to kidnap souls!

Assuredly thou wilt find that the most violent of the people in enmity against those who have believed are the Jews [we read in the Koran, v. 82 of Sūra 5].[...] Look behind every evil that rises against human societies from anywhere, and thou wilt find that it originates with the Jews...both in the past and the present, both today and tomorrow.

Let us not say much more on the beginning of 5:82. As far as the words with which this verse continues are concerned, 'those who practise idolatry', they are creatures of the Jews because the Jews have corrupted the religion of many true believers. The Jews led them away from monotheism, and in spite of their being the first monotheists, and in spite of the messengers which God sent them and the books which He revealed to them, they did not show their fellow-men the road to monotheism or call people to the One God. They withheld from them the things they had received, and hid them from everybody. It is actually even worse: they embellished atheism, and made its ways seem attractive by corruption and evil which they spread through all human societies.

The Christians were not arrogant, isolating themselves from human society; they did not think, as the Jews do, that they are God's chosen people. Hence Christians mixed with the whole world, and let people keep the religion which they had. The Jews, however, were kept isolated by their arrogance and pride. They did not mix with people, and did not call them to God's religion....

The belief persistently expounded in this fragment, viz. that the Jews are behind all evil, can only be an echo of Western anti-semitism. The fundamentalist writer and martyr Sayyid Quṭb (d. 1966) also saw the Jews as being behind all evil.[14] Traditional Islamic anti-Jewish discourse, on the other hand, emphasises instead that 'there is no place for the Jews in the Middle East except as subject to Islamic rule, certainly not as an independent nation.'[15]

When Nasser and Sadat were at war with Israel, the fun-

[14] Nettler, *Past Trials*, 83.

[15] E.g. 'Umar al-Tilimsānī in the monthly *Liwā' al-Islām*, February 1989, 17c.

damentalist opposition to their rule must have looked with special interest to Israel, the main external enemy of their own internal enemy. Is it not written that the enemy of my enemy is my friend? Some individuals within the fundamentalist movement may even have found malicious pleasure in the humiliation of their government and its secret police, which were all-powerful within Egypt, by their Israeli neighbours. Several traces of this attitude can be found in the writings of Islamic fundamentalists. In a fragment which certainly pre-dates the October war of 1973 the popular preacher Sheikh Kishk expresses his admiration for the Jews: they have shown themselves able to create a state around their Torah, and in secondary schools they teach their Talmūd, whereas the Muslims, who have the glorious Koran and the sharī'a which is valid for all places and all times, have been unable to do something similar. The Egyptian defeat of June 1967, he thunders, is due to this inability.[16]

In the aftermath of Sadat's assassination the enigmatic preacher Sheikh Al-Sha'rāwī argued that Sadat's assassins were not on a mission from God because if they had been God would not have permitted them to fail to seize power in Egypt. The Muslim Brotherhood veteran Sheikh Dr Yūsuf Al-Qarḍāwī then quickly pointed out that if this theology was right, God had to be on the Israeli side in the Arab-Israeli conflict.[17] Muḥammad 'Abd al-Salām Farağ, executed in April 1982 for his part in Sadat's assassination, was even more explicit: the liberation of Jerusalem and the Holy Land was a religious command, obligatory for all Muslims, but as long as Egypt was not an Islamic state a victory in Palestine would only benefit the interests of infidel rule. To begin by putting an end to Zionism and imperialism, Farağ argued, was not praiseworthy or useful, but merely a waste of time. 'We must concentrate on our own Islamic situation: we have to establish the Rule of God's religion in our own country first.'[18]

Now it may be argued that this is only an incitement to postpone the war against the Jews, but to do so would be wrong on two counts. First, by postponing it until the moment when Muslim states apply the rules of the God-given sharī'a in their entirety might actually mean putting it off for a long while. Postponing

[16] Kishk, *Tarīq*, 13-17.

[17] Jansen, *Neglected Duty*, 145.

[18] *Ibid.*, 123.

the responsibility for bringing about the destruction of the Jewish state is equivalent to relinquishing it in favour of history.[19] Secondly, one should not underestimate the courage and intellectual independence which an Egyptian citizen needed in the 1970s to raise this point. Egypt felt that it had been militarily attacked and partly occupied by an aggressive neighbour both in 1956 and 1967, and arguing under these circumstances that fighting back was meaningless and useless was close to high treason. The fundamentalist attitude was indeed taken by several Egyptians to imply high treason, as is clear from Fu'ād Zakariyyā's remarks on their stand over the issue of the liberation of Palestine; the fundamentalists 'do not content themselves with being silent on the real problems of the Islamic world, i.e. the danger of Zionism and the [Arab] relationship to the United States, but they even seek to postpone the struggle [against these enemies].[...] In this way, their real message implies an act of high treason.'[20] However, the Egyptian scholar Dr Muḥammad 'Ammāra, whom his enemies have accused of sympathy for the fundamentalists, tried to soften this judgement. He explained that by refusing to go to war for Palestine the men who assassinated Sadat did not differ essentially from the Egyptian Free Officers in 1948 who also believed that the road to the liberation of Palestine *yamurr 'abra taḥrīr al-Qāhira*, 'would pass through the liberation of Cairo.'[21] No doubt 'Ammāra refers here to the words of Colonel Aḥmad 'Abd al-'Azīz, an army hero killed in August 1948.[22] Since in the ideology of the governments of Nasser, Sadat and Mubarak the Free Officers have represented all that is good in Egyptian and Arab politics, 'Ammāra's defence of the fundamentalist position ought to be acceptable to supporters of the Nasser-Sadat-Mubarak regime.

After Sadat's visit to Jerusalem in 1978 things changed. Israel was no longer the enemy of Sadat, the greatest enemy of the religious extremists, but had become a friend of their enemy, and hence, like Sadat, an enemy of Islam itself. The Muslim Brotherhood monthly *Al-Da'wa*, at the time the chief organ of the fundamentalist movement, showed increasing enmity against the Jews and Israel in its 1979 issues. As Bernard Lewis already

[19] Cf. Harkabi, *Fateful Hour*, 3.

[20] Zakariyyā, *Ḥaqīqa*, 72.

[21] 'Ammāra, *Farīḍa*, 46.

[22] E.g., Mansfield, *Nasser's Egypt*, 39.

pointed out, *Al-Da'wa* made no distinction between Zionists and Israelis on the one hand and those professing the Jewish religion on the other.[23] On the magazine's covers in that year this development can be traced. In January the cover asked readers to turn their attention to three enemies of Islam: America, the Rulers of the Muslims and the Jews. The February cover showed Atatürk and Richard Mitchell (see above, p. 40) in the same role. The March issue was devoted to Khomeini who had recently come to power. Attention was also drawn to the conspiracies against Islam by Christian Latter Day Crusaders and Communists, but no mention was made of the Jews. The April issue was silent on the enemies of Islam. *Al-Da'wa* was not published in May, but in June readers were warned against the Syrian Socialist Baath Party and, again, the Christian Crusaders. The Jews were not mentioned in either June or July, but in August earlier warnings against the regime in Syria and the teachings of the Jews were repeated. The September issue was devoted to the 'impossible peace' (*al-salām al-mustaḥīl*) between Egypt and Israel, and the 'realities' of Syria. The October issue was once again devoted to Syria, and it was declared that treaties or pacts with the Jews 'should not be': *lā 'ahd lahum wa-lā dhimma.* Clearly *Al-Da'wa*'s editors regarded the Jews as the greatest enemies of Islam and the Muslims.

The iconography of the Jew on the October cover reminds a Western reader of certain examples of Nazi propaganda. The statement it makes about the impossibility of treaties with the Jews goes against the traditional contents of the handbooks of Muslim law; more important, and more to the point, it contradicted the then current government propaganda in favour of the peace treaty with Israel. Finally, it went against everything the establishment 'Ulamā' were arguing at the time in their campaign to declare the peace treaty legal in terms of Islamic law. If *Al-Da'wa*, the organ of those wanting to apply Muslim law in its entirety, was right that under Muslim law treaties with Jews were impossible, a novel and an important legal development had escaped the notice of many students of Islam.

The November issue continued in the same vein, and in December the Soviet Union, the rulers of the Muslim world and the United States of America were once again identified as the true

[23] Lewis, *Semites*, 192.

enemies of Islam. Thus *Al-Da'wa* in 1979 divided the enemies of Islam into four groups: Crusaders (an obvious codename for the Christians), Jews, Marxists and Secularists. This last group included major political figures like Ḥāfiẓ al-Asad, Ṣaddām Ḥusayn, Nasser, Sadat, Atatürk, Sukarno and many others. The Jews were only one of the four Satanic groups recognised by fundamentalist demonology.

The vehemence of the statement on the September cover concerning the illegality of any form of treaty with Jews was of course mainly directed at those Muslim leaders in Egypt who at the time were defending the treaties which Egypt was in the process of concluding with Israel. The statement had a similar appearance. To quote Bernard Lewis again,

> The Jew is named as 'Jew', and not under any more specific labels such as Zionist or Israeli. Unlike the Christians, the Jews are all bad and there are no good Jews. [...T]he writers of these articles are not concerned with the distinctions made by spokesmen writing in Western languages, between Zionist and Israelis on the one hand and those who profess the Jewish religion on the other. The enemy is simply the Jew.[24]

But however much one might agree with this, this statement on the illegality of treaties with Jews was part of the internal struggle for religious and political authority. The fundamentalists wanted to replace the government, and in order to do so successfully it was one of their many self-imposed tasks to disqualify the 'Ulamā' who supported the government. The first aim of the statement was to undermine the authority of the 'Ulamā' who advocated obedience to the government and peace with Israel, and to drive home the message that true Islam was represented by fundamentalism, not by the establishment 'Ulamā' who, *Al-Da'wa* suggested, were losing their credibility as Muslim leaders by their willingness to compromise with the state and with 'the Jews'.

The small novel religious movement of Shukrī Muṣṭafā propagated views that in many ways deviated from the belief of the mainstream Muslim Brotherhood. The Shukrī group refused to accept the validity of the rules of the sharī'a, which it regarded not as divine but as the work of men. Shukrī himself believed that the world was approaching its end, and that under the leadership

[24] *Ibid.*

of the Jews, *taḥt qiyādat al-Yahūd*, it had reached its greatest corruption ever, *qimmat al-fasād*.[25]

All the same, Shukrī rejected conscription and war against Israel. He held that the Arab-Israeli wars could not be regarded as an Islamic battle, *qitāl islāmī*,[26] and in its defence of present-day Egypt the Egyptian army was not fighting for God, *fī sabīl Allāh*. Of course the Jews who had occupied Palestine were not Muslims, but they were not the only non-Muslims who were illegally occupying a part of the Muslim world. What about the contemporary Arab governments?

What did members of the Shukrī group think about the Jews? 'Abd al-Raḥmān Abū al-Khayr managed to survive the destruction of the group in the summer of 1977 and published his memoirs in Kuwait. Here he claimed that the United Nations, the Rotary Club, the Freemasons and the Jews were running the planet. All the same, he did not actively oppose this arrangement:

> We have no objection to the Palestine problem, *laysa 'alaynā ayy i'tirāḍ 'alā qaḍiyyat Filasṭīn*, or against the Arabs concluding a peace treaty with the Jewish state which took its name from Isrā'īl, the Prophet of God, God's peace be upon Him, whatever the psychological, social, economic or political consequences of that peace treaty may be.[27]

A Western reader of Abū Khayr's memoirs will not always be convinced that the international connections which he unravels are significant: if the Rotarians, Freemasons and Jews are really in charge, how can this state of affairs possibly be verified? At the same time, the formula 'Peace be upon Him' which 'Abd al-Raḥmān Abū al-Khayr respectfully adds to the proper name Isrā'īl, reminds one that for many centuries respectful piety was not as rare as it seems to be today. The last issue of *Al-Da'wa* appeared in August 1980, in the confused weeks before the assassination of President Sadat in October. It had an editorial signed by 'Umar al-Tilimsānī, headed 'Does our misfortune come from Israel or from the leaders of the Muslims?', which demonstrated once more that in the perspective of mainstream Islamic fundamentalism these two entities were roughly equal in unpopularity.

25 Shukrī, *Khilāfa*, in Aḥmad, *Thā'irūn*, 119.

26 Shukrī, *I'tirāfāt*, 98.

27 Abū al-Khayr, *Dhikrayātī*, 123.

At the end of the 1980s, the Egyptian fundamentalists again had their own monthly publication, *Liwā' al-Islām*, which had led a quiet existence since 1947 but changed its character in May 1987. From September 1988 it even printed on its front page the old Brotherhood slogan used by *Al-Da'wa* on its own front page: *ṣawt al-ḥaqq wa-'l-quwwa wa-'l-ḥurriyya*, 'the voice of the truth, of power and of freedom'. A letter to the editor of the *Liwā' al-Islām* in February 1990 had a much less respectful and civilised tone than 'Abd al-Raḥmān Abū al-Khayr had shown. This letter, from one Khālid 'Abd al-Ṣādiq Aḥmad of Suez, called on all Jews to come together in Palestine where, in 'a symphony of war', the Arab-Jewish problem would be resolved. In its second line Mr Aḥmad's open letter 'to the Jews in the whole world' characterises the Jews as *abnā' al-qirada wa-'l-khanādhīr*, 'sons of apes and swine', an erudite quotation from Koran 5:60. However, he mis-spells the Arabic word for 'swine', writing a *dhāl* instead of a *ẓā'*. Somehow this orthographic mistake seems significant though it is difficult to say why. It shows, at least, that the writer lacks a proper Islamic education, since the orthography of classical Koranic Arabic is certainly part of such an education.

Another letter in the same issue of *Liwā' al-Islām* is no less paranoid. Khālid Muḥammad 'Abbās from Al- Manṣūra wants his readers to remember that 'they' still apply the Talmūd faithfully, and carry out the Protocols of the Elders of Zion. 'We', however, read the Koran, in particular Sūra 17, *Sūrat al-Isrā'*, the first verse of which is ambiguous but is usually understood to refer to Mohammed's Night Journey to Jerusalem.

Although the first three issues for 1990 cover the *intifāḍa* and the immigration of Soviet Jews into Israel and its occupied territories, it is obvious that the editors regard Israel and Zionism as only a secondary concern. Much more space is given to Egyptian internal affairs, e.g. the fall of the Egyptian Minister of the Interior, Zakī Badr, or Islamic banking and its problems.

The most complete printed statement of the views of the Egyptian fundamentalists on Israel and Palestine at that time appears on pages 36-7 of the February 1990 edition of *Liwā' al-Islām*. It is an official declaration (*bayān*) of the Muslim Brothers concerning the Emigration of the Jews to Occupied Palestine, *Bayān min al-Ikhwān al-Muslimūn ḥawl Hiğrat al-Yahūd ilā Filasṭīn al-Muḥtallah.* This emigration, according to the statement, is a great crime and a major disaster, and confirms that the leaders of the Jews (*Qādat al-Yahūd*) still believe in a Greater Israel from the Nile to the Euphrates. Beyond this standard rhetoric, the statement has two other major themes. The first concerns the agreement which the authors assumed to exist between the Soviet Union and the United States. These two enemies of Islam had many disagreements, but they agreed on one point: they were allowed to take whatever they want from the things the Muslims in Palestine hold sacrosanct, *tustubāḥ ḥuramāt al-Muslimīn fī Filasṭīn*. The second theme, more concerned with Egyptian and Arab internal affairs, is that the present governments in the Arab world do not handle this affair competently. 'When will our leaders get into action?', *matā yataḥarrak sādatunā wa-kubarā'unā?*

The editors of the statement were certain that the current wave of emigration of Soviet Jews was caused by a Soviet-American agreement to destroy peace in the region, *iḥlāl al-salām fī al-sharq al-awsaṭ*. It was extremely significant that nobody ever talked about the establishment of a Palestinian alternative (*waṭan badīl*) in Jordan, which could only be explained by assuming that Jordan was to be the next stage in the Jewish expansion, *al-maḥaṭṭa al-tāliya li-'l-tawassu' al-yahūdī*.

It can plausibly be argued from these articles and letters that the rank-and-file of the religious activists in Egypt are much more concerned with the Palestine problem than the national leaderships or authorities. The correspondence columns in *Liwā' al-Islām* in particular give this impression, but there are also other indications. For instance, in the fall of 1989 students in the University of Cairo organised a 'Week of the Intifāḍa', but the university authorities prevented a speaker from Qaṭar from addressing the students within the campus. The speaker's theme was to have been 'The Necessity of an Islamic Solution to the Palestine Problem'.[28]

This feeling is reinforced by an incident in 1988. In October of that year *Liwā' al-Islām* gave an account of the Tāba controversy, including a map on which Israel was designated as 'Israel'. The November issue of the monthly apologised profusely for this error, and the editors thanked all who had contacted them or written to them about it. They had only sought to explain the reality,

[28] *Liwā' al-Islām*, December 1989, 48.

but their readers could rest assured that there was no place for a Jewish entity, *kiyān yahūdī*, within the world of Islam.

The rank-and-file activists appeared genuinely worried about Jewish and Zionist influence on the Islamic world, but their fears may, of course, have been influenced by what they read in *Liwā' al-Islām*. In August 1989 we read, for instance, that Zionist organisations were propagating the use of hard drugs among Egyptian Muslim youth in order to undermine Islam. In June 1989 there was a warning against Israeli tourists who introduced AIDS into Egypt. In February 1990 contraception and family planning were denounced as American-Zionist schemes to undermine the health of Muslim women and weaken Islam.[29] It is implicit in their texts that the editors of this Muslim Brotherhood publication regard the arrival of the Jews in Palestine and the establishment of a Jewish state as harmful to Islam and the Muslims as a whole. Why this should be true is only hinted at in allusions like 'Read the verses of the Koran on Mohammed's Night Journey to Jerusalem', and 'Personal rights of Muslims are being violated', which are clearly axiomatic to the largely fundamentalist public who read the paper.

For a full and authoritative discussion of the modern Islamic perspective on Israel and the Jews one has to turn to that most reliable pillar of Islam: the Ulema. Both in 1956 and in 1979 the Egyptian government asked for an official, authoritative fatwā from the state Muftī on the legality of armistice and peace with Israel.[30] In 1956 the fatwā concerned 'an armistice with the Jews in Palestine', *al-ṣulḥ ma'a al-Yahūd fī Filasṭīn*, but in 1979 the then Muftī used a more sophisticated terminology: 'the peace agreement between Egypt and Israel', *ittifāqiyyat al-salām bayna Miṣr wa-Isrā'īl*. In 1956 the fatwā was signed by Sheikh Ḥasan Ma'mūn, in 1976 by Sheikh Ğād al-Ḥaqq 'Alī Ğād al-Ḥaqq. The former consisted of only five pages, the latter of sixteen.

In 1956 the Muftī postulated in the beginning of his fatwā (rule 4) that 'what the Jews have done in Palestine is aggression against an Islamic country [*i'tidā' 'alā balad islāmī*] and it is first of all the duty of the inhabitants of that country to fight back, and secondly it is the duty of every Muslim in [all] Islamic countries to do so.' Palestine is an integral part of Dār al-Islām; it contains

[29] Freijsen, *Banier*, 25.

[30] Ğād al-Ḥaqq, *Fatāwā*, VII, 2645-57, and X, 3621-36.

several religious minorities, but nevertheless *sārat dār al-islām taǧrī ʿalayhā aḥkāmuhā*, the rules of Islam are applicable to it. One of these rules is that such territories cannot be alienated, *tabqā bi-yad ahlihā*.

Muftī Sheikh Ḥasan Ma'mūn, writing in 1956, firmly believed in the supremacy of an international Islamic solidarity. Islamic law in its traditional form has no real place for the governments of modern nation states, which thus have no place in the Sheikh's argument. The present-day activists share his assumptions. They hardly recognise the legitimacy of the modern nation states and national governments within the Islamic world. Thus it would not easily occur to them to abdicate to their own governments the right to sign a peace agreement with foreign invaders of Muslim territory. According to the Muftī, the only possible legal argument in favour of an armistice or any other form of treaty with non-Islamic nations was that to conclude such an agreement was in the interest of the Muslims.

More than twenty years later, Muftī Sheikh Ǧād al-Ḥaqq followed the same line of argument: that a peace treaty was admissible under Muslim law when it averted greater harm. He mentioned as an example of a legally admissible treaty the one concluded by Mohammed with the pagan Meccans at Al-Ḥudaybiyya in March 628, through which Mecca eventually fell into the hands of the Muslims – a fact with which most Muslims are familiar. It was therefore significant that Sheikh Ǧād al-Ḥaqq pointed out that thanks to the treaty with Israel Jerusalem might come back into the world of Islam. The return of the Sinai desert, which was part of the 1979 peace agreement, played an important role in Sheikh Ǧād al-Ḥaqq's argument. 'Does Islam forbid the return of Islamic land?', he rhetorically asked those who opposed the treaty (p. 3631). Egypt stood alone in concluding a peace agreement, the Sheikh admitted (p. 3632), but did not all Arab states want eventually to find a peaceful solution to the problems posed by Israel? Egypt had simply acted more quickly than the other Arab national governments. Opposition by other Ulema is explained away (p. 3634) as an attempt 'to please politicians who do not rule according to what God and His Apostle prescribe'.

Both Sheikh Ḥasan Ma'mūn and Sheikh Ǧād al-Ḥaqq see Israel as just another enemy of Egypt and Islam. They draw no comparisons between the Jews of Medina in the age of the Apostle of Islam Mohammed, and the Jews of present-day Israel. The allegedly special place of Jerusalem in the history of Islam had no place in Ḥasan Ma'mūn's fatwā of 1956, because Jerusalem proper was not conquered by Israel till 1967. Sheikh Ğād al-Ḥaqq mentioned Jerusalem, but assumed that his readers would know why Jerusalem was special. It is difficult not to conclude that both these 'Ulamā' saw the Arab-Israeli conflict as essentially a profane one that needed to be solved peacefully since this was in the interest of Islam and the Muslims. Other 'Ulamā', however, held other views. In a speech in the mosque of the University of Cairo in early 1990, a Muslim Brotherhood veteran, Sheikh Muḥammad al-Ghazālī, declared that once the Jerusalem Aqṣā mosque was lost it would be the turn of the Ka'ba, in *ḍā'a al-masğid al-aqṣā... yakūn al-dawr 'alā al-Ka'ba.*[31] This illustrates – if such an illustration is needed – that not all Egyptian 'Ulamā' quietly support the policies of the Egyptian government.

Since the 1970s Sheikh 'Abd al-Ḥamīd Kishk has been one of the most eloquent critics of the Egyptian regime, and his verbal virtuosity is a source of constant embarrassment to officialdom. In the mid-1970s he explained that the victory of the Muslims in Medina over their Meccan enemies at the battle of Badr (traditionally dated March 624 AD/Ramaḍān 2 AH) filled the hearts of the Jews of Medina with the 'snakes of hatred and the scorpions of hostility'. The historical truth of this claim is uncertain and its relevance to the peace agreement between Israel and Egypt may be minor, but it is well known that traditionally the outstanding characteristic of the Jews, as they were seen and treated in the classical Islamic world, was their lack of importance, their weakness and their insignificance.[32] However, Sheikh Kishk seems to be a traditional preacher for whom this had already changed. Although the scorpions-and-snakes passage is ambiguous, it is possible that the Sheikh's public understood it as referring to the recent conclusion of peace, particularly because of the Koran quotation which he added – 'If thou fearest treachery at all from any people, cast back to them [thy covenant] equally'[33] – in conjunction with his assurance that the Jews are the Jews in all times and places.[34]

[31] *Liwā al-Islām*, January 1990, 47.

[32] Lewis, *Semites*, 126 and 129.

[33] Koran 8:58.

[34] Jansen, 'Kishk', 63.

In an interview in April 1989, Sheikh Kishk identified the three biggest problems of the Islamic world as, first, world imperialism;[35] secondly, the fall of the Caliphate;[36] and thirdly, the 'poisonous dagger in our back which is called Israel'. When explaining this, he made it clear that Palestine falls in the same category as Spain, Crete, Sicily and Cyprus – territories lost to Islam, a fact which Sheikh Ḥasan Ma'mūn overlooked in his fatwā of 1956. In a fatwā[37] of Sheikh Kishk on the question 'What is Zionism?' the historical data given were uncontroversial, but it concluded with the claim that the aim of Zionism was to destroy the Arab states (*al-duwal al-'arabiyya*). All Muslims and Arabs were thus asked to unite against these enemies of humanity. There is no reason to think that Sheikh Kishk and his public do not sincerely believe that their religion and their co-religionists are in danger from world imperialism, national governments in the Arab world and Israel. However, in this list Israel is ranked third.

This is in contrast to the list of a certain Fu'ād al-Sayyid, the outspoken commentator of the Egyptian Ṣūfī monthly, who (in its March 1990 issue) ranks Israel first: 'The most dangerous of these [imperialist] conspiracies is the Zionist conspiracy.'[38] But it is significant that he too sees Zionism as an offshoot of world imperialism; in his view, it is simply an extreme case of Western enmity against Islam and the Muslims.

Moreover, his terminology carefully distinguishes between Israel, Zionism and Jews, and his concern at the immigration of Soviet Jews does not sound paranoid or irrational.

In the same issue of this monthly, Sheikh Ğād al-Ḥaqq, no longer in his former capacity as Muftī of the Republic but now *Shaykh al-Azhar*, and carefully using a terminology which makes all distinctions one could possibly wish for, expressed his anxiety over the status of the Muslim holy places in Jerusalem and the immigration of Soviet Jews. But in the same interview he showed much greater concern over other things, above all the rise of religious activism and extremism in Egypt.

Within Israel there are no problems as important as those of Israel's relations with the neighbouring Arab states, and of its

[35] *Liwā' al-Islām*, April 1989, 34–5.

[36] This implies criticism of the present regime.

[37] Kishk, *Fatāwā*, 121.

[38] *Mağallat al-Taṣawwuf al-Islāmī*, March 1990, 10.

behaviour towards the Palestinian Arabs within Israel whose lives it controls. This is not true of countries like Syria and Egypt, where Israel and the Palestinians count as only one among many problems that beset them. Indeed, for a long time they followed policies based on the pretence that Israel did not exist. Religion of course, plays a major role when this problem is considered by those large groups of the populations of the Middle East who will formulate any problem as a religious problem, but among opinion-formers and even among religious leaders the problem of Israel is often viewed rather pragmatically.

In reality, fundamentalists aim their verbal attacks on Israel at the political and religious leaders of their own countries, who are known to be in favour of peace with Israel, even if on their own terms. However, many members of the public are convinced that a conspiracy exists involving the United States, the former Soviet Union, certain Arab governments and Israel, with the aim of harming Islam and the Muslims, especially in Palestine. For example, in February 1990 there was a demonstration at the University of Cairo in which more than 6,000 students decided to send telegrams to the Ministers of Foreign Affairs of the United States, the Soviet Union and Egypt. According to *Liwā' al-Islām*[39] the telegrams declared these ministers 'guilty' and demanded support for the *intifāḍa*. The feelings of powerlessness which such demonstrations and such telegrams betray are an excellent basis for fundamentalist propaganda and recruitment. There is no short-term policy that can change this; the only remedy is political participation and education.

Although Muslim and fundamentalist views on Israel, Palestine and the Jews vary considerably, there is a common factor: Muslim inhabitants of all persuasions in the region feel that the arrival of the Jews and the establishment of a Jewish state in Palestine have turned out to be an act of aggression against the Muslims. It is only natural that the fundamentalist movements should exploit these ideas and try to persuade the public that the real cause of all this misery is the government which refuses to follow the rules which Islam supplies. Mainstream Muslim views on Israel and the Jews are, with few exceptions, no more sinister than can be expected after three decades of open war and war propaganda,

[39] February 1990, 49.

and do not reach the level of paranoia of traditional Western anti-Semitism.[40]

In December 1994, as in any other month, most Egyptian weeklies and monthlies carried articles on Israel and the Jews, which again contained extremely varied opinions. The monthly *Al-Mukhtār al-Islāmī* was then the official organ of the Egyptian fundamentalists, and its editorial for December 1994 is full of Palestinian blood, the Zionist enemy and 'Arafat's men who by attacking Ḥamās and al-Ğihād are being used as a protective wall around the Zionist entity'. This was accompanied (p. 44) by quotations from 'the Hebrew half of the Torah' – these were some of the more bloody passages concerning the conquest of Canaan. Nevertheless, most of the periodical's ninety-six pages are devoted to the Algerian struggle ('From Within the Prison Camps') and polemics against the Egyptian government.

The December 1994 issue of the Sufi monthly *Al-Islām Waṭan* is devoted to 'the Return of the Glory which the Muslims have lost and which will not be realised without the return of the Caliphate'. On the cover is a picture allegedly from an El Al Airlines journal showing a reconstruction of how the Temple Mount in Jerusalem supposedly looked when the Temple was still there. No explanatory article was necessary, since readers would understand the picture's significance. The Al-Azhar journal *Mağallat al-Azhar* for December 1994 (p. 1000) routinely calls the Jews and Israel 'the enemy', but asks the Muslims to emulate the respect the Jews show for their own language, their national unity etc. Such an example should inspire them.

The enlightened weekly *Rūz al-Yūsuf* gives much more space to female circumcision, but criticises the Saūdī State Muftī Ibn Bāz, whose fatwās 'have long been the chief support of terrorists' but who now, also in a fatwā, happily defends peace with Israel. What, the paper asks, is the use of such fatwās? However, it is clearly more unhappy with the Ulema and the fatwā system than angry with Israel. Elsewhere in the same issue there is reasonably objective writing on Israel and the Algerian Jews there.

Printed sources suggest that opinion in the Arab world about

[40] Nevertheless, heavy leather-bound copies of the Arabic version of the spurious Protocols of the Elders of Zion, *Ḥukamā' al-Ṣahyūn*, are found in many bookshops in the Arab world, usually of Sa'ūdī origin. It is difficult to regard these volumes as an authentic expression of Islamic sentiment or scholarship. On the diffusion of the *Brūtūkūlāt* in the Arab world: Lewis, *Semites*, 208–11, 265, 271.

Israel and the Jews is no longer determined by any single theological, political or ideological point of view. However, the traditional political, theological and ideological loyalties still exist. In the worldview of many, the Jews – after centuries of *dhimma*, 'protection, co-existence on the basis of recognising the superiority of Islam', are finally back where they belong in the Koranic perspective, that is the perspective of the earliest, golden age of Islam: the Jews who allegedly were once Mohammed's greatest enemies, are today the greatest enemy of the modern Muslims as well.

7

WOMEN AND THE IMPLEMENTATION OF ISLAM

Modern Muslim fundamentalists want to seize power in order to be able to see Islamic law implemented in full. How does Islamic law appear when applied and implemented?

Fundamentalists, despite censorship, manage to publish and distribute books, pamphlets and journals. These rarely give a clear idea of how fundamentalist rule would look, and perhaps this is unnecessary: not being too specific helps to attract individuals who oppose the existing order but have no ready recipe for change. Moreover, handbooks and detailed studies on the implementation of Islamic law abound in all bookshops and libraries in the Islamic world, and it would be extraordinary if a Muslim fundamentalist regime did not intend to apply these laws and regulations as they are described in these books in some form. Any revolutionary Muslim fundamentalist regime that omitted to do so would immediately be confronted with an Islamic opposition movement demanding the application of these or similar laws. The Western world only regards subjects like crime, family and ownership as the proper concern of the law. The laws of Islam have a much wider range, and encompass all civil and religious matters. Thus they make provisions for etiquette, prayer, ritual purity, clothes and so on.

The return by women (though not by men) to certain kinds of full traditional Islamic attire is one of the most notable developments in the contemporary Islamic world.[1] Female attire, women, gender and sex are definitely not excluded from being discussed in the handbooks of Islamic law. What do Islam and Islamic law have to say on such subjects, and what are the rules for which the fundamentalists are ready to kill and to die?

[1] Lewis, *The Middle East*, 318.

The Koran is the foremost book of Islam. It is often ambiguous[2] but, like the New Testament,[3] it is unusually clear on the position of women. Men, we read, have authority[4] over women, and rank[5] above them. Moreover, they are allowed to beat women.[6] Women are not allowed to draw attention to themselves, especially not by stamping their feet.[7] They are ordered to remain in their houses,[8] which is unfortunate when they want to study, work, shop or vote. However, here as elsewhere, a well-known and much-discussed and studied exegetical problem arises. The context of Koran 33:33 suggests that the command to remain at home, which is embodied in that verse, is exclusively addressed to the wives of the Prophet. This is how a number of modernist Muslim scholars have understood it, but over the centuries mainstream Muslim scholars have assumed that the command was addressed to Muslim women in general.[9]

It goes without saying that the wives of the Prophet have been important 'role models' in Islam; thus when the Koran in verse 33:59 prescribes a veil, this has usually been understood as a general prescription and to apply to all Muslim women, even if it may have been addressed only to the Prophet's wives.[10] However, the aim of veiling is to prevent temptation, and it could be argued that if the wives of the Prophet, who were naturally above all suspicion, already had to be veiled, how much more necessary it must be today for ordinary women, the wives of ordinary men.

On the surface all the Koranic verses about women[11] seem to belittle them, but professional exegetes can work wonders, and

[2] See, e.g., Koran 3:7, in Bell's translation: 'in it [the Koran] are clearly formulated verses; these are the essence of the Book; other [verses] are ambiguous [Ar.: *mutashābihāt*]'.

[3] 1 Tim. 2:12, 'I permit no woman.. to have authority over men'; and 'Wives, be subject to your husbands....', repeated three times: Eph. 5:22; Col. 3:18; 1 Pet. 3:1.

[4] *Al-riğal qauwāmūn*, Qur'ān 4:34; cf., e.g., 'Ukāsha al-Tībī, *Tabarruğ*, 153: *'nāmūs min nawāmīs Allāh al-thābita'*, and Ascha, *Statut*, 87.

[5] *Darağa*, Qur'ān 2:228 (end); cf., e.g., 'Ukāsha, *Tabarruğ*, 155: *'huwa al-riyāsa'*, and Ascha, *Statut*, 87.

[6] *Wa-ḍribūhunna*, Qur'ān 4:34; Ascha, *Statut*, 103.

[7] *Lā yaḍribna bi-arğulihinna*, Qur'ān 24:31; Ascha, *Statut*, 138.

[8] *Qarna fī buyūtikum*, Qur'ān 33:33; Ascha, *Statut*, 133.

[9] Ascha, *Statut*, 132 and references.

[10] However: *wa-nisā' al-mu'minīn*, 'and the wives of the believers', Qur'ān 33:59.

[11] An overview of these verses: *EI* (2nd edn), VI, 466b; or Ghassan Ascha, *Statut*, esp. pp. 34–6; and elsewhere.

are easily able to transubstantiate these verses into psalms that sing the glory of the equality of men and women. For an outsider it is difficult to escape the conclusion that the Koran simply repeats prejudices concerning women that were typical of the time and place of its revelation.

The Koran's authenticity and timelessness, many Muslims believe, are crucial to the validity of the claims of Islam. Safety from the fires of hell cannot be guaranteed if the Koran is not God's uncreated word. Man can be certain that the promises and threats of the Koran are true, but only if the Koran as we know it today and as it was revealed through Muhammad (d. 632 AD) is God's word in the most literal sense imaginable. Consequently, the Koran's teachings should be free of the limitations and defects of the time and place of its revelation, the Arabian peninsula in the early seventh century of the Christian era. It might become difficult to believe that the Koran is the word of God if it could be shown to reflect and repeat prejudices, or even false beliefs, that were of that place and period. Believers might then conclude that they had to abandon their hopes of being admitted to Paradise and its eternal life, which is not easy to do.

Such considerations give special importance to the Koranic teachings about women. Because, no matter how much of what men and women do to each other is dictated by biology, some of it is dictated rather by culture and custom. In literalists' eyes the credibility of Islam and the Koran would be almost irreparably damaged if the Koran were to prescribe, in the name of God, that man should perpetuate possibly unfair and even unjust rules that were part of the culture and custom of Arabia in the seventh century AD.

There are four possible ways of resolving the dilemma. The first is to interpret the Koran in such a way that its teachings conform to the modern, newly-discovered, politically correct belief, prevalent in our present age, that men and women are equal. Secondly, it is possible to pay lip-service to the modern ideology of equality but at the same time to interpret women's rights in such a way that they become meaningless and men are indeed given preeminence over women.[12] The third strategy – of accepting that part of the Koran reflects the local prejudices of the period

[12] Ghassan Ascha's *Du statut inférieur de la femme en Islam* is an eloquent indictment of this strategy.

and place in which the Koran took its present form – does not seem compatible with the status of a believer. And the fourth strategy is simply to acknowledge that men are superior to women, whatever foolishness Western modernity may teach at the moment. The rarity, if not the absence, of this strategy reflects how much moral authority Western values have in the Islamic world. Muslims definitely do not want to be outdone by the West in respect for women.

The Koran, which to Muslims is the word of God, is not alone in addressing the subject of women and their rights. The multiple Traditions, which many regard as representing the words of the Prophet, also discuss it. Thousands of Traditions are ascribed to the Prophet, and they are collected in a number of canonical collections. Some of these Traditions are specifically concerned with women[13] and their rights and obligations. It is generally agreed that not all the Traditions attributed to the Prophet of Islam are really and historically words that he once uttered. But even those Traditions created by the generations that lived in the decades after the Prophet reflect a point of view which Muslims at the time must have believed to be true, authoritative and important. So even when not all Traditions can be said with absolute certainty to reflect the teachings of Mohammed and his generation, they do reflect the opinions of later generations of Muslims.

In this vast corpus of Traditions we again meet a considerable number that belittle women, a few of which must be mentioned. Women, we are told, form the majority of the inhabitants of Hell. Another complementary Tradition informs us that in Heaven women are a minority.[14] The testimony of a woman is only half a testimony,[15] a community ruled by a woman cannot prosper,[16] and a man should not be asked why he beats his woman.[17] Only within a specific set of cultural and religious values the truth or justice of such statements can be a subject of debate. Modern Muslim fundamentalists, however, do not want to apply verses of the Koran or individual Traditions. Their aim is more precisely

[13] See, e.g. Wensinck, *Concordance*, vi, 186-96, *mar'a*; and vi, 433-10, *nisā'*.

[14] *Al-nār akthar ahl^{i}hā al-nisā'*, and *aqall sākinī l-ğanna al-nisā'*.

[15] *Shahādat al-mar'a niṣf shahāda.*

[16] *Lan yufliḥ qawm*^{un} *tamlik*^{u}*humu mra'a*^{tun} and *lan yufliḥ qawm*^{un} *wallaw amr*^{a}*humu mra'a*^{tan}.

[17] *Lā yus'al al-rağul fīmā yaḍrib*^{u} *mra'at*^{a}*hu.*

defined: to implement the laws of Islam fully. Does Islamic law in its traditional handbook form speak slightingly of women, or give rulings that presuppose their inferiority to men?

Divorce (*ṭalāq*) is an absolute right reserved to the husband. He does not have to consult his wife or explain his decision to her. Moreover, he has the right to ask the authorities to bring back a wife who has left the conjugal home; this male prerogative is known as *bayt al-ṭā'a*. The presence of witnesses, or a form of registration, is not necessary when a husband pronounces a divorce. Nor even is the repudiated wife required to be present during the quashing of the repudiation. Thus a malicious husband may create confusion over whether a repudiation has taken place or not. This is a serious problem, because when the supposedly repudiated wife remarries she may unknowingly be guilty of adultery and risk being sentenced to death.

A married man may call his wife exclusively his own, whereas the reverse is not possible: Islamic law permits a man to marry four wives but a woman may not be married to more than one man. The rule about a woman's testimony having only half the value of a man's has become part of Islamic law, and a woman inherits half of what a man in her position would inherit. It sometimes appears as if under Islamic law a woman is only half a man. Married women may own property, and this right has been taken over by most systems of law in Islamic countries. It is often advanced as one of the (for women) positive points of Islamic law, but it is doubtful whether this is genuinely so. Whereas women may indeed be the rightful owners of their property, they are not always in control of their own possessions; the relevant decisions about administering a woman's property can usually only be made with the husband's permission. This is a problem, since according to Islamic law a woman cannot easily choose her own husband: her family, or actually her nearest male relative, her *walī*, may object to the marriage if, according to the *walī*, the prospective bridegroom is not his future wife's equal by birth.[18] Dr Ghassan Ascha has pointed out that within prosperous families the combined effect of these rules has often been that women had to remain celibate by the orders of their male relatives.[19] A second effect of this state of affairs is that, in order to keep

[18] See, e.g., Schacht, *Islamic Law*, 161-2.

[19] Ascha, *Statut*, 215-16 and references.

authority over property within the family, girls are often married off to relatives.

Islamic law, again, is more than what its handbooks say it is. The collections of fatwās[20] are also sources of great importance for those desiring guidance on points of law. A Saʿūdī fatwā collection of about 1,000 pages, reprinting fatwās from the 1970s and later, has a special chapter of almost 50 pages 'concerning women'.[21] Here we can expect to find what Muslim women need to know about Islam's teachings on their situation, and we can see how their questions are answered by men who have devoted their lives to Islam and are appointed by their government to expound its teachings. The first point the muftīs wish to consider is a woman's freedom of movement. They assure their constituency that a woman has to inform her husband where she wants to go when she wants to leave his house. The husband may then give her permission to go to places where no harm can befall her, since he knows her interests best, *fa-huwa adrā bi-maṣāliḥ^i^hā*. The scholars substantiate this by simply invoking the two familiar passages on women from the Koran: 4:34, 'Men have authority over women', and 2:228, 'Men have pre-eminence over women'. It may be coincidence that these two important verses on women are quoted on the first page of the chapter, or the muftīs may consciously have arranged their material in this way. Whatever is the truth, at least two modern muftīs understand these verses literally, deem them important, and make no attempt to explain them away.

What other examples of divine wisdom does this fatwā collection divulge?[22] Women may not shake hands with men, except for certain close relatives. They may not wear high heels. They may go unveiled[23] – but only in the presence of blind men. They may not cut their hair. They may not wear a wig. They may not wear *libās^an^ ḍayyiq^an^ yuḥaddid ğism^a^hā*, literally 'tight clothes that

[20] A *fatwā* is an opinion on a point of law. The person who gives a fatwā is a muftī.

[21] Ibn Bāz, *Fatāwā*, 825-73.

[22] All questions and answers from pp. 825-74 and 607-18 are paraphrased below in the order in which they occur in the Arabic original. Two or three short questions were omitted because they were repetitive, or because an explanation in English of the point of the question would take up much more space than the relative unimportance of its topic could justify.

[23] The text of the fatwā is unambiguous: *takshif an wağ^i^hā*. On the veil in Saudi Arabia: Kamla Nath, 'Education', 176-7, in Beck and Keddie, *Women*.

define [the contours of] her body'. They may not wear white clothes. They may not address men who are not close relatives.[24] A woman is forbidden to make her voice heard except when answering a judge or somebody who knocks on the door or calls on the telephone, or of course, as always, close male relatives.

A woman should choose her husband because of his piety and his morals, not because of his wealth or his family. Women may not dress in trousers – nor even may little girls dress in 'short clothes'. Women's clothes should cover the whole of their bodies. They are allowed to pray in the mosque, but may not use perfume before doing so. To pray at home, needless to say, is preferable. Also in the circles for which these muftīs write, tensions arise between married men and their mothers-in-law. A woman does not want to take off her veil in front of her son-in-law, but is this correct? Should a woman have to veil herself in front of her son-in-law? The muftīs decide that a son-in-law is a close male relative before whom a woman need not hide herself.

A girl is accused by her friends of having complexes if she does not participate in reprehensible girlish behaviour like gossiping or listening to songs. When she asks her state-appointed spiritual mentors what she should do, they advise her: be patient and brave, God will reward the steadfast. Show your disapproval and do not join the gossiping; tell the other girls of the heavenly rewards that await them.

A teacher may hit his female pupils (*ṭālibāt*) when circumstances require it because being kind, as the muftīs know well, is sometimes of no avail. May a woman pluck her eyebrows? No. May she varnish or paint her fingernails? No, because nail-varnish will interfere with ritual purity before prayer. How long may a girl let her fingernails grow? Not for more than forty nights, or she will look like an animal or like certain non-Muslims, *bahā'im wa-ba'ḍ al-kafara*. May a woman be alone with a male driver in a car? The answer is more complete than the question: whether travelling by land, sea or air she may not be alone with the man who drives, sails or flies the conveyance. According to the opinion of Shaykh Muḥammad al-Ṣāliḥ al-Ithīmīn, passed down in early March 1986, this is confirmed by several utterances of the Prophet.

24 'A close male relative', here and below, is a clumsy attempt to reproduce in English the Arabic technical term *maḥram*, 'non-mar iageable person' (because of consanguinity). See, e.g., Schacht, *Islamic Law*, 162.

And except in cases of extreme necessity no woman should talk with a man by telephone. May a Muslim woman wear a brassière? Not when the aim is to deceive people into, for example, thinking that she is young or a virgin; in order to prevent bodily harm it is, of course, allowed. Does a Muslim woman have to wear a veil in the presence of non-Muslim women? No. Does Islam allow non-Muslim female servants to wash the clothes of a Muslim woman, since these clothes are worn during prayer and have to be pure? Yes. But the proud owner of the clothes should explain to these women who do the washing that their religion is mistaken, and that Islam is true and has replaced all earlier religions.

My family ridicule me for having begun to wear a veil and Muslim dress, and to fast and pray regularly. What should I do? You must thank God for your conversion. My family mock me for my piety and prevent me from dressing in the Islamic way. Do I have to leave them? Explain to your parents what the Koran and the Traditions of the Prophet teach about Islam. May I show myself without a veil[25] to my husband's brothers? No, not even when your husband wants you to. May I go unveiled when travelling outside my own country? No. Is a man allowed to see the face of his brother's wife? Is he a close relative in front of whom veiling and suchlike are not necessary? No. The sisters of your wife should cover their faces in front of you since you are not their husband; you may not be alone with them. May a woman lift her veil to kiss the black stone of the Ka'ba?[26] No, men may see her. May very young children go out unveiled? No. May a Muslim woman allow her hair to be visible in the presence of non-Muslim women? Perhaps.

A couple pay a friendly visit to another couple to whom they are related. The evening is spent in quiet conversation, and enlivened by the consumption of tea and coffee. In the jargon of Islamic law such an extravaganza gives rise to the following question: 'One of my girlfriends said to me "my husband allows me to show my face when in the company of a relative who in turn permits his wife to sit with my husband." Is such a thing allowed?' The answer: 'You are not allowed to obey your husband when this means being unveiled in the presence of one of his male relatives.'

[25] The text is unambiguous: *ṭalab minnī allā astur^a waǧhī*, 860.

[26] Ibn Bāz, *Fatāwā*, 870.

Many of the questions arise from confusion over the proper definition of a close relative, a *maḥram*. By the strict rules of Islamic law, only those whom one is precluded from marrying because of a certain degree of consanguinity[27] can be regarded as close relatives with whom free social contact, without the veil, is allowed. In everyday life a number of people seem to have begun seeing the official Islamic definition as too restrictive. They tend to want to reshape their social lives, at least within their own families, and in this to follow the American and European examples which have become familiar to them. When the representatives of Islamic scholarship tell their flock that Islam forbids a couple to have tea with another couple – in the way that they were accustomed to do when they studied in the United States, England or France – then their credibility may be at stake.

Some of the questions are asked by non-Saudi Muslims returning from residence in Saudi Arabia to their native countries. The insights into Islam which they gained when working or studying in Saudi Arabia – so their letters and questions show – are seldom appreciated at home. In particular the desire to wear Islamic attire appears to create a problem. The fatwās that are requested by letter from outside Saudi Arabia make it clear, albeit implicitly, that the families of young people who had taken the step of wearing Islamic attire often found difficulty in treating it seriously because they rejected the strict views advocated by the muftīs. No doubt many modernised Muslims also reject the views of these muftīs, and it goes without saying that many in the West will have the greatest difficulty in taking seriously the advice which the muftīs give so freely. However, the muftīs themselves want these views made public, in the belief that they represent much more than their own limited human viewpoints; rather, they represent the laws of God, which is why they are written down, edited, indexed, printed and put on the market. The opinions of these muftīs are decidedly not a secret which it is dishonourable to disclose.

The (*circa*) 1,000 pages of Ibn Bāz's fatwā collection discuss gender questions not only in the chapter on women but in many other chapters. For example, women and their bodies are important in the fatwās on ritual purity. Nor should the chapters on inheritance, divorce, a wife's disobedience (*nushūz*), and a husband

[27] Schacht, *Islamic Law*, 162, lists these degrees.

cursing his wife should be overlooked. Of those which discuss gender questions special attention should be given to the one[28] on the rules of seeing [women], being alone [with women] and keeping company [with them], *aḥkām al-naẓra wa-'l-khalwa wa-'l-ikhtilāṭ*. May men look at the faces or bodies of actresses and female singers when these are shown on television, the movie screen, videos or the printed pages of magazines? No. May a man look at magazines that are 'interested in news about actors and actresses', and read such magazines, work for them, distribute or publish them? No, the Koran and the Prophet have repeatedly warned against such practices. May a medical student preparing for his gynaecology exams look at (pictures of) the female reproductive organs? Only if he would otherwise fail his exams. This intricate point is one which the muftīs feel they have to explain. There must be a sufficient number of Muslim doctors, and if the study of modern gynaecology were forbidden to Muslim medical students, Muslim women would be dependent on non-Muslim doctors, which self-evidently no one wishes to happen.

The daughters of my mother's sister and the wives and daughters of my father's brothers are my best friends. A woman asks if they may visit each other and sit together without being veiled. The experts answer that this is a bad habit, *'āda sayyi'a*, and to kiss or shake hands with them is forbidden by the laws of Islam, they explain, invoking Koran 33:53, '....from behind a veil;[29] that is purer for your hearts and for theirs...'[30] May male students attend lectures given by a woman who is not veiled? No. May a man be alone with a woman to whom he is not related in such a way that marriage would be precluded? No. May men and women mingle in factories or offices? No, they should be strictly separated. May a Muslim enter a market where, as he knows, he will inevitably see men and women selling and buying? He may not, except to admonish the public who visit such a market and explain to them the laws of Islam. May a father kiss his daughter? Only on her cheek. May a male university student say 'hello' to female classmates? You cannot have female classmates, because education should be segregated. However, greeting someone is in principle allowed, provided you do not shake hands. May I look at pictures

[28] Ibn Bāz, *Fatāwā*, 609-17.

[29] Arabic: *ḥiǧāb*, usually translated as 'veil' or 'screen, curtain'.

[30] Adapted to the context from Bell's translation.

of women in newspapers? Not under any circumstances. May I read magazines that show pictures of nude women? No.

The last fatwā in this chapter is of great interest, since it shows once again the tension between customary behaviour and the demands of the divine law. In a letter[31] a student asks for a fatwā:

> Every now and then I visit my family after absences of half a year or sometimes even a full year. When I arrive at the house the women, big and small, come up to me and kiss me. I find this embarrassing. It must be said that with our family this habit is widespread and means nothing, because according to their views it does not represent anything that is forbidden by Islam. I have now acquired a considerable amount of Islamic culture and this whole matter confuses me. How can I avoid being kissed by the women of my family, knowing that if I only shook hands with them on such an occasion they would become extremely angry and would say 'He does not respect us, he dislikes us, he does not love us any more'? I have no bad intentions when I kiss them. Do I commit a sin when I kiss them?

Seen through the eyes of an expert on Islamic law this is a simple problem. A Muslim is forbidden even to shake hands with, let alone to kiss, women other than his own wife and a number of close female relatives with whom marriage is precluded because of consanguinity. One should greet people with words, the fatwā says, not by kissing or shaking hands. Society must take heed since such seemingly innocent behaviour is one of the commonest ways to spread permissiveness. Does this answer do justice to the emotional and social problem expressed by the letter quoted above?

The chapter on the making of marriages contains a number of interesting points. May a man marry a virgin he has seduced? Only after she has given birth or has had her period, the experts say. This solution is not as benign as it sounds, since families will never accept that a girl who has given birth out of wedlock can marry into their family, whose honour such a marriage would irreparably damage. Another question discussed in the marriage chapter is 'the secret habit',[32] *al-'āda al-sirriyya.*[33] This is very

[31] Ibn Bāz, *Fatāwā*, 616.

[32] A common Arabic euphemism for 'masturbation'.

[33] Ibn Bāz, *Fatāwā*, 631.

dangerous, as it takes away a person's strength and weakens the nerves. It is absolutely forbidden by Islamic law because it is harmful, and Islamic law forbids anything that causes harm. The Egyptian fundamentalist monthly *Al- I'tiṣām*[34] goes further and claims that 'only an Islamic society is able to achieve a victory over this problem'. Masturbation is also discussed twice[35] in the chapter devoted to 'General Questions'. The first time the fatwā is not given in answer to a question but in answer to a cry of desperation: 'How can I quit the secret habit?' The Muslim scholars, like their Christian colleagues in earlier decades, know the answer: fasting is exceptionally effective. The second question on masturbation may be a subtle form of protest against the supremacy of the Muslim clerics over personal matters:

> I am a boy of eighteen years old. For the past three years I have resorted to the secret habit because of the spiritual calm[36] I find in it. I often feel remorse. And in winter, because of the cold, I have many times omitted to wash afterwards. Also, during Ramaḍān in the summer of 1982 I did it during the day when I was fasting.... How does this affect my prayers and my fasting? Isn't sperm ritually pure? And somewhere I heard a story of how during morning prayer one of the Prophet's wives rubbed sperm from the Prophet's robe....

Spiritual calm? By masturbation instead of by fasting and praying? Rubbing sperm from clothes? What is the world coming to? Certainly the idea that spiritual calm can be attained through masturbation is a dissenting opinion among Muslim 'Ulamā'. There can be little doubt that the world will hear more from the eighteen-year-old who managed to get this minority view eternalised in the 'Ulamā's own official law books.

The equality of men and women comes up again in a question on how pupils in school should behave.[37] Must they rise when the teacher enters? Whether the teacher is male or female is of no importance, the Muftīs answer, but rising is not advisable; the Prophet did not like it.

[34] *Al-I'tiṣām*, August 1981, 20: *akbar mushkila tuwāğih al-shabāb*, 'the biggest problem with which youth is confronted'.

[35] Ibn Bāz, *Fatāwā*, 951, 974.

[36] *rāḥa li-'l-nafs*.

[37] Ibn Bāz, *Fatāwā*, 993.

The chapter on general questions furthermore routinely forbids bathing suits,[38] even innocent photographs[39] 'for remembrance only', listening to music etc. Somehow all these detailed rules seem to have given a sense of urgency to a general questions with far-reaching implications[40] which is discussed near the end of the Saudi fatāwā volume. When we want to characterise proper Muslim behaviour, it is asked, may we use the formula 'in accordance with the customs and traditions of Islam'[41]? Does the use of such a formula in such a context not implicitly belittle the prescripts and provisions which God gave to his elect? It is indeed preferable, the Muftīs declare, to say 'in accordance with the law of Islam and its just provisions'. The Muftīs, obviously, are convinced that they are not teaching merely human, local conventions but the laws of God.

Nevertheless, the rules for proper Islamic behaviour as written down by one of the most authoritative Egyptian experts on Islamic law, Sheikh Dr Yūsuf al-Qarḍāwī, in his widely distributed book *Al-Ḥalāl wa-'l-Ḥarām fī al-Islām*, literally 'The Allowed and the Forbidden in Islam', are not always identical to those propounded by the Saudi Muftīs. This volume, written on the initiative of the Azhar university in Cairo and first published in 1960, has often been reprinted all over the Muslim world. It has been translated into Turkish and other languages and, like the Saudi fatāwā, is as official and authoritative as an Islamic book can be. According to this source, a Muslim woman has to cover her hair, her breast, her throat and the back of her neck – but not her face.[42] No veil or gloves are necessary, because according to the definitions of the Arabic term '*awra* used by Dr Al-Qarḍāwī,[43] the face and hand may be visible. Literally '*awra* means 'shame' and hence, in the jargon of Islamic law, 'the part of the body that may not be uncovered without bringing shame'. Obviously, a difference of opinion on the question whether or not the face is legally part of the '*awra* has important practical consequences. According to the Saudi scholars who represent the Ḥanbalī school

38 *Ibid.*, 809.

39 *Ibid.*, 936.

40 *Ibid.*, 992.

41 *al-'ādāt wa-'l-taqālīd al-islāmiyya*

42 Al-Qarḍāwī, *Ḥalāl*, 152.

43 E.g. Al-Qarḍāwī, *Ḥalāl*, 149: *Mā laysa bi-'awrat al-mar'a – ay... wağhihā wa-kaffayhā.*

of Islamic law,[44] the face is part of a women's '*awra* and therefore has to remain covered before strangers. Dr Al-Qarḍāwī, on the contrary, represents the viewpoint of the Shāfiī and Ḥanafī schools of Islamic law which deny that a woman's face is part of her '*awra*.[45] The development, within a system of law, of different schools is a perfectly natural and universal phenomenon. The origin of such schools usually goes back to geographical factors, sometimes of great antiquity, and their spread follows the vicissitudes of dynasties and political power. But no matter how natural the formation of schools may be, it follows that Islamic fundamentalists in the coming years have a problem when they demand the application of Islamic law. Are the interpretations of the law of the four different schools of equal practical value? Is the veil God's command or not? Which interpretation of the sharī'a will be followed? Farağ Fōda may have been accurate in his prediction[46] that when fundamentalist movements are left free, as they are in Afghanistan, they will start to fight each other.

The veil is personal and visible. Female circumcision[47] is much less visible, but very much more personal. Islam prescribes male circumcision, but does it prescribe female circumcision too? Here the respective schools of Islamic law are again not fully in agreement. Around 1950 the Egyptian State Muftī Ḥasanayn Muḥammad Makhlūf defined female circumcision[48] as 'the amputation of the upper part of the skin of [the clitoris], not the removal of the [whole] clitoris'. The Muftī, like all the others who quote this definition, derive it ultimately from a fifteenth-century source, Ibn Ḥağar al-'Asqalānī's authoritative commentary, entitled *Fatḥ al-Bārī*, on Al-Bukhārī's canonical collection of prophetic Traditions. This commentary was completed in 1438 AD.

The same definition can be found more than five centuries later in a twentieth-century Western study of the subject,[49] according to which the orgasm is delayed for circumcised women.

44 E.g. Ibn Bāz, *Fatāwā*, 867: *wağh al-mar'a al-ḥurra 'awra*.

45 See, e.g., Ḥasanayn Muḥammad Makhlūf, Muftī of Egypt in 1946-50 and 1952-4, writing in 1950, repr. in his *Fatāwā*, I, 136-43; Al-Ğazīrī, *Al-Madhāhib al-Arba'a*, V, 54; and, e.g., Ğād al-Ḥaqq, *Al-Fatāwā*, XX, 7796-8.

46 Fōda, *Suqūṭ*, 159-66.

47 See the article 'Khafḍ' in *EI* (2nd edn), IV, 913 (1977).

48 Makhlūf, *Fatāwā Shar'iyya*, I, 145.

49 Soheir A. Morsy, 'Sex Differences and Folk Illness in an Egyptian Village' in Beck and Keddie (eds), *Women in the Muslim World*, 610-11.

Moreover, circumcised women 'generally report that they enjoy sex' and 'their conversation and joking often centre around this topic'. The contrary view is represented by, e.g., Yūsuf al-Maṣrī, who is categorical that female circumcision makes the life of a circumcised woman and her husband hell: according to him, clitoridectomy does not delay orgasm but makes it almost impossible under normal circumstances. Yūsuf al-Maṣrī, furthermore, believes that the consumption of soft drugs and perhaps even hard drugs is directly linked to the problematic character of orgasm and arousal[50] for women who have undergone clitoridectomy. The discussions of this subject are repetitive, and most of the arguments exchanged are summed up in a chapter on 'Selected Issues of Coptic Ethics', pp. 318-41 of Otto Meinardus, *Christian Egypt: Faith and Life*, Cairo 1970. Circumcision is practised not only among Muslims but also among Egypt's Christian minority, the Copts. This has led many to believe that the custom is pre-Islamic –the more so since in several solidly Islamic regions it appears to be unknown.

The Egyptian State Muftī Makhlūf, writing in the 1950s, believed that the Shāfi'ī school of Islamic law put clitoridectomy in the category 'obligatory', whereas the Ḥanbalī school only recommended it. Ḥanafīs, Mālikīs and a number of Shāfi'īs teach that it is a custom to be recommended but not a religious obligation.[51] In 1980 the Egyptian State Muftī Ǧād al-Ḥaqq 'Alī Ǧād al-Ḥaqq[52] saw female circumcision as 'something Islam calls for', *da'ā ilayhi al-islām* – which, in his balanced vocabulary, is not the same as something which Islam prescribes. But, he warns, it was certainly not a practice that should be abolished on the authority of 'one or more medical men whose opinions cannot be regarded as scientific or empirically tested'. Muftī Ǧād al-Ḥaqq recognised that the other schools have different opinions, but he suggests that a number of (unnamed) Ḥanbalīs agree with the Shāfi'īs and hold circumcision to be obligatory. Regrettably this is one of the few statements in the fatwā that does not have a Western-style footnote.

During the UN world population conference held in Cairo

[50] Youssef El Masry, *Le drame sexuel de la femme dans l'orient arabe*, Paris 1962; German translation: *Die Tragödie der Frau im arabischen Orient*, Munich 1963.

[51] Makhlūf, *Fatāwā*, I, 145-6.

[52] Ǧād al-Ḥaqq, *Al-Fatāwā*, IV, 3119-25.

in September 1994, the CNN network broadcast worldwide the scene of a ten-year-old girl undergoing circumcision. According to the reports, the operation was carried out by a hairdresser assisted by a plumber, and the world witnessed the hairdresser cutting off the child's clitoris with a razor, and heard her agonised screams. The Egyptian authorities at once began a publicity campaign to repair the damage done to Egypt's image of modernity by the broadcast. A number of the people involved were arrested, a campaign against clitoridectomy was started, and a ban on it was announced.

A committee of experts was established to advise the government on this sensitive matter, and one of its members was Sheikh Muḥammad Sayyid Ṭanṭāwī, the State Muftī. Sheikh Ṭanṭāwī stated that female circumcision had nothing to do with Islam, and was unknown in many strictly Islamic countries, including Saudi Arabia. To this the former Egyptian State Muftī, now *Sheikh al-Azhar*, Sheikh Ǧād al-Ḥaqq 'Alī Ǧād al-Ḥaqq, had to react, which he did by saying that Islam did not want Muslims to neglect to perform this 'embellishment' of women. The Egyptian government now decided that the operation, if it was to be performed at all, had to take place in a hospital, arguing that, because of the medical skills required, clandestine operations were even more harmful to the health of the 'embellished' girls. The Egyptian Organisation for Human Rights, EOHR, then took the *Sheikh al-Azhar* to court in April 1995, accusing him of harming Muslims in Egypt by spreading untrue religious opinions concerning female circumcision.[53]

Again we are left with a fundamental uncertainty. Is clitoridectomy, or female circumcision, part of the divine laws of Islam which fundamentalists want to enforce and implement after the Islamic revolution?

There is some concern among both government officials in the Middle East and fundamentalist activists that the reputation of Islam among non-Muslims is not being enhanced by women's issues. In 1989 Egypt's fundamentalist monthly *Liwā al-Islām* published a letter from Saudi Arabia containing a bitter complaint about 'their' opinions on women and Islam, though without an explanation of who 'they' were:[54]

[53] See, e.g., the Dutch daily *NRC*, April 15, 1995.

[54] October 1989, 50.

> They say that in the world of Islam women are unjustly treated [*maẓlūma*]. What is the nature of this mistreatment? That they are repressed, and have no liberty? When you ask them what kind of liberty they are deprived of, you will get a stupid answer: [the liberty] to unveil and to intermingle.[...] However, man and woman form two poles of electricity, positive and negative.[...] When two such poles get into contact with each other in any other way than properly, everybody knows the result....

The electricity metaphor is apt: it suggests that the two poles have no will of their own and simply have to follow natural laws once they have touched each other. Does the writer of this letter really argue that a young Muslim boy and girl, when they see each other face to face have no more brains than two electric poles? However, the editors clearly think that the comparison is worth printing and, together with large segments of their public, judge that to intermingle, in Arabic *ikhtilāṭ*, is dangerous, immoral, un-Islamic, shameful and unmanly.

In the late 1980s, in the same journal, the Brotherhood veteran Zaynab al-Ghazālī (b. 1936[55]) addressed women's problems under the heading 'Muslim Sisters'. Besides 'personal answers', *rudūd khāṣṣa*, to personal questions, she also made more general observations on the hard facts of life her Muslim sisters had to face. In September 1989 she mentioned how the Cairo vice squad arrested 100 men and women who 'were involved in committing indecencies' in the Muqattam hills outside Cairo – 'as if the government hasn't known about this offence for years'. The government, she continues, professes to be worried about the political reliability of people who frequently go to mosques, but should it not rather be worried about men and women who commit indecencies in furnished apartments and night clubs, and drink alcohol? In October 1989 she contributed an editorial reporting on the spread of drugs. Again she ridiculed the worries of the government: what else but drug abuse could be expected when the school curricula were empty and wanting? The natural solution was to include more Koranic study in the school curricula. However, the government had other plans – to open clinics for the treatment of addicts: 'Do you want to open clinics and hospitals for drug addicts? We,

[55] *Liwā' al-Islām*, November 1989, 51.

on the contrary, demand that you open the mosques that were closed down and that are surrounded, day and night, by soldiers.'

It cannot be denied that since the 1960s the authorities in Egypt have on occasions laid siege to mosques, arrested the faithful praying there, then closed them down. But it could well be asked why the writer brings such happenings to the attention of her Muslim sisters. Are they really supposed to form a judgement on public matters at all? Although Zaynab al-Ghazālī's editorials suggest that they must do the former, a women's primary task appears none the less to be at home. (The family values which Muslim fundamentalists advocate differ hardly at all from those promoted by American Christian fundamentalists, and apart from the rather technical difference that Islam allows and Christianity forbids polygamy, one could imagine a tactical coalition on those values between the two fundamentalist camps.)

Zaynab al-Ghazālī writes[56] one particularly elaborate reply to a letter:

> A wife has the responsibility to make her husband really feel at home. A husband wrote to me, telling the story of the tragedy of his home. He and his wife are both university graduates. She has no duties but the house, and she does not work. The house is sixty square meters, and consists of a living room and two bedrooms. It is elegantly and well furnished, but it is not clean or kept in order. There are two small girls whose clothes and appearance are as one would expect of young children. When he comes home from his work he has to clean the house and often even to prepare the meal. He is unhappy because [his wife] is not dressed well and her appearance is bad. He is unhappy because the children are dirty. He is unhappy about the chaos in the house which nobody takes care of apart from himself. He is unhappy when he struggles to travel back to Cairo every week, hoping that a change will take place in the thirty-six hours which he will spend at home, but everything is always the same. Chaos in the house, the children dirty, the furniture not arranged, his wife not elegant or taking care of herself.[...] She has elegant clothes in the wardrobe but does not put them on.[...] When

56 *Liwā' al-Islām*, November 1989, 50.

he orders her to do so, she does, but then she does not take them off unless he orders her again....

A Westerner reading such a story would be likely to think that psychiatric help, family therapy or marriage therapy are probably the only way to break the deadlock which the couple and their two dirty children have reached. Not so Zaynab al-Ghazālī:

> I am amazed at his letter, and ask myself: what kind of university education is that? An illiterate wife would be better at keeping her husband happy, preparing his food, putting on the clothes he likes, cleaning his house, and taking care of his children, than such a university graduate. What kind of university did she go to? We can only be sorry for our men and women who are the victims of such educational systems. A wife should be an elegant flower.[...] Only fools will equate the education of women with the education of men.[...] We need special programs that will prepare women for their tasks...to create a loving motherhood...and build happy families..

Such words are rarely heard in the decadent West. However, the magazines that must be seen as the voice of the fundamentalist movements abound with such admonitions. In the 1970s too, the fundamentalist monthly *Al-Da'wa*[57] also published articles entitled 'Towards a Muslim home', *Naḥw Bayt Muslim*, arguing in favour of the same family values.

Because Islamic attire has always been associated with fundamentalism, it may seem somewhat contradictory that its adoption has enabled women to play a greater number of social roles than was possible before and hence to spend less time as a housewife. In particular women (dressed properly) can travel all over town without being pestered by men, and they can study. This advantage of Islamic attire may have contributed to its popularity, and it may also explain why its adoption has recently been much more common among women than among men. The number of social roles men are able to play when they start to dress in a conspicuously Islamic fashion does not increase; indeed, it may decrease. In one of the letters to Zaynab al-Ghazālī we read:[58]

> [I am] a student in one of the faculties of the University but

[57] E.g. October 1977, p. 44; November, p. 44; November, p. 43; December, p. 52.

[58] *Liwā' al-Islām*, December 1989, 50.

> I cannot find any of my teachers willing to encourage me and my colleagues in the pursuit of Islamic activities. When we put up a notice on the wall, the only reaction was a request to appear at the office of the state security police.[...] Especially the veil causes much mockery from teachers and students.[...] What must we do? Is our religion so frightening to others? I fear for my religion, and myself, and my sisters....

That fear may be much more general than the writer of this letter realised at the time.

8

A POLITICAL CULTURE DEALING WITH FUNDAMENTALISM

On the eve of the war of June 1967, Cairo abounded with posters demanding the death of the poisonous viper of imperialism, Arab reaction and Zionism. The authorities wished the public to believe that a mortal danger to the Egyptian people was represented by this trinity – which has become much better known to the outside world than it was in the 1960s. Thanks to Baathist Iraqi propaganda and the Kuwait war of 1990–1 few Western journalists today are unfamiliar with this threefold slogan, and it is generally recognised as being essentially nationalist in character.

Nationalism has always been and still is the most influential ideology in the independent modern nation-states of the Arab world,[1] where in one or other of its many forms it is the ideology of the ruling élite. Not many years before the June war, in April 1963, Arab nationalism appeared to be on the threshold of a major political triumph when Syria, Iraq and Egypt signed a charter of unity, *mīthāq al-waḥda*, and Cairo was chosen as the capital of this projected United Arab Republic.[2] This and other similar developments soon turned out to be disappointments,[3] but the newspapers of Nasser's Egypt gave ample space to nationalist thinkers like 'Alī Ṣabrī[4] to familiarise the public with the ideology of Arab nationalism, the local Egyptian form of which was named 'Arab socialism'. Competing ideologies were poorly represented, or rather not represented at all, in the Egyptian journals, newspapers

[1] Kedourie, *Nationalism in Asia and Africa*, 1970.

[2] See, e.g., Ra'ûf 'Abbās Ḥâmid, *Thawrat Yulyû*, 215.

[3] Hopwood, *Egypt*, 66.

[4] Secretary-General of the only legal political organization, the Arab Socialist Union, and prime minister until October 1965. See, e.g., his *al-Taḥawwul al-Ishtirākī*.

and magazines of the period or in the books on the news-stands with which Cairo traditionally abounds.

Nevertheless, there were other ideologies available. The Egyptian Free Officers, who represented the nucleus of the July 1952 revolution, were undeniably in power but ideologically they were weak.[5] They had dissolved all Egyptian political parties in January 1953, but the Wafd party in particular still presented a problem. The Wafd lost much of its appeal after British military pressure forced the King of Egypt to appoint a prime minister from that party in February 1942. In the eyes of the Egyptians, this tarnished the reputation of democracy, the parliamentary system, the King, the Wafd party and the British themselves. However, the popularity of the Wafd was such that when the 1953 dissolution decree was revoked in November 1976[6] and political parties became legal again, it managed to re-emerge.

The two other opposition movement that existed in the Nasser era were the communists, who constituted no serious threat, and the Muslim Brotherhood. The Brotherhood had influence in the universities and in the *niqābāt*, the 'guilds' or 'unions'. This influence worried the authorities. Consequently, in the wake of disturbances in which its members were involved on 13 January 1954, the Egyptian government dissolved the Brotherhood on the following day, and this has not been revoked up till the present day.[7] The long and bitter struggle which followed the dissolution has claimed many lives, and led to many others being sent to prison or to concentration camps, sometimes for long periods.[8] Seen in the perspective of the history of ideologies, it was a remarkable struggle in that both Nasser and the Egyptian Muftī declared, in the early 1960s, when nationalisations and sequestrations became an increasingly common occurrence,[9] that Islam and socialism were in complete accord. The Brotherhood wanted Islam, while the government wanted socialism, so if everything was as it seemed, how could there be a struggle between them?

In June 1961 the Egyptian government promulgated law no. 603, which introduced a reform of Al-Azhar University. The

[5] See, e.g., Hāla Muṣṭafā, *Al-Dawla*, 112.

[6] *Ibid.*, 313.

[7] See, e.g., *Rūz al-Yūsuf*, August 14, 1995, 18.

[8] Mitchell, *Muslim Brothers*, esp. 105-62.

[9] See, e.g., Hāla Muṣṭafā, *Al-Dawla*, 136.

new, reformed structure brought Al-Azhar even further under government control than it had been before. At the same time, the number of lower- and medium-level Al-Azhar institutes was increased, and such institutes were opened in the countryside as well. Even Al-Azhar institutes for girls were opened.[10] The inception of these institutes created a large number of state-funded jobs for people who, the regime suspected, would otherwise be susceptible to fundamentalist ideas. The radio, newspapers and book publishers expanded their 'Islamic' activities in this period. All newspapers started to have religious supplements at the weekend, a new radio station was opened that broadcast Koran recitation for most of the day, and the number of state-funded mosques grew. It seemed that the world was becoming a more Islamic place.

Yet at the same time as all these Islamic measures were being taken, the Brotherhood and the Egyptian government were involved in a running battle. Outside the Arab world the sequence of small and large struggles taking place in the 1960s between the authorities and the religious opposition movements was not regarded as very important. They might have been bloody at times, but they were after all the internal affairs of a Third World state, and religious affairs at that. The West at the time felt threatened by communism, and the Islamic menace was still to be discovered. For example, when Sayyid Quṭb was executed in August 1966, the non-Muslim world paid little or no attention.[11] This, after all, was the time of the Cultural Revolution in China, and one of the most exciting things that happened at Cairo University in that year was the sudden return to China of approximately fifty Chinese students of Arabic who had been seized with a patriotic urge to participate in the great revolutionary events taking place in their own country. However, these were not the only students who disappeared suddenly from the campus. Every now and then, it was whispered, students were taken away for questioning about Muslim Brotherhood activities, and not all of them were seen again. Gradually an atmosphere of oppression and suspicion gripped the campus. Could those who had returned from questioning

[10] *Ibid.*, 137.

[11] Mansfield, *Nasser's Egypt*, 244: 'Most of the Muslim Brothers imprisoned in 1965 have now [1969] been released.'

still be trusted? What had happened to the ones who had not returned?

The regime which created this atmosphere lost all its credibility after the defeat by Israel in June 1967. Observers like Yvonne Haddad are certain that the rise of Islamic consciousness was in no small part the result of the Arab-Israeli wars of 1967 and 1973.[12] Farağ Fōda thought that the defeat of June 1967 was seen by many Egyptians not as a defeat for Egypt or the Egyptian leadership, but as a condemnation of the way that Egypt had adopted Western culture and civilisation. This perception gained support, he wrote, from the idea that Israel was in essence a religious entity. In the wake of the 1967 defeat, he observed, violent Islamic movements appeared in all Arab countries.[13]

Many Egyptian intellectuals see a direct connection between the defeat of June 1967 and the revolution of July 1952. It would be too simple, an Egyptian sociologist[14] wrote in 1992 'to assign the blame for the June defeat, as many do, to the a-religious character of the July revolution [*al-bu'd 'ani 'llāh*]'. Nevertheless, he too thinks that the main flaw of Nasserism was its neglect (*'adam al-intibāh*) of the 'Egyptian cultural heritage in which Islam plays such a central role [*al-turāth wa-'l-islām fi-'l-qalb^{i} minhu*']. As other factors he mentions the absence of freedom of expression and the all-embracing bureaucracy. The revolutionary lack of freedom of expression and the staleness of the ideological discussions concerning Arab unity and imperialism, even the very way in which Nasser used to pronounce the Arabic word for imperialism (as *isti'mārrr*, with a prolonged final consonant) displeased and greatly irritated many Egyptians. In the later 1970s the Egyptian writer Ibrāhīm 'Abduh[15] asked his readers, not without sarcasm, what the revolutionary progress of Nasserism had actually consisted of. 'Abduh recalled that before the Nasser/Naguib revolution of 1952, students in Egypt often demonstrated, and vehemently discussed democracy and freedom. Under the Nasser regime, on the contrary, they discussed the subtleties of imperialism, *isti'mārrr*, and knew better than to demonstrate. Ibrāhīm 'Abduh wondered

12 Yvonne Haddad, 'The Arab-Israeli Wars'.

13 Farağ Fōda, *Qabl al-Suqūṭ*, 51, 168-9.

14 Ḍiyā' Rashwān, in Qindīl, *Al-Nāṣiriyya*, 92-3.

15 Jansen, 'Ibrāhīm 'Abduh'.

if this change from freedom to imperialism could be seen as progress.

Nevertheless, in the first hours of the June war, the students were not without enthusiasm. On one wall they painted *sawfa nadkhulu tall abīb al-yawma*, 'We will enter Tel Aviv today', apparently impervious to the contradiction hidden in the two adverbs of time which the Arabic phrase contains, *sawfa* ('in the future') and *al-yawm* ('today'). When, at the end of the week of the war, Nasser announced his resignation in an official speech to his people, the students could still be roused into joining the crowds that demanded his return to office. Nasser, as we now know, obeyed the will of the masses, and the lorries crowded with people who had demonstrated with calls for his return to office went back to the government buildings from where they had started their spontaneous circumambulations.

However, a little later, in April 1968, new and different reasons for enthusiasm appeared: the Virgin Mary was seen above the Zaytuna Coptic church in Old Cairo[16] – on her second appearance fifteen children were trampled to death. Muslim and non-Muslim authorities made a great national cause of this vision, *qaḍiyya waṭaniyya kubrā*, and the official newspaper *Al-Ahrām* even published scientific photographs, *suwar 'ilmiyya*, of the apparition; these showed a white cloud, or at least a white spot, beside the tower of the church. Only research in Egyptian archives can reveal whether it was at this point in time that the Egyptian authorities consciously took the decision to encourage religion and religious enthusiasm as an antidote to the general feeling of despair and malaise brought about by the June 1967 defeat. There is considerable circumstantial evidence for this conclusion.

The identification of the celestial object above the Zaytuna church in the spring and summer of 1968 as Mary the mother of Jesus must have been politically welcome. Mary is important to Christians and Muslims alike. She has appeared regularly at several places in Europe, and Christian liturgy, the New Testament (Luke 1:42) and the Koran (3:42) all call her 'blessed among women'. Even in less troubled times it would have been difficult to find another religious figure who would be a better symbol of the national unity between Egypt's Muslims and Copts. The

[16] See, e.g., S. Wild, 'Ṣâdiq al-'Aẓm's book'; and Usrat Kanīsat Ghabriyāl, *Mu'ğiza*, II, 5.

Zaytuna apparition was followed by encouragement of religious enthusiasm directed more specifically at a Muslim audience, and in the following years Egyptian specialists on interpretation of the Koran published some spectacular findings on its scientific contents.[17] For example, the Western science and technology that had so harmed the Muslim and Arab cause was already foretold in the Koran. Understood correctly, it referred not only to evolution theory and twentieth-century cosmography but also to tanks, aircraft, helicopters and machine-guns.

Islam might recently have lost a few battles, but it was to Islam that one has to look for ammunition and inspiration in the war between it and the enemies of God. Some Egyptian Muslim writers sought to refute the ideas behind this brand of Koran interpretation, called *tafsīr ʿilmī*, 'scientific exegesis', but in general the idea that the Koran predicted the results of modern science and technology came to be accepted.[18] This, of course, greatly contributed – as it still does – to the awe in which the Koran and Islam are held by the general public.

Did the nationalist rulers realise that in this way the nationalist ideology which justified their power might become undermined? Whether they did or not is no longer important: the long list of elaborate measures taken by the Egyptian authorities in the Nasser era in relation to Islam and Islamic institutions had already created an indissoluble link between Islam and politics, which were now unseparable. Ironically it has turned out that these measures, taken by the Nasser regime in order to pre-empt the religious opposition, served mainly to whet the appetites of the Islamic fundamentalists, many of whom soon became insatiable.

In 1971 the Sadat regime went even further. It amended article 2 of the constitution so that it now stipulated that 'the principles of the Islamic sharīʿa [are] a main source of the [country's] legislation', *mabādi' al-sharīʿa al-islāmiyya maṣdar ra'īsī li-'l-tashrīʿ*. This gesture was intended to have a double effect: to win over Egyptians who might otherwise have sympathised with a fund-amentalist opposition movement or even joined it, and to create

[17] An outsider's understanding of the phenomenon of *tafsīr ʿilmī* might benefit from an explanation why in a similar way certain Hindu scholars also believe that atom bombs, rockets and aeroplanes were invented by ancient Indians and are mentioned in ancient Hindu holy texts (see V.S. Naipaul, *India: a Million Mutinies Now*, 153).

[18] See, e.g., Jansen, *Interpretation*, 35-55.

a new, religious legitimacy for the regime.[19] However, the effect, has probably been the opposite to what was intended. Many understood the formula to be a surreptitious way of saying that the regime did not intend to apply the sharīʿa.

Other measures calculated to win friends among the religiously inspired opposition movements in general and the Muslim Brothers in particular may have been more effective: Brotherhood prisoners from the Nasser era were freed, and in July 1972 all Soviet advisers were expelled from Egypt. These two measures also strengthened the self-confidence of the religious opposition. When students demonstrated in the summer of 1972 the regime was certain that the communists were behind it; the *ǧamāʿāt islāmiyya* were now heard of for the first time. When the Ramadan/October war of 1973 broke out, the regime again used a number of Islamic symbols: the operation of crossing the Suez canal was called *Badr* after the first Islamic military victory, which took place near Medina in March 624. It appeared possible to present the outcome of the 1973 war against Israel as a victory for Egypt. The self-confidence of the regime was never greater.

The regime now permitted its traditional rival in the struggle for power, the Muslim Brotherhood, to resume some of its activities. These included resuming publication of its two monthlies *Al-Daʿwa* and *Al-Iʿtiṣām*, which from the start showed a strong bias against communism. 'Where will the communist advance be stopped?', the first issue of *Al-Daʿwa* asked on its front page in June 1976. Today we know the answer, but in the mid-1970s this must have been an important question, certainly to the oppositional Muslim Brotherhood and the ruling nationalist military élite which both felt threatened by local leftist and Nasserist movements. Even without access to government archives one can safely assume that in this period the Muslim Brotherhood and its monthlies were loyal allies in the battle against Marxism and Communism. However, the Brotherhood had its own agenda in which the battle against both the local Egyptian communists and world communism were only minor points, as the June 1976 issue of *Al-Daʿwa* made clear. The Koran, the journal stated, was above the constitution; Islamic law was to be applied in its totality, and Islamic banks had to be established. It was an agenda that few people could then take seriously. Yet by the mid-1990s it was obvious that

[19] See, e.g., Hāla Muṣṭafā, *Dawla*, 150.

this agenda had deeply influenced the political culture of Egypt and other Arab countries where the Islamic movement was able to speak up.

In an attempt to enlarge the religious basis of its legitimacy even further, the government promulgated in 1976 its law concerning the Ṣūfī Brotherhoods, *Qānūn al-Ṭuruq al-Ṣūfiyya*, and a little later the authorities decided to found the Ṣūfī monthly *Mağallat al-Taṣawwuf al-Islāmī*, 'the journal of Islamic mysticism', the first issue appearing in May 1979.[20] This publication did not win them many new friends. Already in October 1979 the Ṣūfīs felt confident enough to attack Judge Muḥammad Sa'īd al-'Ashmāwī[21] in their new journal. In July 1978 Al-'Ashmāwī had published articles in the daily *Al-Akhbār* that were extremely critical of the favourite fundamentalist slogan 'Application of the Sharī'a'. These articles, the Ṣūfīs wrote, had been an attempt 'to dilute Islam', 'to replace the Text with the spirit of the Text', and 'an attack on Islam in the name of Islam itself'. Tensions in January 1980 led to a new constitutional amendment aimed at reconstituting the political equilibrium between Marxists, Nasserists and fundamentalists. The new text of article 2 of the April 1980 constitution now stipulated that 'the principles of the Islamic sharī'a are the main source of the [country's] legislation', *mabādi' al-sharī'a al-islāmiyya hiya al-maṣdar al-ra'īsī li-'l-tashrī'*.[22] The effect of twice adding the Arabic article *al* to the constitution will be felt long after Nasserists and Marxists have been forgotten. With the addition of the definite article, Islam and its laws had ceased to be just one of the sources of legislation, maybe according to expediency, but had become, at least according to constitutional theory, the exclusive source of all legislation in Egypt. Genuine fundamentalists could not but be encouraged by such an amendment. In the following years sympathisers with Islamic fundamentalism who wanted to emphasise the legitimacy of their aspirations only needed to point to article 2 of the Egyptian constitution.

Then on 6 October 1982 came the assassination of Sadat by a group of fundamentalists. Contrary to popular belief at the time, it had nothing to do with his peace initiative towards Israel.[23] In

[20] See, e.g., Jansen, *Neglected Duty*, 65-70.

[21] See Chapter 5, above.

[22] Hāla Muṣṭafā, *Dawla*, 214.

[23] The judge who tried and sentenced Sadat's assassins again confirms this explicitly in

the last week of September 1981 the group who murdered Sadat was brought together by Muḥammad 'Abd al-Salām Farağ, who has explained his ideas in a document entitled *Al-Farīḍa al-Ghā'iba*, The neglected duty [of Ğihād].[24] Sheikh Dr 'Umar 'Abd al-Raḥmān, now known all over the world for of his alleged involvement in the bombing of the World Trade Center in New York in early 1993, had extensive contacts with the group in the months before the assassination, but not in the final stages.

The prosecutors and the judges were careful not to make a martyr of Sheikh 'Umar[25] who was, after all, an 'Ālim, a professional man of religion and a representative of official Islam. Like the actual assassins, Sheikh 'Umar told his interrogator that a head of state, such as Sadat, who ruled by his own laws and not by the laws of Islām should as a matter of course be seen as an apostate from Islam. The Sheikh explained that whether or not such an apostate should be killed, as the assassins believed, was another question. First a council of 'Ulamā' should 'discuss' with the President what Islam prescribed for the running of the country. Only if the President then persevered in his refusal to rule according to what God had sent down would 'his blood become *ḥalāl*'.[26] The initiated are well aware that the Arabic expression concerning his blood becoming *ḥalāl* means 'Islam permitted his murder'. The Sheikh said that it was not certain whether such discussions with 'Ulamā' had taken place; hence he could not (yet?) give his blessing to the assassination of Sadat. An outsider can only admire the subtlety of this argument, which saved the Sheikh's neck.

Vice-President Mubarak, who took over from Sadat, tried to introduce a new businesslike atmosphere of rationality, efficiency and matter-of-factness. To those who remember them, Nasser's romanticism and thirst for the Kingdom of Politics suddenly looked alien. Nevertheless, Mubarak too became the victim of the way the Egyptians have treated their rulers since time immemorial.

---

his memoir *'Camp David lam taqtul al-Sādāt'* (Camp David did not kill Sadat), in Fāḍil, *Mudhakkirāt*, 107-10.

24 See Jansen, *The Neglected Duty*.

25 The considerations of 'Umar 'Abd al-Raḥmān's acquittal are reprinted in Fāḍil, *Mudhakkirāt*, 159-63.

26 Ṣalāh, *Hākadhā*, 144: *lam a'rif anna mağlis^{an} min al-'ulamā' nāqashahu wa-rafaḍ al-ḥukm bi-Kitāb Allāh; Ibid.*, 158: *aftā.. bi-ḥall dam al-ra' īs shar^{an}? lā, innamā aftā bi-kufrihi faqaṭ.*

Gradually, like the Pharaohs, he became deified, no longer always received the relevant information from his entourage, and was then seen as a god that had failed. However, his regime has been the most pragmatic ever to rule Egypt.

However all this may be, in 1983 Egypt saw a new electoral law which among other things laid down that political parties should win at least 8 per cent of the votes in order to be represented in parliament. Moreover, the government would appoint a number of members of parliament from among the groups that would get less than 8 per cent of the votes. Thus it became necessary for pre-election coalitions to be formed. Consequently, in the 1984 elections the Muslim Brotherhood formed a coalition with the Wafd party, and out of a total of 448 seats the Wafd won fifty-one and the Brothers seven. The government party *Al-Ḥizb al-Waṭanī al-Dīmūqrāṭī*, the National Democratic Party or NDP, got 390 seats.

In the 1986 elections the Brotherhood formed a coalition with leftist parties which had only obtained four seats in the 1984 elections. The new coalition won sixty seats, including thirty-four for the Brotherhood, plus four independents. This time the leftists did well, winning twenty-six seats. The share of the Wafd fell to thirty-five. The NDP got 348 seats out of the unchanged total of 448.[27] The conclusion is obvious. A coalition with the Muslim Brotherhood guaranteed electoral success. At the same time, the May 1984 elections indicated that the Islamic movement had become divided into two: one wing dominated by the old Muslim Brotherhood and another consisting of an unknown number of irreconcilables. Several of the Brotherhood leaders appeared ready to collaborate, perhaps even co-operate loyally, with the regime. Any danger from then on only seemed to come from small and isolated radical splinter groups.

Due to Brotherhood pressure, 1984 saw two measures that were calculated to appease the Islamic fundamentalists: Egypt's national airline was forbidden to offer its passengers alcoholic drinks; and the new edition of the medieval classical Arabic prose text, *1001 Nights*, was taken off the market because it contradicted Islamic values. The authorities hoped that these measures would lessen the pressure for the application of the sharī'a, but of course their effect was the opposite. Nor did the presence of the Brother-

[27] Hāla Muṣṭafā, *Al-Dawla*, 316–17.

hood in parliament cause a decline in fundamentalist terrorist activities. In 1987 there were three notorious assassination attempts: two on former Ministers of Internal Affairs, Al-Nabawī Ismāīl and Ḥasan Abū Bāshā, and one on Makram Muḥammad Aḥmad, editor-in-chief of the weekly *Al-Muṣawwar.*[28] In 1989 yet another former Minister of Internal Affairs, Zakī Badr, was the target of an assassination attempt, but it too failed although the means adopted by the would-be assassins were technically a little more sophisticated than those of 1987. In October 1990 Rif'at al-Maḥğūb, president of the *mağlis al-sha'b*, the parliament, was actually murdered. Dr Farağ Fōda was murdered in 1992, and in 1993 there were three significant murder attempts that failed: on Ṣafwat al-Sharīf, the Minister of Information in April, on Ḥasan al-Alfī, the Minister of Internal Affairs, in August, and 'Āṭif Ṣidqī, the Prime Minister, in December.[29] Several attempts were made on the lives of security service officials. Thus senior Egyptian government figures who worry about assassination cannot be regarded as paranoid.

The years 1992-3 witnessed a novelty: terrorist attacks on tourists in Egypt. These attacks were directly aimed at weakening the Egyptian economy, and cannot have gained many converts for fundamentalism among the many Egyptians who are economically dependent on tourism. A second novelty of the early 1990s, at least for Egypt, was that attacks were made on individuals, often women who were regarded as not conforming to Islamic norms, especially in their dress, and there were random attacks in crowded neighbourhoods. This last form of terrorism was probably aimed at creating a general atmosphere of insecurity. Lastly, aggression against shops that sell alcohol and their owners, destruction of video clubs, the breaking up of festive meetings and ceremonies of Muslim mystical fraternities, and so on, have been widely reported.[30] Nevertheless, these attacks were a convincing demonstration to many that the state could not guarantee public safety.

The Egyptian authorities have taken a number of measures to counter and perhaps even to solve these problems. Some of these were direct and others indirect.[31] Both confrontation and dialogue

28 *Ibid., Dawla*, 320-1; 385.

29 *Ibid.*, 386, lists the assassinations and assassination attempts.

30 *Ibid.*, 388.

31 *Ibid.*, 389-401.

have been used. However, the Mubarak regime inherited the new text of article 2 of the constitution from its predecessors, and a state professing to have the principles of the Islamic sharīʿa as the main source of its legislation definitely has an ideological problem when it needs to fight those who want to see this sharīʿa applied. In the present climate of opinion it is unimaginable that the article should be revoked.

However, a confrontational measure was taken for the first time with the state of emergency being declared immediately after the assassination of President Sadat in October 1981; it has not been revoked up till the time of writing, and a fine legal point is whether the government is entitled to allow the state of emergency to continue for so long. It can be argued that after more than ten years the situation can no longer be regarded as exceptional. The liberal viewpoint is that the state of emergency was exclusively created to enable exceptional situations to be confronted, and that it should therefore now be lifted. A second measure is the Law on Terrorism, *Qānūn al-Irhāb*, passed in 1992 with the object of coping with the increasing fundamentalist terrorism of the time. However, laws are a poor weapon for fighting the lawless – or those armed with a higher Law. Increasingly the government has transferred cases of fundamentalist violence to military courts. The result of all these measures has been an increase in the number of (political) prisoners.

There were some more subtle indirect measures, but they too had unwelcome side-effects. The government tried to contain the fundamentalist ideology by relying on Al-Azhar and its branches, which should help to make the people familiar with 'real Islam' as opposed to the fundamentalist variety. The newspapers of this time were full of articles on *al-fahm al-ṣaḥīḥ*, 'the correct understanding', of Islam. Here too the government propagandists sometimes made a connection between religious correctness and worldly success:

> Islam can only be victorious with the help of a correct faith.[...] Why are Muslims weak when their numbers are so large...? Only a correct faith, *īmān ṣaḥīḥ*, can make Islam victorious.[32]

In its context such an argument could only be understood as a warning that false ideas about Islam would guarantee the con-

[32] *Liwāʾ al-Islām*, 12 March 1987, front page editorial.

tinuation of present misery and inferiority, whereas obediently listening to the 'Ulamā' would result in great rewards. Some of the proper-understanding-of-Islam articles that appeared in the 1980s and early '90s can only be called very boring, but they fulfilled an important function in the political context in which they were published. However, internal quarrels between the Ulema, who suddenly discovered their own importance, became unavoidable, and perhaps somewhat lessened the prestige of the official Islamic institutions.

As a reward for its help to the government in the struggle against fundamentalism, Al-Azhar obtained from about 1985 on increasing authority over Egyptian intellectual life. It acquired the power to forbid books, and the 'Ulamā' used this new power in the way that their colleagues in the Vatican had used the Index of Forbidden Books in the good old days of unquestioned clerical hegemony over the minds of believers. Imitating Vatican practice, Al-Azhar experts now forbade novels, poetry, essays, plays, scholarly books, books about themselves, the interpretation of the Koran, history, politics and much more.[33] Never had they been busier reading dangerous materials. Because the government, quite simply, needed Al-Azhar and its authority in the struggle against fundamentalism, it could ill afford to take measures against this sudden spirit of righteousness. Moreover, Al-Azhar showed more and more clearly a desire to have a degree of independence from the government. Its scholars were tired of having been obliged to listen to the fundamentalists calling them *'Ulamā' al-Sulṭa*, 'government clergy', and were now determined to show who they really were: better censors of art and morals than any other religion or regime had ever produced.

Al-Azhar showed that it was apparently developing into a problem almost as great as the fundamentalists themselves when one of its prominent scholars, Muḥammad al-Ghazālī, declared in June 1993:

> Whoever declares publicly that he demands the non-application of the sharī'a is an apostate and has to be killed. Whoever kills such a person commits *ifti'āt* against the government. Islam knows no punishment for *ifti'āt*.[34]

[33] An (incomplete) list of books forbidden by Al-Azhar: Hāla Muṣṭafā, *Dawla*, 313-14, and in *Rūz al-Yūsuf*, 10.5.92.

Islamic law and a number of the modern and classical Arabic dictionaries are silent about the Arabic word *ifti'āt*, which is perhaps best translated as 'hostility'. The Egyptian government none the less understood the phrase perfectly. Since Muḥammad al-Ghazālī was not alone in his views, it decided in the fall of 1993 to make the Prime Minister himself (and not the Minister for Awqāf and Azhar Affairs) responsible for Al-Azhar and all its affairs.

The assassinations, assassination attempts and disturbances of the 1980s and '90s are generally seen as the work of extremely small and isolated groups. This impression may be correct, but it is impossible to be sure. On the other hand, violence committed by a small group has no less effect than violence committed by a large group. Moreover, a group that does not hesitate to use force need not be large in order to take power. It is striking that the violence has been aimed not only at the regime and its representatives but also at two other powerful symbols of modernity and modernism in Egypt: the Copts and Israeli diplomats. Some see these as an affront to Islam. Many Copts, as individuals, have embraced modernity with eagerness, without forsaking solidarity with their church and its leaders. The way of life of a number of them suggests that it is possible to be Egyptian and modern at the same time. The same can be said of a number of highly sophisticated Egyptian Muslims – and it is precisely these Muslims whom the fundamentalists most frequently attack. Furthermore, the Israeli diplomatic presence in Cairo is felt by a number of people as confirming that the modern world is having its way without regard for traditional Muslim sensitivities. This suggests that fundamentalism is an ideology that wants to fight the modern world, but to do so effectively it naturally does not shrink from using modern methods. It is only the value system of modernity that it attacks, not its technical possibilities.

Zakī Badr, the Minister of the Interior till January 1990 who was the object of an assassination attempt in 1989, is far from certain that the fundamentalist movement has really been split into a broad movement that cooperates with the state and a small one that has 'degenerated into primitive rebellion'.[35] He seems

[34] Hāla Muṣṭafā, *Dawla*, 395; *Al-Ḥayā* 23.6.92. Cf. *iftiyāt*, 'offence'.

[35] Fouad Ajami, 'In the Pharaoh's shadow'.

to realise that religious extremism is not due only to economic factors but is a truly religious phenomenon:

> The greatest danger is these extremist *ǧamāʿāt*. They express themselves in religious jargon, and since the culture of the people of Egypt is deeply religious, they are certain to find fertile ground for their activities.[36]

Another Minister of the Interior of the Mubarak era, Aḥmad Rushdī, holds the opposing, reductionist view:

> Religious extremism started in the 1940s.... It is due to particular economic and social circumstances.[...] Religious extremism is escapism, getting away from bigger problems. Some people take to drugs, others to religious extremism.[37]

This calls for two comments. First, Aḥmad Rushdī gives a totally secular, this-worldly explanation of religious extremism, and obviously does not even consider the possibility that some of it may have other than economic grounds. Many modern observers will hesitate to agree to such a view of this complex religious phenomenon. If it were true, religious extremism would be expected to have a much stronger following than it actually has. Secondly, measures dictated by the IMF and the World Bank in order to direct the state-controlled economies of many Third World countries towards an open market will, in the near future, make the poor even poorer. Is this likely to lead to more religious extremism, in Egypt as well as elsewhere?

On the effects of imprisonment Aḥmad Rushdī also takes the sociologist's view:

> I have always been against the use of force in the confrontation with extremist groups.[...] Imprisonment leads to growth of the phenomenon. Prison camps were the only places where the extremists were safe: they got to know each other there, and became even more extremist. I consider the prison camps to be a hatchery (*mafrakha*) of extremist thought.[38]

If it is true that imprisonment turns the moderate Islamists into extremists, it is of course important to keep the moderates

[36] Muḥammad Muṣṭafā, *Wazīr*, 213.
[37] *Ibid.*, 167.
[38] *Ibid.*, 167.

away from prison. But is the distinction between moderate and radical Islamists a valid one? Zakī Badr, the eloquent Minister of the Interior whose biting remarks against his opponents were widely regarded as exceeding the limits of what could be tolerated in Egypt, has his doubts:

> The Muslim Brothers are no Muslims.[...] They are enemies of what Islam stands for.[...] From the very day of their foundation by Shaykh Ḥasan al-Bannā they have had a secret faction, *farīq sirrī*, that occupied itself with intimidation and worse, from the murder of Al-Nuqrāshī up till the murder of Sadat.[39]

Ambassador Ḥusayn Aḥmad Amīn takes a milder view. He examines the differences and similarities between the radicals and the Muslim Brotherhood on the one hand and the radicals and secular intelligentsia on the other.[40] According to him the mainstream Muslim Brotherhood wants to change society, whereas the radical fringe wants to leave it. When the radicals use the traditional Islamic term *hiǧra*, 'emigration', they discuss their wish to leave the world of paganism, a choice of words which is significant: in the history of Islam the same term is used to describe Muḥammad's emigration from pagan Mecca to Yathrib/Medina in 622.

Whereas the radicals believe that their society is un-Islamic and evil and that it is religion which requires them to leave it (*takfīr al-muǧtama'*), the secular intelligentsia also want to leave since they despise the society (*taḥqīr al-muǧtama'*) that gives them so few possibilities to build themselves a future. Ḥusayn Amīn's wordplay on *takfīr/taḥqīr*, 'charge of unbelief'/'contempt', adds to the force of this observation. When a society and its ways are rejected *in toto* both by its religious activists and its secular intelligentsia, things look bleak, and it is difficult to envisage the rise of a healthy political culture. Moreover, Ḥusayn Amīn's observation is valid not only for Egypt but for the whole Arabic-speaking world.

Nevertheless, it was in Egypt that the government meted out collective punishment in the first days of September 1981 to both the secular intelligentsia and the religious activists by ordering the precautionary arrest of 1,536 individuals on the charge of

39 *Ibid.*, 217.

40 Ḥusayn Aḥmad Amīn, *Dalīl*, 21-24.

inciting religious civil war and destroying national unity. It later seemed as if President Sadat had left only two groups at large: his courtiers and those who were to assassinate him before the television cameras during a parade on October 6.

The former Minister of the Interior Al-Nabawī Ismā'īl, on whom an assassination attempt was made in 1987, justifies the wide-ranging September arrests as follows:[41]

> It was obvious in 1981 that many were attempting to change Egypt into a second Lebanon and a second Iran at the same time. The late President, however, gave all priority to the Israeli withdrawal from Sinai which was to take place on April 25, 1982. The President then decided to use the powers which the constitution gave him to take measures against anyone threatening national unity or social peace. These measures are nowadays known as the September Decisions.
>
> I have to emphasise that if some of the elements who were arrested in September 1981 had been at large when the President was assassinated, many things would have turned out worse than they did. Some of these people we had put behind bars possess great demagogic powers of persuasion, and it has since become evident that Sadat's assassins took this into account in their plans.

What would have happened if the authorities had failed to repress the disturbances following Sadat's assassination? And what would happen if the religious activists were to take power in Egypt today? Would they create a Saudi-style state? Would Pakistan or Sudan be their example, or would it be worse? Egyptian newspapers abound with wild speculations on this topic. These speculations may merely serve to scare the public away from the fundamentalists.

However, on August 31, 1992, under the title 'What if the extremists rule Egypt?', *mādhā law ḥakam al-mutaṭarrifūna Miṣr*, the Cairene weekly *Rūz al-Yūsuf* presented a list, compiled by outside experts, of possible measures which the religious extremists might be expected to take if they came to power. The list contained ten items: 'the end of national unity (a euphemism for civil war between Muslims and Copts); the death penalty for secularists (the fundamentalists' favorite code term for their opponents); the

[41] Muḥammad Muṣṭafā, *op. cit.*, 33-4.

razing of the Pyramids and all other pre-Islamic pagan archaeological sites; mass killings (of anyone opposing the new revolutionary fundamentalist government); clubs (like the famous Nadi al-Gezuira Sporting Club, with its restaurants, swimming pool, tennis courts, theatre and playgrounds) would be closed; television programmes would be abolished; the existing curricula at the universities would be abolished; the leftists would be murdered; the Islamic money management institutions (see above pp. 3, 61, 73 etc.) would come back; and the veil would become obligatory.

The different fundamentalist factions according to *Rūz al-Yūsuf*, are widely expected to fight each other bitterly if ever the possibility arises of their taking power. Once they are in power, only a military *coup* could rid Egypt of these people, in the opinion of one expert consulted by the newspaper. Certainly the experts cited can not be regarded as spokesmen for the religious radical movement, and we cannot be certain that their predictions are correct, but their guesses are probably better informed than ours. The list of items perhaps contains one hopeful element: namely that the fundamentalists are not expected to declare war on Israel or any of Egypt's other neighbours. A local Islamic revolution, optimistic diplomats and experts hope, can perhaps be expected to be only an internal affair with few foreign policy consequences, or none.

The question to which everyone would like to know the answer is whether such an Islamic revolution in Egypt, or any other Arab country, is a realistic possibility. Most foreign and Arab observers think it improbable, but the religious activists themselves obviously think otherwise. In May 1992 local officials of Egypt's ruling National Democratic Party in Asyut seemed to have joined those who take such a possibility seriously when they established contacts with the leaders of the Ǧihād movement, who bear the title *amīr*, 'prince'. The NDP officials went into elaborate secret negotiations with these *umarā'* (plural of *amīr*) hoping to prevent further bloodshed in their region. A detailed account in the Cairo weekly *Rūz al-Yūsuf*[42] reports how they explained to the *umarā'* that if in their region the Copts continued to be attacked, and if the Egyptian government showed itself unable to protect them, the United Nations might want to intervene, as in Bosnia. Was this what the *umarā'* wanted? It was

[42] August 31, 1992.

not. However, the negotiations broke down when the main negotiator on behalf of the Ğihād movement, a medical student called 'Alā' Rağab, was arrested.

Fouad Ajami's warnings, published in the early 1980s,[43] are still valid, and not for Egypt only:

> The schizophrenia between the new culture of Egypt... and the retreat into old pieties is a dangerous combination. A society's professed symbols cannot war with its realities for very long. Sooner or later the gap will be turned into an intolerable chasm, which will be filled either by terror or by an appalling slide into mediocrity and cynicism.

None the less, in the mid-1990s the prestige of the 'Ulamā' in Egypt has never been greater. They are driven around in impressive government limousines, and their expert advice on all aspects of life fills the television screens and the bookshops. This contrasts strangely with the great 'Ulamā' of the past who often spent a large part of their lives in government prisons.[44]

It is, perhaps, slightly worrying that writers who fight the ideology of fundamentalism with intellectual and religious arguments, like Farağ Fōda and Al-'Ashmāwī, have been hit by anathemas pronounced on them by the official 'Ulamā'. The political culture of Egypt has put the 'Ulamā' in the position to pronounce effective anathemas: will they turn out to be the actual beneficiaries of the struggle between Islamic fundamentalism and the authorities?

[43] Fouad Ajami, 'In the Pharaoh's Shadow', 31.
[44] Farağ Fōda, *Qabl al-Suqūṭ*, 32.

CONCLUSION

At the end of the nineteenth century, the Middle East perceived itself as being inferior to the West. Even today, many inhabitants of that region believe that Western Europe, North America, East Asia and South-East Asia have taken the lead in many fields – technological, military, economic and others. To measure such perceived inferiority is, of course, impossible. Middle Eastern writers themselves sometimes point to the number of Nobel Prizes and Olympic medals that have been awarded to scientists and athletes from the region.

Where power, science and scholarship are concerned, the Arab world still strongly feels that it has missed opportunities. In the minds of many – but of course not all – these feelings have turned to hatred, directed mainly at an internal enemy: Muslims who are seen as westernised. However, external enemies – the West and Israel – are not completely forgotten, and there can be little doubt that the account with the West will at some point have to be settled.

Only in one field does the Muslim Middle East have no doubts about its superiority: religion. But here we find an awkward problem: this religious superiority cannot easily compensate for other perceived inferiorities, because the Islamic religious superiority failed to translate itself, as it should have done,[1] into worldly triumphs. The reason for this failure, many believe, is not hard to discover: Islam is not being applied and implemented.

Since the second half of the nineteenth century more and more Muslims have started to believe that to implement Islam can mean only one thing: Muslims must be ruled by Muslim governments, which apply the laws of God. The laws of God are the laws of Islam, and the laws of Islam have been fixed in the traditional handbooks of the Islamic sharīʿa. Many believe that not to rule by these laws implies apostasy from Islam.

The majority of the inhabitants of the Arab world are Muslim.

[1]Ḥusayn Aḥmad Amīn, *Dalīl*, 15.

Hence, the governments of the region have not been able to refrain from taking measures that concerned Islam. Mosques have been built, radio and television programs devoted to Islam broadcast, institutes for the teaching of Islam (where pious Muslims could find jobs) founded, and so on. Even the Nasser regime (1952-70), generally perceived as not very religious, took so many measures of this nature that at the end of it the separation between politics and religion, if it ever existed, had become history.

Many Muslims have narrowed Islam down to the demand for the introduction of the application of Islamic law. It is both political and religious at the same time, and it is the dual nature of this demand that gives Islamic fundamentalism its distinctive character. Muslims who have thus reduced Islam to the single demand for the implementation of Islamic law often accuse their fellow-Muslims of the crime of apostasy from Islam. In their eyes anyone who neglects to apply (any of) the traditional prescripts of Islam is not only a lax Muslim but an apostate. In Islamic law apostasy is a capital crime, and thus the demand for the application of Islam and Islamic law becomes a political as well as a religious demand, which is frequently supported by terrorism and death threats.

Since the late 1970s, this particular Islamic mixture of politics, violence and religion has been known as Islamic fundamentalism, which like all fundamentalisms has narrowed a religious tradition down to an ideology. Nevertheless, Islamic fundamentalism is fully religion and at the same time fully politics. The number of Muslims who have some degree of sympathy with the fundamentalist ideological positions, and indeed have come to believe that only the strictest application of their religion can put things right, again seems to be increasing, and mainstream religious leaders have reflected these feelings in their sermons and writings. Moreover, Islamic fundamentalism has little or no consistent and organised intellectual opposition. The governments of the region try to reach compromises with the fundamentalists, but these often have no effect other than to whet the fundamentalists' appetite for power. At the same time, governments and their 'lackeys' fight the more violent forms of fundamentalism with modern police methods.

One of the first internationally notorious Muslim 'fundamentalists', Muṣṭafā Shukrī (d. 1978), may have believed that some Muslims were in reality apostates who ought to be killed. However, unlike most of his kind in recent times, he did not believe that the implementation of Islam was identical to the implementation of Islamic law in its traditional handbook form. He regarded the contents of these books as the work of men, whereas mainstream fundamentalist Islam sees the rules which these books supply as divine guidance.

Modern fundamentalist Muslims do not have uniform views on Israel and the Jews. They sometimes express their admiration for the Jews, who they believe have succeeded in creating a Jewish state in the religious, and what they think of as the political, sense. Many fundamentalists believe that Muslims should follow this example and create a Muslim state. Rashīd Riḍā, writing at the end of the First World War, denied the existence of enmity between Islam and Judaism. In doing so he could point to centuries of Jewish-Muslim coexistence in the Middle Ages. Many modern fundamentalists, on the other hand, see the Jews and Israel in the light of the Koran – which came into being in a period of bad relationships between the Jews and the Muslims in the town of Medina between 622 and 632. The way the Koran qualifies the Jews of Medina ('apes and swine', 5:60) is thus applied, at least by some modern writers, to the Jews of the twentieth century.

The return of a variety of forms of Islamic female attire is one of the most remarkable sights in the Middle East since the 1970s. Many believe that when women apply Islam in their daily lives, this should be visible in the way they dress. Since Islamic law is not totally uniform but divided into schools, it is difficult to say which form of attire is the correct and proper one. Does God want women to veil their faces or not? Whereas the veil and the *ḥiǧāb* are visible in public, the opposite is the case with clitoridectomy or female circumcision. Again it is not fully clear what Islamic law prescribes concerning *khitān* and *khifāḍ*. The different schools prescribe slightly different procedures and practices, and qualify the operation in slightly different ways. The discussions on this topic may give a hint of the difficulties Islamic regimes will have to face once they come to power. Does God want women to be circumcised or not? Men would derive less benefit than women from returning to forms of traditional attire: it would reduce, not increase, the number of social roles they can play –as long as secularist governments are in power. Women, on the contrary, can be certain that the number of social roles they can play increases when they adopt Islamic attire.

Islam will survive into the next century in two forms: a reinterpreted form and a form that attempts to apply the varieties of Islam that are codified in the Islamic sharī'a and its handbooks. The precise terms of this dilemma were first formulated by Ğamāl al-Dīn al-Afghānī. The representatives of the tendency to reinterpret have little popular support; their force is the force of reason and arguments. On the other hand, not every Muslim thinker who has to be classified as a re-interpreter is an intellectual giant. This has sometimes been to the disadvantage of the reinterpretation movement.

Those Muslims who want to apply the traditional rules from the books of Islamic law are out for power. They want to rule in place of the existing regimes. However, Middle Eastern governments have not only used force in the battle against the fundamentalists; they also have used diplomatic means, and by all sorts of concessions have been able to win over many people who otherwise might well have succumbed to the seductive clarities of Islamic fundamentalism. This has resulted in parts of society and parts of the state being Islamised, which for certain regimes has meant the loss of part of their secular character. From this development it is possible to argue that what is at stake in the conflict between the existing regimes and the fundamentalists is in reality the Islamisation of the modern nation-state, and that this Islamisation – whatever it may mean in practice – is inevitable.

A number of small fundamentalist groups have degenerated into a state of primitive rebellion. Their total lack of doubt concerning God and the Last Things is possibly to be envied, but it cohabits with murderous designs on less favoured Muslims. This desire for murder has received its theological framework from Sayyid Quṭb, who was hanged in Cairo in 1966. He died with a smile on his lips. The time may be coming when citizens of the Middle East who are not willing to die smiling will have to decide whether it is worthwhile to die fighting in order to forgo the privilege of being killed by men who are ready to die smiling.

BIBLIOGRAPHY

Muḥammad '**Abduh**, *see* Al-Afghānī.

Abu-Amr, Ziad, *Islamic Fundamentalism in the West Bank and Gaza: Muslim Brotherhood and Islamic Jihad*, Bloomington: Indiana University Press 1994.

— [Ziyād Abū 'Amr], 'Nash'at wa-Taṭawwur Ḥarakat Al-Ǧihād al-Islāmī fī al-Ḍiffa al-Gharbiyya wa-Ghazza' in Mūsā Zayd al-Kīlānī, *Al-Ḥarakāt al-Islāmiyya fī al-Urdun*, Amman 1990, pp. 168–89.

'Abd al-Raḥmān **Abū** al-**Khayr**, *Dhikrayātī ma'a Ǧamā'at al-Muslimīn 'Al-Takfīr wa-'l-Hiǧra'*, Kuwait 1980.

Naṣr Ḥāmid **Abū Zayd**, *Naqd al-khiṭāb al-Dīnī: Ṭab'a Ǧadīda ma'a Ta'līq Muwaththaq 'alā mā Ḥadath*, Cairo: Madbūlī, 3rd edn July 1995 (228 pp.).

—, *Al-Tafkīr fī Zaman al-Takfīr: Ḍidd al-Ǧahl wa-'l-Zayf wa-'l-Khurāfa*, Cairo: Madbūlī, 2nd edn July 1995 (404 pp.).

—, *Mafhūm al-Naṣṣ: Dirāsa fī 'Ulūm al-Qur'ān*, Cairo: Al-Hay'a 1993 (360 pp.) See also 'Uṣfūr, *Hawāmish*, 35.

—, *Al-Ahrām*, 15 June 1995, front page: *'Qaḍat Maḥkamat al-Isti'nāf bi-'l-Qāhira ams bi-'l-tafrīq bayn al-ustādh al-ǧāmi'ī Naṣr.. wa-zawǧatihi.. li-ittihāmihi bi-'l-irtidād 'ani 'l-dīn al-islāmī'*.

—, *Minbar al-Islām*, July 1995/Ṣafar 1316, pp. 22–7: *'Riddat Abū Zayd'*. An example of the strong emotions the case evoked.

— (Khālid al-Sharīf, ed.), *Du'ātun 'alā Abwāb Ǧahannam: Asbāb al-Ḥukm fī Qaḍiyyat Naṣr Abū Zayd*, Cairo 1995. Contains a number of documents, *inter alia* the text of the judgement on the dissolution of Abū Zayd's marriage delivered by the Court of Appeal, June 14, 1995.

Adams, Charles A., *Islam and Modernism in Egypt*, 1933, repr. New York: Russell and Russell 1968.

Al-**Afghānī**, Ǧamāl al-Dīn, and Muḥammad 'Abduh, *Al-'Urwa al-Wuthqā: Al-Maqālāt wa-'l-Fuṣūl*, taqdīm: Muṣṭafā 'Abd al-Rāziq. Beirut: Dār al-Kitāb al-'Arabī 1970 (454 pp.).

Ahady, Anwar-ul-Haq, 'The Decline of Islamic Fundamentalism', *Journal of Asian and African Studies*, XXVII, 3–4 (1992), 229–43.

Rif'at Sayyid **Aḥmad**/Rifaat Sayed AHMED, *Al-Nabiyy al-Musallaḥ (1): Al-Rāfiḍūn*, London: Riyāḍ Al-Rayyis/Riad El-Rayyes 1991.

—, *Al-Nabiyy al-Musallaḥ (2): Al-Thā'irūn*, London: Riyāḍ Al-Rayyis/Riad El-Rayyes 1991.

——, *Tanẓīmāt al-Ghaḍab al-Islāmī fī al-Sab'īnāt*, Cairo: Madbūlī 1989 (202 pp.).

Ajami, Fouad, *The Arab Predicament: Arab Political Thought and Practice Since 1967*, Cambridge University Press 1992.

——, 'In the Pharaoh's Shadow: Religion and Authority in Egypt' in Piscatori, *Political Process*, 12-35.

Ḥusayn Aḥmad **Amīn**, *Fī Bayt Aḥmad Amīn wa-Maqālāt Ukhrā*, Cairo: Madbūlī 1989[2].

——, *Al-Islām fī 'Ālam Mutaghayyir wa-Maqālāt Islāmiyya Ukhrā*, Cairo: Madbūlī n.d. (1988).

——, *Dalīl al-Muslim al-Ḥazīn fī Qarn al-'Ishrīn*, Cairo: Madbūlī 1987[3] (1st edn Cairo 1983), 404 pp.

Muṣṭafā **Amīn**, *Lā*, Beirut 1985[2], 932 pp. Contains a bibliography of the books written by Muṣṭafā Amīn on pp. 929-32.

——, *Shakhṣiyyāt Lā Tunsā*, Cairo 1988, 2 vols. See also under Fawzī.

Muḥammad **'Ammāra**, *Al-Farīḍa al-Ghā'iba: 'Arḍ wa-Ḥiwār wa-Taqyīm*, Cairo 1982.

Ghassan Ascha, *Du statut inférieur de la femme en Islam*, Paris: Harmattan 1989.

Muḥammad Sa'īd al-**'Ashmāwī**, *Ḍamīr al-'Aṣr: Khulāṣa 'ani 'l-Fikr al-Dīnī*, Cairo/Beirut 1979[2].

——, *Al-Ribā wa-'l-Fā'ida fī al-Islām*, Cairo 1988.

——, *Ma'ālim al-Islām*, Cairo 1989, 304 pp. [pp. 264-99: interviews with the author].

——, *Al-Islām al-Siyāsī*, Cairo 1987.

——, *Ḥaqīqat al-Ḥiğāb wa-Ḥuğğiyyat al-Ḥadīth*, Cairo: Madbūlī al-Ṣaghīr 1995[2].

'Abd al-Ghaffār **'Azīz** (ra'īs qism al-da'wa bi-ğāmi'at al-Azhar), *Man Qatala Farağ Fōda?*, Cairo 1992, 216.

Bannā: Ḥasan al-Bannā, Aḥmad Muḥ. Al-Sukkarī and Ḥāmid 'Abduh 'Askariyya, *Mudhakkira fī al-Ta'līm al-Dīnī*, Cairo: Maṭb. al-Salafiyya 1348 (the Muslim year between June 9, 1929, and May 28, 1930 AD). Leiden University Library 8157 C 9.

——, *Mudhakkirāt al-Da'wa wa-'l-Dā'iya bi-Qalam al-Imām al-Shahīd Ḥasan al-Bannā*, n.p., n.d., Dār al-Shihāb, 272 pp.

——, *Mağmū'at Rasā'il al-Imām al-Shahīd Ḥasan al-Banna*, Beirut: Al-Mu'assassa al-Islāmiyya li-'l-Ṭibā'a etc. n.d., several reprints, 382 pp.

Barreau, Jean-Claude, *De l'Islam en géneral et du monde moderne en particulier*, Paris: Belfond-Le Pré aux Clercs 1991.

Muḥammad 'Abd al-'Aziz ibn **Bāz** and Muḥammad ibn Ṣāliḥ al-'Ithīmīn, *Fatāwā Hay'at Kibār al-'Ulamā' wa-Fatāwā al-Lağna al-Dā'ima wa-Ghayrihim*, Makt. al-Turāth al-Islāmī, 'Abdīn 1990, 1002 pp. in 2 vols; Fatwās from Saudi Arabia.

Beck, Lois, and Nikki Keddie, eds, *Women in the Muslim World*, Cambridge, MA: Harvard University Press 1978.

Bell, Richard, *The Qur'ān* Translated, 2 vols, Edinburgh 1960^2.

Binchy, D.A., *Church and State in Fascist Italy*, London 1970^2.

Bloom, Harold, *The American Religion: The Emergence of the Post-Christian Nation*, New York: Touchstone 1992.

Brockelmann, C., *Geschichte der Arabischen Litteratur*, Leiden: E.J. Brill 1942.

Burridge, Kenelm, *New Heaven/New Earth: A Study of Millenarian Activities*, Oxford: Blackwell 1980.

Carré, Olivier, and Michaud, Gérard, *Les Frères Musulmans (1928-1982)*, Paris: Gallimard/Julliard 1983.

Chidester, David, *Salvation and Suicide: An Interpretation of Jim Jones, the People's Temple, and Jonestown*, Bloomington: Indiana University Press 1991^2.

Cooper, Artemis, *Cairo in the War, 1939-1945*, London: Penguin Books 1995. Relies largely on Charles Tripp, 'Ali Mahir and the Palace in Egyptian Politics, 1936-1942', unpubl. Ph. D. thesis, University of London 1984, for its information on Ḥasan al-Bannā and Muslim Arab Egypt in general.

Quṣayy Ṣāliḥ al-**Darwīsh**, *Rāshid al-Ghanūshī: Ḥiwārāt*, London 1992, 192 pp.

Muḥ. Ḥusayn al-**Dhahabī,** *Mādhā Qāl al-Shaykh al-Dhahabī wa-Li-mādhā Qatalūhu?*, n.p., n.d. (Cairo: Wizārat al-Awqāf 1978-9), 48 pp. Pamphlet, separate reprint of Al-Dhahabī's article on the Shukrī group.

EI ^{2}: H.A.R. Gibb, J.H. Kramers, E. Lévi-Provençal, J. Schacht, B. Lewis and Ch. Pellat, eds, *The Encyclopaedia of Islam*, new edition, Leiden: E.J. Brill 1960.

Karim Al-**Gawhary**, *Islamische Banken in Ägypten*, Berlin: Arabische Buchvertrieb 1994.

Samīr **Fāḍil**, *Kuntu Qādiy*^{an} *li-Ḥādith al-Minaṣṣa: Mudhakkirāt Qāḍ*^{in} *'Askarī min Ḥarb al-Yaman ilā Ightiyāl al-Sādāt*, Cairo: Sphinx 1993, 164 pp. & ill. Memoirs of the military judge who presided over the trial of Sadat's assassins, and who was prosecutor in the case of Shukrī.

Maḥmūd **Fawzī**, *'Umar 'Abd al-Raḥmān: Al-Shaykh al-Amrīkī al-Qādim!*, Cairo 3rd edn 1993, 168 pp.

—, *'Abūd al-Zumur: Kayfa Ightalnā al-Sādāt?!*, Cairo 3rd edn 1993, 240 pp.

—, *I'tirāfāt Muṣṭafā Amīn*, Cairo: Sphinx 1992, 128 pp. & ill.

Muḥammad 'Abd al-Salām **Farağ,** *Al-Farīḍa al-Ghā'iba*, English translation in Jansen, *Neglected Duty*, 159-234; edition (uncritical) of Arabic text in e.g. Ğād al-Ḥaqq, ed., *Fatāwā*, X (1983), 3762-92. See also Maḥmūd Ṣalāḥ, *Qatalnā*, 155.

Farağ **Fōda**, *Qabl al-Suqūṭ*, Cairo 1985.

—, *Ḥattā Lā Yakūn Kalām*[an] *fī al-Hawā'*, Cairo 1992, 264 pp. See also Munīr Shafīq; 'Abd al-Ghaffār 'Azīz.

Freedman, L., and E. Karsh, *The Gulf Conflict, 1990-1991*, London: Faber and Faber 1993.

Freijsen, I.H., *De Banier van de Islam. Het Nieuwe Elan van de Egyptische Moslimbroederschap, een Analyse van haar Huidige Orgaan 'Liwā' al-Islām'*, Leiden: CNWS 1990.

Ǧād al-Ḥaqq 'Alī Ǧād al-Ḥaqq; Ibr. al-Dasūqī; 'Abd al-Laṭīf Hamza; and Ǧamāl al-Dīn Muḥ. Maḥmūd, eds, *Al-Fatāwā al-Islāmiyya min Dār al-Iftā' al-Miṣriyya*, vols. I-XX, Cairo 1980-93/1400-13. The 20 volumes contain 7,799 consecutively numbered pages, plus indexes. Continues to appear.

'Abd al-Raḥmān al-**Ǧazīrī**, *Al-Fiqh 'alā al-Madhāhib al-Arba'a*, Cairo, date of preface 1939/1358. Many reprints, e.g. Istanbul 1986, 5 vols.

Gellner, Ernest, *Postmodernism, Reason and Religion*, London: Routledge 1992.

El-**Ghanouchi**, see Darwīsh and al-Ghanūshī.

Rāshid al-**Ghanūshī**, *Min al-Fikr al-Islāmī fī Tūnis*, 2 vols, 174 & 168 pp., 2nd edn Kuwait 1992.

Goitein, S.D., *Jews and Arabs: Their Contacts through the Ages*, New York: Schocken 1974.

Hadar, Leon T., 'What Green Peril?' *Foreign Affairs*, Spring 1993, 27-41.

Yvonne **Haddad**, 'The Arab-Israeli Wars, Nasserism, and the Affirmation of Islamic Identity' in John L. Esposito, ed., *Islam and Development: Religion and Sociopolitical Change*, Syracuse University Press 1980, 107-21.

Ra'ūf 'Abbās **Ḥāmid**, ed., *Arba'ūna 'Ām*[an] *'alā Thawrat Yulyū*, Cairo: Ahrām 1992, 312 pp.

Ḥasan **Ḥanafī** and Al-Imām al-Khumaynī, *Al-Ḥukūma al-Islāmiyya*, I'dād wa-Taqdīm dr Ḥasan Ḥanafī, Cairo, 2nd edn September 1979, 32 + 150 pp[2].

—, *Ǧihād al-Nafs aw al-Ǧihād al-Akbar*, Taqdīm wa-I'dād dr Ḥasan Ḥanafī, n.d., n.p. (Cairo 1980-1) 92 pp.

Harkabi, Yehoshaphat, *Israel's Fateful Hour*, New York: Harper and Row 1988. Originally in Hebrew: *Hakhra'ot Goraliyot*, Tel Aviv: Am Oved, 3rd imp. June 1986.

Ḥamid **Ḥassān**, Muḥ. 'Abd al-'Aẓīm 'Alī, 'Abd al-Fattāḥ Yaḥyā Kāmil Aḥmad, *Muwāǧahat al-Fikr al-Mutaṭarrif fi-'l-Islām*, preface by Yaḥyā Kāmil Aḥmad, n.p. Cairo: Maṭb. al-Ǧabalāwī 3rd edn 1980.

D. **Hopwood**, *Egypt: Politics and Society, 1945-1981*, London: Geo. Allen and Unwin 1982.

Hottinger, Arnold, *Fellachen und Funktionäre. Entwicklungswege im Nahen Osten*, Munich: Kösel 1967.

—, *Islamischer Fundamentalismus*, Munich: Ferdinand Schöningh/Wilhelm Fink 1993.

Hunter, Shireen T., *The Algerian Crisis: Origins, Evolution and Lessons for the Maghreb and Europe*, Brussels: Centre for European Policy Studies, 1996.

Fahmī **Huwaydī**, *Al-Qur'ān wa-'l-Sulṭa: Humūm Islāmiyya Mu'āṣira*, Cairo: Shurūq 1981, 2nd edn 1982, 3rd edn 1991, 248 pp.

—, *Al-Tadayyun al-Manqūṣ*, Cairo: Ahrām 1987, 2nd edn 1988, 312 pp.

—, *Al-Islām wa-'l-Dīmuqrāṭiyya*, Cairo: Ahrām 1993, 280 pp.

—, *Iḥqāq al-Ḥaqq*, Cairo: Shurūq 1994, 256 pp.

Ibn Taymiyya, *Daqā'iq al-Tafsīr*, ed. Dr Muḥ. Al-Sayyid Ğulaynid, 4 vols, Cairo: Dār al-Anṣār 1977-81.

—, *Mağmū' Fatāwā... b. Taymiyya*, ed. 'Ar. b. Muḥ. Qāsim Al- 'Āṣimī..., n.p., n.d., (repr. Saudi Arabia, ca. 1970- 80).

—, *Al-Siyāsa al-Shar'iyya*, Cairo: Al-Sha'b 1971.

—, *Mağmū'at Fatāwā... b. Taymiyyah*, ed. Farağ Allāh Zakī al-Kurdī, Cairo: Maṭb. Kurdistān al-'Ilmiyya 1329 (1911).

Jansen, Johannes J.G., *The Neglected Duty: The Creed of Sadat's Assassins and Islamic Resurgence in the Middle East*, New York: Macmillan 1986.

—, *The Interpretation of the Koran in Modern Egypt*, Leiden: E.J. Brill 1974.

—, 'Muḥammad Abū Zayd', in *EI* (2nd edn), VII, 420-1 [1991].

—, 'The Voice of Sheikh Kishk (b. 1933)', in Ibr. A. El-Sheikh, C.A. van de Koppel and R. Peters, *The Challenge of the Middle East*, Amsterdam: IMNO 1982, 57-66, 189-91.

—, 'Ḥasan al-Bannâ's Earliest Pamphlet', *Welt des Islams* 32 (1992), 254-8.

—, 'The Preaching of Shaykh Al-Sha'rāwī: its Political Significance' in W.A.L. Stokhof and N.J.G. Kaptein, eds, *Makalah-Makalah yang Disampaikan dalam Rangka Kunjungan Menteri Agama R.I.H. Munawir Sjadzali M.A. ke Negeri Belanda (31 Okotober-7 November 1988)*, Seri INIS, Jilid VI, Leiden/Jakarta 1990, pp. 179-93.

—, 'Ibrâhîm 'Abduh (b. 1913): His Autobiographies and his Polemical Political Writings', *Bibliotheca Orientalis*, XXXVII (1980), pp. 128-32.

Jomier, J., *Le Commentaire Coranique du Manâr*, Paris: Adrien-Maisonneuve 1954.

Mağdī **Kāmil**, *Al-Khurūğ min al-Sulṭa*, Cairo 1994, 196 pp.

Keddie, Nikki R., *Sayyid Jamāl ad-Dīn 'al-Afghānī': A Political Biography*, Berkeley: University of California Press 1972.

Kedourie, Elie, *Democracy and Arab Political Culture*, London: Cass 1994.

Kerr, Malcolm H., *Islamic Reform: The Political and Legal Theories of Muḥammad 'Abduh and Rashīd Riḍā*, Berkeley: University of California Press 1966.

'Amr **Khafāğī**, *Milaff 'Abd al-Ḥalīm Mūsā*, Cairo: Sfinks 1993, 184 pp.

Al-**Khālidī**, Ṣalāḥ 'Abd al- Fattāḥ, *Sayyid Quṭb: Min al- Mīlād ilā al-Istishhād*, Beirut/Damascus 1991, 608 pp.

Khomeini: Al-Marğa' al-Dīnī al-A'lā al-Imām al-Muğāhid al-Sayyid Rūḥallāh al-Khumaynī, *Al-Ḥukūma al-Islāmiyya: Durūs Fiqhiyya alqāhā...'alā Ṭullāb 'Ulūm al-Dīn fī al-Nağaf al-Ashraf Taḥt 'Unwān* 'Wilāyat al-Faqīh' 13 Dhī Qa'da-1 Dhī Ḥiğğa 1389 (*ca.* 21 January-*ca.* 8 February 1970), n.d., n.p., 154 pp. (bought in Damascus, February 1989).

—, *see also* Ḥasan **Ḥanafī**.

Muḥ. 'Abd al-Ḥamīd **Kishk**, *Ṭarīq al-Nağāh*, Cairo n.d.

—, *Fatāwā al-Shaykh Kishk: Humūm al-Muslimīn al-Mu'āṣira*, Cairo n.d. (1989?).

—, *Fī Riḥāb al-Tafsīr*, Cairo n.d., 8 vols. Each *ğuz'* has its own dated *nihil obstat* from the Department for Research, Writing and Translation of the Azhar. The *nihil obstat* for the first *ğuz'* is dated March 15, 1987. In August 1995 vol. 8 had not yet appeared. Vols 1-7 contain 6,746 consecutively numbered pages, and go up to the end of *ğuz'* 28. Indexes and title-pages are not numbered.

Kramer, Martin, *The Moral Logic of Hizballah*, Tel Aviv University: Dayan Center for Middle Eastern and African Studies, Occasional Papers no. 101, August 1987.

Lapidus, Ira, 'The Separation of State and Religion in the Development of Early Muslim Society', *International Journal of Middle East Studies*, 1975, 363-85.

Lawrence, Bruce B., *Defenders of God: the Fundamentalist Revolt Against the Modern Age*, San Francisco: Harper and Row 1989.

Lewis, Bernard, 'The Return of Islam', *Commentary* (New York), vol. 61, no. 1, January 1976, 39-49; repr. in Michael Curtis, ed., *Religion and Politics in the Middle East*, Boulder, CO: Westview Press 1981, 9-29.

—, *Semites and Anti-Semites: An Inquiry into Conflict and Prejudice*, New York: W.W. Norton 1986.

—, *The Jews of Islam*, Princeton University Press 1987.

—, *The Middle East: 2000 Years of History, From the Rise of Christianity to the Present Day*, London: Weidenfeld and Nicolson 1995.

Linton, Ralph, 'Nativistic Movements', *American Anthropologist*, NS, 45 (1943) 230-40.

Lodge, David, *Write On: Occasional Essays, 1965-1985*, London: Penguin Books 1988.

Mağma' al-Lugha al-'Arabiyya, *Mu'ğam Alfāẓ al-Qur'ān al-Karīm*, Cairo: Hay'a 1970, 2 vols, 641 and 918 pp.

Muṣṭafā **Maḥmūd**, *Al-Islām wa-'l-Mārkisiyya*, Cairo: Dār al-Ma'ārif 1975, 84 pp.

Ḥasanayn Muḥammad **Makhlūf**, *Fatāwā Shar'iyya wa-Buḥuth Islāmiyya*, Cairo: Muṣṭafā al-Ḥalabī 2nd edn 1965, 2 vols, 392 and 212 pp. The author was Muftī of Egypt in 1946-50 and 1952-4.

Peter **Mansfield**, *Nasser's Egypt*, rev. edn 1969, Harmondsworth: Penguin Books.

Mar'ī (d. 1624): *Kitāb al-Kawākib al-Durriyya fī Manāqib al-Imām... Ibn Taymiyya li-'l-Imām al-Shaykh Mar'ī b. Yūsuf al-Karmī al-Ḥanbalī*, Cairo: Maṭb. Kurdistān al-'Ilmiyya 1329/1911.

Marty, M.E., and R.S. Appleby, eds, *Fundamentalisms Observed*, University of Chicago Press 1991.

——, eds, *Fundamentalisms and Society: Reclaiming the Sciences, the Family and Education*, University of Chicago Press 1993.

——, eds, *Fundamentalisms and the State: Remaking Polities, Economies, and Militance*, University of Chicago Press 1993.

Abū al-A'lā al-**Mawdūdī**, *Al-Ḥukūma al-Islāmiyya*, tr. Aḥmad Idrīs, Cairo (Al-Mukhtār al-Islāmī) 2nd edn 1980. Date of translator's preface to 1st edn: 25 August 1976. 318 pp.

Miller, Judith, 'The Challenge of Radical Islam', *Foreign Affairs*, spring 1993, 43-56.

——, 'Faces of Fundamentalism: Hassan al-Turabi and Muhammed Fadlallah', *Foreign Affairs*, November/December 1994, 123-42.

Mimouni, Rachid, *De la barbarie en général et de l'intégrisme en particulier*, Paris: Belfond-Le Pré aux Clercs 1992.

Mitchell, Richard P., *The Society of the Muslim Brothers*, Oxford University Press 1969.

Mortimer, Edward, *Faith and Power: The Politics of Islam*, London: Faber and Faber 1982.

Anwar **Muḥammad**, *Ğanrālāt al-Islām: Khafāyā Tanẓīm al-Uṣūliyyīn al-Duwalī*, Cairo 1992, 184 pp.

——, *Khumaynī Miṣr: 'Umar 'Abd al-Raḥmān*, Cairo 1993, 152 pp.

Nāyil **Mukhaybir**, 'Aṣbaḥat Īṭāliyā.. Markaz.. al-Uṣūliyya.. Al-Ittifāq al-Sirrī bayn al-Mutaṭarrafīn wa-'l-Māfiyā..', *Al-Waṭan al-Arabī* (Paris/London) 937 (17 February 1995) 16-18. Eloquent testimony to the fear of fundamentalism and fundamentalists felt by the non-fundamentalist westernised Muslim citizens of the Middle East.

Hāla **Muṣṭafā**, *Al-Dawla wa-'l-Ḥarakāt al-Islāmiyya al-Mu'āriḍa bayn al-Muhādana wa-'l-Muwāğaha fī Ahday al-Sādāt wa-Mubārak*, Cairo: Al-Maḥūrsa 1995, 444 pp. The most important secondary source available.

——, *Al-Islām al-Siyāsī fī Miṣr min Ḥarakat al-Iṣlāḥ ilā Ğamā'āt al-'Unf*, Cairo 1992.

Muḥammad **Muṣṭafā**, *Kuntī Wazīran li-'l-Dākhiliyya*, Cairo: Akhbār al-Yawm n.d. (preface dated 1992).

Shukrī Aḥmad **Muṣṭafā**, 'Kitāb al-Khilāf' in Aḥmad, *Al-Nabiyy al-*

Musallah (2): *Al-Thā'irūn*, 115-60. Probably the only edition extant; uncritical, incomplete, contains misprints, but still very valuable.

—, Al-Naṣṣ al-Kāmil li-Aqwāl wa-I'tirāfāt Shukrī Aḥmad Muṣṭafā, Amīr Ǧamā'at Al-Takfīr wa-'l-Hiğra, amām Maḥkamat Amn al-Dawla al-'Askariyya al-'Ulyā 1977, in Aḥmad, *Al-Nabiyy al-Musallaḥ (1): Al-Rāfiḍūn*, 53-109 (interrogation by the court, 3rd edn November 1977).

—, 'Afkār Shukrī Muṣṭafā al-Ḥaqīqiyya', *Al-Siyāsa* (daily, Kuwait), second half October 1979, at least 8 long articles, quoting and summarising the November 1977 interrogation.

Nagel, Tilman, *Geschichte der islamischen Theologie. Von Mohammed bis zur Gegenwart*, Munich: C.H. Beck 1994.

V.S. **Naipaul**, *India: A Million Mutinies Now*, London: Minerva 1992.

Nettler, Ronald L., *Past Trials and Present Tribulations: A Muslim Fundamentalist's View of the Jews*, Oxford: Pergamon Press, 2nd edn 1989. Translation with commentary and introduction of Sayyid Quṭb's pamphlet on the Jews, *Ma'rakatunā ma'a al-Yahūd*.

Oxf. EMIW: John L. Esposito, *The Oxford Encyclopaedia of the Modern Islamic World*, New York: Oxford University Press 1995, 4 vols..

Pfaff, William, *The Wrath of Nations*, New York: Touchstone 1994.

Piscatori, James P., ed., *Islam in the Political Process*, Cambridge University Press 1983.

Polk, William R., *The United States and the Arab World*, Cambridge, MA: Harvard University Press 1965.

Yūsuf al-**Qarḍāwī**, *Al-Ṣaḥwa al-Islāmiyya bayn al-Ǧuḥūd wa-'l-Taṭarruf*, Cairo, 2nd edn 1984.

—, *Al-Ḥalāl wa-'l-Ḥarām fī al-Islām*, Cairo: Wahba, 10th edn 1976. Many reprints, e.g. Beirut and Damascus, 14th edn 1985. Preface dated 1960.

'Abd al-Ḥalīm **Qindīl**, ed., *Al-Nāṣiriyya wa-'l-Islām*, Cairo 1992.

Sayyid **Quṭb**, *Fī Ta'rikh: Fikra wa-Minhāğ*, Cairo, 4th edn 1980.

—, *Ma'ālim fī al-Tarīq*.

—, *Ma'rakat al-Islām wa-'l-Ra'smāliyya*, Cairo, 7th edn 1980.

—, *Fī Ẓilāl al-Qur'ān*.

—, *Al-Mustaqbal li-Hādhā al-Dīn*, Cairo 1981, 100 pp.

—, *Al-Salām al-'Ālamī wa-'l-Islām*, Cairo, 5th edn 1980.

Quṭb's bibliography: Al-Khālidī, 515-92.

Rekhess, Elie, 'The Iranian Impact on the Islamic Jihad Movement in the Gaza Strip' in D. Menashri, ed., *The Iranian Revolution and the Muslim World*, Boulder, CO: Westview 1990, 189-206.

Fu'ād b Sayyid Abd al-Raḥmān al-**Rifā'ī**, *Al-Nufūdh al-Yahūdī fī Ağhiza al-I'lāmiyya wa-'l-Mu'assasāt al-Duwaliyya: Al-Af'ā al-Yahūdiyya Istawlat 'alā Wasā'il al- I'lām..* etc., Cairo (Naṣā'iḥ Islāmiyya 7) n.d.; preface dated Rağab 1407 (March 1987), x+160 pp. A remarkable example of paranoid anti-semitism.

Ğābir **Rizq**, *Madhābiḥ al-Ikhwān fī Suğūn Nāṣir*, Cairo, 2nd edn 1978.

Ruthven, Malise, *The Divine Supermarket*, London: Chatto and Windus 1989.

—, *Islam in the World*, London: Penguin Books 1991.

Roy, Olivier, *The Failure of Political Islam*, London: I.B. Tauris 1994.

'Alī **Ṣabrī**, *Sanawāt al-Taḥawwul al-Ishtirākī*, Cairo n.d. (1966), 200 pp.

'Adnān **Sa'd al-Dīn**, 'Min Uṣūl al-'Amal al-Siyāsī li-'l-Ḥaraka al-Islāmiyya al-Mu'āṣira' in 'Abdallāh al-Nafīsī, *Al-Ḥaraka al-Islāmiyya: Ru'ya Mustaqbaliyya: Awrāq min al-Naqd al-Dhātī*, Cairo: Madbūlī 1989, pp. 269-98.

Ḥasan **Ṣādiq**, *Ğudhūr al-Fitna fī al-Firaq al-Islāmiyya mundhu 'Ahd al-Rasūl hātta Ightiyāl al-Sādāt*, Cairo: Madbūlī 1993², 604 pp. pp. 275-598 discuss the twentieth century. Contains (parts of) documents, often regrettably in incomplete and uncritical editions. See esp. pp. 529-82 on the 'dialogue' between official Ulema and supposedly repenting extremists.

Muḥammad Bāqir al-**Ṣadr**, *Buḥūth Islāmiyya wa-Mawāḍī Ukhrā*, Beirut, 3rd edn 1983.

Maḥmūd **Ṣalāḥ**, *Hākadhā Qatalnā al-Sādāt: I'tirāfāt Khālid al-Islāmbūlī wa-Zumalā'ihi fī Ḥādith al-Minaṣṣa*, Cairo: Madbūlī al-Saghīr 1995, 164 pp. Texts from the police interrogations in October 1981 of Sadat's assassins.

Schacht, Joseph, *An Introduction to Islamic Law*, Oxford University Press 1964.

Munīr **Shafīq**, *Bayn al-Nuhūḍ wa-'l-Suqūṭ: Radd 'alā Kitāb* Qabl Suqūṭ *li-Farağ Fōda*, Tunis 1991, 136 pp.

Muḥammad **Shaḥrūr**, *Dirāsāt Islāmiyya Mu'āṣira fī al-Dawla wa-'l-Muğtama'*, Damascus 1994, 376 pp.

Sharon, Moshe, 'The Islamic Factor in Middle East Politics', *Midstream* (Theodor Herzl Foundation, New York), XXXX, 1 (January 1994) 7-10.

Munīr Ṭāhir al-**Shawwāf**, *Tahāfut al-Dirāsāt al-Mu'āṣira fī al-Dawla wa-'l-Muğtama'*, Riyadh 1995, 224 pp.

Shirley, Edward G. (pseudonym of a former Iran specialist for the Central Intelligence Agency), 'Is Iran's Present Algeria's Future?' in *Foreign Affairs*, 74, 3, May/June 1995, 28-44.

Muṣṭafā Faraghlī al-**Shuqayrī**, *Fī Wağh al-Mu'āmara 'alā Taṭbīq al-Sharī'a al-Islāmiyya*, Al-Manṣūra: Al-Wafā' 1986.

Shusman, Awīwa, 'HaYakhas Be'Itonut HaMitzrit LeShī'a **'al Reqa'** HaMahpekha HaIslamit BeIran', *HaMizrakh HeKhadash*, XXXI (1986) 138-51 (in Hebrew).

Shukrī, see Shukrī Aḥmad **Muṣṭafā**.

Sivan, Emmanuel, *Radical Islam: Medieval Theology and Modern Politics*, New Haven: Yale University Press 1985.

Stark, R., and W.S. Bainbridge, *The Future of Religion: Secularization, Revival and Cult Formation*, Berkeley: University of California Press 1985.

Stillman, Norman A., *The Jews of Arab Lands: A History and Source Book*, Philadelphia: Jewish Publication Society 1979.

—, *The Jews of Arab Lands in Modern Times*, Philadelphia: Jewish Publication Society 1991.

Ḥaydar **Ṭāhā**, *Al-Ikhwān wa-'l-'Askar: Qiṣṣat al-Ğabha al-Islāmiyya wa-'l-Sulṭa fī Sūdān*, Cairo 1993.

'Umar al-**Tilimsānī**, *Al-Ḥukūma al-Dīniyya*, Cairo (Dār al-I'tiṣām) n.d. (1994).

Shawkat al-**Tūnī** al-Muhāmī, *Muḥākamāt al-Diğwī*, preface by Muṣṭafā Amīn, Cairo: Al-Sha'b 1975.

Ḥasan al-**Turābī**, *Tağdīd al-Fikr al-Islāmī*, n.p., 3rd edn 1993, 206 pp.

—, 'Abd al-Fattāḥ Maḥğūb Muḥammad Ibrāhīm, *Al-Duktūr Ḥasan al-Turābī wa-Fasād Naẓariyyat Taṭwīr al-Dīn*, Cairo 1995, 248 pp.

'Ukāsha 'Abd al-Mannān al-Ṭībī, *Al-Tabarruğ: Akhṭar Ma'āwil al-Hadm wa-'l-Tadmīr fī al-Muğtama' al-Islāmī*, Cairo: Makt. al-Turāth al-Islāmī, Abdīn, date of preface Ramaḍān 1409/April 1989.

'Umar Aḥmad, *Asyūṭ Madīnat al-Nār: Asrār wa-Waqā'i' al-'Unf*, Cairo (Sfinks) 1994, 224 pp. On the disturbances in Asyut in 1993; contains a small number of photocopied reproductions of communiques from *Al-Ğamā'a al-Islāmiyya fī Miṣr* and *Tanẓīm al-Ğihād-Miṣr*.

Uṣfūr, Ğābir, *Hawāmish 'alā Daftar al-Tanwīr*, Cairo 1994.

Usrat al-Tarbiya al-Kanasiyya bi-**Kanīsat** al-Malāk **Ghabriyāl** bi-(Ḥārat) al-Saqqāyīn (Abdin, Cairo), *Arba'ūna Mu'ğiza li-'l-Sayyida al-'Adhrā'*, vol. 2, Cairo, 5th edn 1990, 100 pp. Preface dated August 1977. Starts with the appearance of Mary on the evening of April 2, 1968. Miracles numbered from 40 to 80.

Wallace, Anthony F.C., 'Revitalization Movements' *American Anthropologist*, NS, 58 (1956) 264-81.

Wasserstein, Bernard, 'Writing on the Wall' (review of Norman A. Stillman, *The Jews of Arab Lands in Modern Times*), *Times Literary Supplement*, June 14, 1991, 9-10.

Webster, Richard A., *The Cross and the Fasces*, Stanford University Press 1960.

Wensinck, A.J., 'The Oriental Doctrine of the Martyrs' in *Mededeelingen Koninklijke Akademie van Wetenschappen*, Afd. Letterkunde, 53, A, 6, Amsterdam 1921; reprinted in *Semietische Studiën uit de Nalatenschap van Prof. dr A.J. Wensinck*, Leiden: A.W. Sijthoff 1941, 90-113.

—, *Concordance et Indices de la Tradition Musulmane*, 7 vols, Leiden: E.J. Brill 1936-69.

Wielandt, Rotraud, *Offenbarung und Geschichte im Denken Moderner Muslime*, Wiesbaden: Steiner 1971.

Wild, S., 'Ṣâdiq al-'Aẓm's book "Critique of Religious Thought" ', in *Actes* Ve *Congrès International d'Arabisants et d'Islamisants* (1970), *Correspondance d'Orient* no. 11, Bruxelles (1971), pp. 507-13.

Woodward, Bob, *Veil: The Secret Wars of the CIA 1981-1987*, London: Headline, 1987.

Zakariyyā, Fu'ād, *Al-Ḥaqīqa wa-'l-Wahm fī al-Ḥaraka al-Islāmiyya al-Mu'aṣira*, Cairo 1986.

—, *Al-Ṣaḥwa al-Islāmiyya fī Mīzān al-'Aql*, Cairo 1989, expanded edn n.d.

Zubaida, Sami, *Islam, the People and the State: Political Ideas and Movements in the Middle East*, rev. paperback edn, London: I.B. Tauris 1993.

GENERAL INDEX

INDEX OF KORAN QUOTATIONS